OREGON'S DRY SIDE

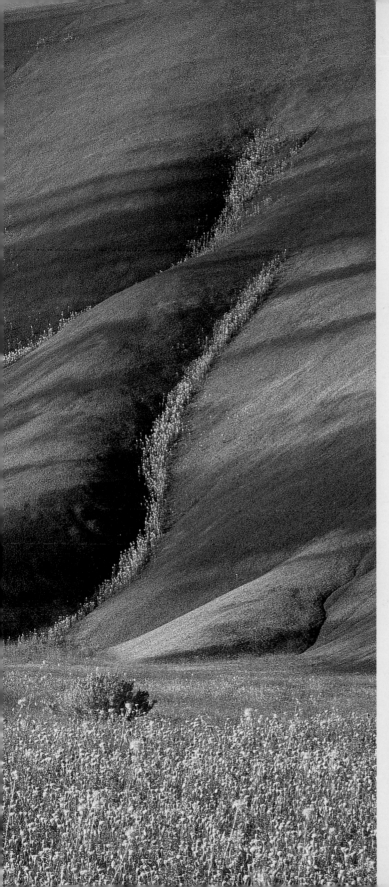

OREGON'S DRY SIDE

Exploring East of the Cascade Crest

Alan D. St. John

Timber Press

To my father, Glenn St. John,
and my grandfather, Orville St. John,
maverick outdoorsmen of the American West.
They passed on to me their genetic dispositions for an unquenchable need
to explore and savor the freedom of wild places. I value this inheritance
more than any imaginable wealth of gold.

CAUTION: Before exploring remote backcountry roads, always remember the cardinal rule: top off your gas tank and bring full drinking water containers. Also, please be aware that the maps provided in this book are not adequately detailed for navigating routes beyond the primary interstate and state highways. When planning a trip into the remote sections of Oregon's dry side, acquire up-to-date maps that clearly delineate all secondary and unpaved roads, along with showing the geographic contours and general lay of the land. In especially wild, little-traveled places, the rough roads that access these rugged landscapes usually require high-clearance, four-wheel-drive vehicles. During wet weather, beware of many dirt roads that become muddy quagmires—the Owyhee Canyonlands of far Southeastern Oregon are particularly noted for this hazard. When in doubt, don't go. During the extreme heat of summer, running out of gas or becoming stranded by mechanical failure in the desert can be dangerous. And never drive off road, causing environmental damage.

Library of Congress Cataloging-in-Publication Data

St. John, Alan D.
    Oregon's dry side: exploring east of the Cascade Crest/Alan D. St. John.
        p. cm.
    Rev., expanded ed. of: Eastern Oregon: portrait of the land and its people. Helena, MT: American Geographic Pub., c1988.
    Includes bibliographical references and index.
    ISBN-13: 978-0-88192-829-7
    1. Oregon—Guidebooks. 2. Natural history—Oregon—Guidebooks. 3. Automobile travel—Oregon—Guidebooks. 4. Oregon—Description and travel. 5. Oregon—Geography. 6. Geology—Oregon. I. St. John, Alan D. Eastern Oregon. II. Title.
    F874.3.S695 2007
    917.9504′44—dc22
                                        2006024588

PAGE 1: Abandoned farm on The Nature Conservancy's Clear Lake Ridge Preserve, near Joseph. PAGES 2–3: Spring wildflowers at the Painted Hills. John Day Fossil Beds National Monument, Central Oregon. Inset: Golden bee plant (*Cleome platycarpa*). OPPOSITE: Jefferson Park on the crest of the Cascades. Mount Jefferson Wilderness, Central Oregon. PAGE 6: Autumn storm along the eastern escarpment of Steens Mountain, Southeastern Oregon. PAGE 9: Alvord Desert playa detail, Southeastern Oregon. PAGE 300: Moonset at sunrise, Alvord Desert.

Photography by the author unless otherwise noted.
Maps by Allan Cartography, Medford, Oregon

This revised, expanded work incorporates portions of the book published in 1988 by American Geographic Publishing as *Eastern Oregon: Portrait of the Land and Its People.*

Published in 2007 by
Timber Press, Inc.
The Haseltine Building
133 S.W. Second Avenue, Suite 450
Portland, Oregon 97204-3527, U.S.A.
www.timberpress.com

For contact information regarding editorial, marketing, sales, and distribution in the United Kingdom, see www.timberpress.co.uk.

Designed by Susan Applegate
Printed in China
Reprinted in 2007

Have you wandered in the wilderness, the sagebrush desolation,
The bunch-grass levels where the cattle graze?

Have you whistled bits of rag-time at the end of all creation,
And learned to know the desert's little ways?

Have you camped upon the foothills, have you galloped o'er the ranges,
Have you roamed the arid sun-lands through and through?

Have you chummed up with the mesa? Do you know its moods and changes?
Then listen to the Wild—it's calling you.

ROBERT SERVICE, *The Call of the Wild*, 1907

Contents

Acknowledgments

THIS book's wide-ranging overview of so many subjects required me to repeatedly seek help from those knowledgeable in the various aspects of Oregon's dry side. Writing the text with any degree of accuracy would have been impossible without their able and generous assistance. However, I alone shoulder the blame for any inaccuracies that have crept in—not the fine folks acknowledged here. Undoubtedly, I have accidentally left someone out, and sincerely apologize for any such oversights. Similarly, many was the time I phoned an unidentified worker at a chamber of commerce, county office, national wildlife refuge headquarters, Native American tribal administration, or other such agencies to seek information. Anonymous though you may be, know that you are appreciated.

First of all, kudos to Eve Goodman and the staff at Timber Press. Thank you all for believing in my vision for this book, for your understanding when it took longer than anticipated, and for your hard work bringing it to fruition. Editor Patrice Silverstein contributed a New York City transplant's fresh viewpoint—her many suggestions brought different approaches to crafting sections of text that never would have occurred to me.

Special gratitude goes to Buck Jenkins, connoisseur of the arts and sciences, bon vivant, and philanthropist. Without his generous funding for this project's film processing and a good portion of the general supplies and research materials, completion would have been nearly impossible. He also contributed many hours reading through the entire text. His formidable editing abilities as a retired professor of English literature were especially appreciated in the slaying of tenacious dangling participles.

Others who reviewed sections of text, contributed helpful suggestions, and offered general encouragement were Jim and Sue Anderson, Ellen Bishop, Bob Boyd, James Chatters, Larry Chitwood, Stacy Davies, Ted Fremd, Stu Garrett, Doc and Connie Hatfield, Lucile Housley, Doug Knutsen, Ed Park, Gayle Parlato, and Tom Rodhouse.

Many people took time from their busy schedules to answer my questions on any number of subjects that pertained to their individual expertise, and came to my aid in various other ways: Steve Arnold, Phyllis Badgley, Fred Barstad, Ralph Berry, Jay Bowerman, Chad Boyd, Doug Calvin, Chris Carey, Paul Claeyssens, Gary Clowers, Bobbie Conner, Monty

Cook, Tom Crabtree, Amy Jo Detweiler, Eric Eaton, Mark Eberle, Jeff Elsasser, Tom Ferron, Brian Ferry, Steve George, Jo Hallam, Linda Hardison, Ray Hatton, Sarah Herve, Gary Huckleberry, Richard Jenkins, Dave Jensen, Charles Johnson Jr., Jimmy Kagan, Clair Kunkel, Jim LaBonte, Dan Luoma, Don Mansfield, Bill Marlett, Chris Marshall, Pete Martin, Rick Miller, Jason Miner, Judy Rae Parrish, Rich Pyzik, Jim Riggs, Eric Scheuering, Matt Smith, Brad Spence, Terry Spivey, Lorraine St. John, Marty St. Louis, Bruce Taylor, Sue Vrilakas, and Rich Wandschneider.

I had the able help of several historical archivists in hunting down images from the past and producing quality prints of them. Their enthusiasm concerning local history was contagious: Robert Applegate (Nez Perce National Historic Park), Gary Deilman (Baker County Library), John Frye (Deschutes County Historical Society), Emory Ferguson (Harney County Historical Society), Gordon Gillespie (Bowman Museum), Ann Hayes (Wallowa County Museum), and Lesli Larson (University of Oregon Libraries). On two occasions, the services of a studio photographer were required to create fresh, new prints from old, fading photographs: Jon Croghan made the Baker County Library reproductions, and Ruthie Miller produced those from the Harney County Historical Society collection.

I cannot praise enough the skills of Lawrence Andreas and his talented staff at Allan Cartography. Working from my color felt-pen sketches, they accurately created maps that not only visually inform, but are works of art as well. The results exceeded my expectations.

I give heartfelt thanks to my wife, Jan, and my son, Matthew, for once again enduring the inconvenience of a long-term book project in our home. Your patience was appreciated during the many months I was monkishly sequestered in my study, pecking at a keyboard, alternating with frenetic comings and goings at all hours in my photographic quests. Jan is also to be praised for reading every word of the text and giving me the unique blend of honest criticism and encouragement that only a loving spouse is capable of.

Lastly, I want to convey to all the people of Oregon's dry side my great appreciation for your warmth and friendliness in sharing your love and pride for the land and your communities. And deepest gratitude of all goes to the Maker of this vast region and all of its marvelous diversity.

Regions of Oregon's Dry Side

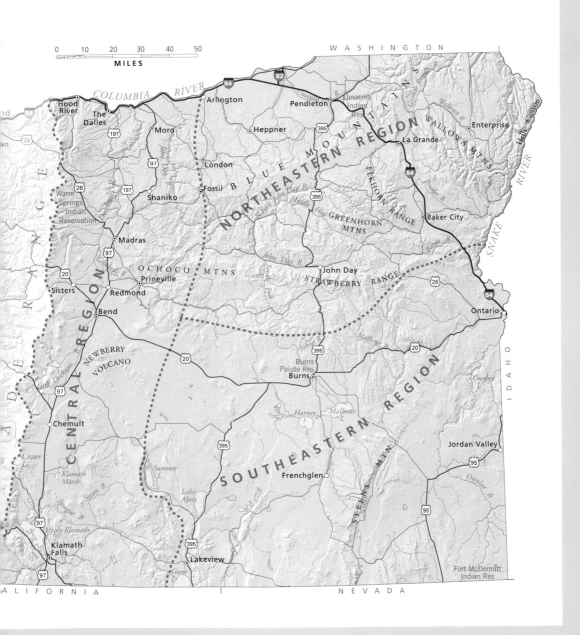

An Invitation to Explore the Dry Side

Somehow the wide free sageland, the spacious desert and all its creatures, seems a fitting introduction to the mountains, a contrast yet a harmony, for it is all the natural free earth.

MARGARET MURIE, *Wapiti Wilderness*, 1966

Anyone traveling across Oregon will marvel at the variety of topography within this one state's boundaries. In reality, the famed monoclimate of dank mosses and misty, green rain forests that supposedly carpet the entire state exists only in the geography of the imagination.

East of the Cascade Range lies a high and dry land of sunny, open landscapes under seemingly limitless skies. What sometimes pleasantly surprises newcomers is the extent of this interior plateau country—two thirds of the state has a climate and terrain similar to Idaho and Nevada. And the scenic diversity is astounding—ranging from sweeping sagebrush plains, to lofty, pine-clad peaks that are eternaly crowned with snow.

To senses accustomed to lushly wooded, greenly serene countryside or manicured, leafy city surroundings, the rugged, often harsh landscapes and climate of this region can take some getting used to. But with greater familiarity, the desire to see and know more of the intriguing qualities and beauty of Oregon's dry side proves irresistible.

Although all of these landscapes are often conveniently lumped as "Eastern Oregon," three differing geographic regions are apparent: Central Oregon, Southeastern Oregon, and Northeastern Oregon—each with its own distinctive

Alice Elshoff hiking through sagebrush steppelands near Paisley, Southeastern Oregon

Dawn at the Alvord Desert below the fault block
upthrust of Steens Mountain, Southeastern Oregon

geology, flora, fauna, human culture, and flavor. Creating an explorer's guidebook for all of this variety through research, writing, photography, and personal experience has been a daunting task.

By necessity, to cover everything that I felt was important, my approach has required painting in rather broad brushstrokes. Many readers, already familiar with Oregon's dry side as residents or frequent visitors, might be disappointed that some of their favorite places have been omitted. Conversely, some folks will no doubt be happy that their "secret" spots are not included here. I can sympathize with this sentiment, as everyone needs special retreats away from crowds where quietude prevails. To be honest, I purposely left out a couple of my own favorite, obscure camp-sites and trails. Other locations that are fragile and cannot withstand heavy use are not to be encountered in these pages as well. Along with most of the state's well-known signature attractions east of the Cascades, I have also described many lesser-known locations that offer unfrequented trails with fresh vistas, wildlife viewing opportunities, tiny outposts that consist only of an old-fashioned mercantile, lonely ghost towns, and unusual festivals (how about a rattlesnake- and bear-meat barbecue, for instance?).

This book is designed to serve dual purposes: the history of the people and land can provide informative armchair reading at home; on the road it can be used as a general guide while exploring, and you'll also find that elements of a natural history field guide

Young coyote. Malheur National Wildlife Refuge, Southeastern Oregon

Autumn reflections in Cottonwood Creek. Pueblo Mountains, Southeastern Oregon

have been included. Toss *Oregon's Dry Side* on the backseat of your auto for your next outing east of the Cascades.

Along with regional maps that show the basic geography and vegetation zones, you'll also see, scattered throughout the book, close-up features (flagged in light blue) about the geology, typical plants and animals, notable points of interest, and historical sites, as well as "Trailposts" that suggest some good places to hike. Wildflowers, perennial favorites of outdoor enthusiasts, have been afforded an extensive section to aid you in the identification of the most commonly seen and unique species native to the sagebrush country. A checklist of the plants and animals included herein, providing both common and scientific names, appears at the end of the book.

Cushion buckwheat. Summit of Steens Mountain, Southeastern Oregon

Backpacker camp at Mirror Lake in the Eagle Cap Wilderness. Wallowa Mountains, Northeastern Oregon

Be advised: this book is not an in-depth travelogue that micromanages every mile of your explorations. Before launching off, the reader is expected to be a self-starter who acquires additional maps that are detailed and specialized guidebooks for each area (see "Resources"). Throughout the book, when describing remote backcountry that is only reachable via rough jeep roads, I emphasize the need to use a motor vehicle with high clearance, equipped with extra gas, and stocked with water and food. This is just common sense stuff. In out-of-the-way districts where gas stations, grocery stores, and cafés are few and far between, I've mentioned where supplies can be obtained, or give warning of a total lack thereof. When specific restaurants, hotels, and other businesses are named, this does not necessarily indicate an endorsement by the author or publisher: as time passes, ownerships transfer, names change, quality may decline, and some places go out of business. My listings merely represent examples of establishments typical for a region, or ones that are historically significant and unique in some way.

It will soon become readily apparent during your travels that the land itself, comparatively sparsely settled in most places, is the dominant influence. Reflecting this, the residents are largely hardy, robust, outdoor-oriented folk with attitudes and values strongly shaped by their surroundings. And like the multifaceted region, its peoples range from tribal Native American Indians to cattle ranchers, farmers, loggers, computer programmers, stockbrokers, doctors, artists, teachers, among others, and the retired elderly who come to the area for its healthful climate. For Oregonians and visitors alike, the exceptional fishing, hunting, skiing, mountain-biking, river-running, and other outdoor sports inspire passionate devotion.

As the population increases and more people grow to appreciate and enjoy this land, debates have arisen in recent years over how best to manage the region's diverse resources. Strongly worded clashes between environ-

October in Bend's Drake Park, Central Oregon

mental groups and the beef and timber industries have become frequent, among various other contentious issues. Oregon's famed, fiercely individualistic, pioneer spirit is freely expressed east of the Cascades!

Whether lobbying for expanded wilderness protection or guarding the continuity of a traditional ranching or logging lifestyle, residents of the region vigorously protect their "elbow room." This maverick attitude was shared by former Oregon governor Tom McCall, who grew up on a ranch in the sagebrush and rimrock country of Central Oregon. Outspoken and unconventional during his two terms (1967–1975), the tall, gravelly voiced Republican drew national media attention when he rumbled, "Come visit us again and again . . . but for heaven's sake, don't come here to live."

McCall's provocative comments were part of a welcoming message to thousands of Jaycees from across the nation, assembled at a 1971 convention in Portland's Civic Auditorium. His words, humorous but deadly seri-

Kayaking the Deschutes River in Bend, Central Oregon

ous, conveyed a dedication to protecting Oregon's environment and livability from unlimited, poorly planned development. These sentiments reveal a native affinity for the freedom afforded by wide, open spaces where neighbors are few and far between—a gritty viewpoint that matches the landscape.

While doing photography for this book in

An Invitation to Explore the Dry Side   **19**

Evening fishing in the Wallowa Valley, Northeastern Oregon

Farmland near Richland, Northeastern Oregon

rural districts, I was pleased to see that many formerly faltering communities, perhaps at one time bypassed by a freeway or economically crippled by the closing of their local lumber mill, are coming back to life. Citizen volunteers have pulled together and devised survival strategies that are proving successful. Some have acquired National Historic District status for their downtown areas, resulting in financial grants to refurbish beautiful brick buildings dating from the turn of the last century. Resultantly, this has attracted new residents seeking slower-paced, affordable places to live that provide a sense of traditional community.

I greatly enjoyed stopping at small cafés in these villages to eat and chat with the locals, while soaking up the atmosphere. I remember a chilly late afternoon in November 2004 when I drove through Union, scouting for photogenic storefronts. Glancing to my right, I noticed a sign in the window of the Main Street Eatery: "Our clam chowder voted best in Union County!" Being a chowder fan, I quickly parked and went inside, choosing a table with a view of Main Street. Soon a steaming bowl of some of the best clam chowder I've ever tasted was placed in front of me by the friendly head chef and owner, Richard Loose. His wife, Venice, joined us for a conversation about the gratifications of small-town life. While we talked, families strolled the sidewalk outside, their arms laden with full shopping bags from the nearby mom-and-pop grocery store. Children cruised up and down the street on their bicycles, and pickup trucks passed by, driven by farmers in town for a Friday evening. It was easy to see that Union is alive and well.

Whenever possible, it's preferable to geardown and get off the interstate freeways. Meandering secondary highways can lead

June rainstorm over Zumwalt Prairie and the distant Wallowa Mountains, Northeastern Oregon

to charming interludes like the one I had in Union. Each turn in the road brings changing vistas and the unexpected. Combining such excursions with the impressive scenery and bracing climate, you'll be compelled to venture outdoors and explore enticing hiking trails. Indeed, with an intensely blue sky above, the heady aroma of sagebrush in the air, and the beckoning calls of magpies in the junipers, who could resist becoming better acquainted with Oregon's dry side?

If you are a first-time explorer here, I'm somewhat envious. Many surprises and wonderful adventures await you. Hopefully, the descriptions and illustrations in this book will prove valuable for your excursions. It's easy to overuse adjectives when trying to impart a sense of what it's like to experience these unfettered landscapes—gazing off the rim of Steens Mountain's Kiger Gorge; rafting the rapids of the Deschutes River; sitting by a sagebrush campfire under a starry high desert firmament; cresting Glacier Pass on a Wallowa backpacking trip; watching transfixed as hundreds of snow geese suddenly take to startled flight at Malheur National Wildlife Refuge. Words often seem frustratingly inadequate and only hint at the real thing.

Nevertheless, perhaps it was all summed up best by a visitor from Japan. While doing consulting work in 1984 for Fuji Broadcasting during the filming of a television series in Central Oregon, I happened to ride out to the location with one of the directors. I speak no Japanese and he spoke very little English.

After ascertaining through short, monosyllabic conversation and sign language that he had toured some of Oregon's most scenic areas east of the Cascades, I asked him what he thought of it all. There was a moment of silence while he intently searched his mind for a way to express his impressions. Then he decisively spread his arms wide and said with strong conviction, "Big!"

PART I

The Dry Side: A Natural History

Why is Oregon's Dry Side Dry?

The Cascade Range successfully blocks a large portion of the wet, moderating air that moves inland from the Pacific Ocean, creating to the east of the mountains a pronounced rainshadow—a leeward dry side. While some locations in the humid coastal forests of Oregon can record nearly 130 inches of precipitation in a year, the arid Alvord Desert in Southeastern Oregon may sometimes receive as little as five inches. Milder temperatures generally prevail to the west of the Cascade crest, whereas the intermountain region of Oregon claims a typical continental climate with warm, dry summers and cold, snowy winters. Consequently, much of this area supports scant vegetation.

Although it is popularly referred to as the high desert, many botanists and ecologists would say this regional colloquialism is inaccurate. Places with less than ten inches of annual precipitation are commonly called deserts, but things are a bit more complex than this. Experts postulate various technical delineations explaining the conditions that create a true desert. But if we cut through the complexity and focus on the common denominators in these scientific treatises, two key factors emerge—very low rainfall, paired with evaporation that is always greater than precipitation.

By this definition, some of the seriously dry basins in the southeastern corner of the state are bona fide true deserts. Most of Oregon's open country east of the Cascades, however, lacks this severe degree of aridity and actually falls under the ecological classification of sagebrush steppe. The rather nebulous, catch-all high desert designation gathers together an enormous drylands area of the American West containing sagebrush plains, grassy prairies, alkali flats, sand dunes, brushy salt scrub, extensive marshes, fault block mountains, sparse juniper woodlands, and bordering pine forests. Thus, although not strictly correct, the vivid "high desert" label provides a handy package for an otherwise unwieldy collection of ecosystems. And the natural heritage of this diverse section of the Northwest is a rich one to explore.

Whatever the proper terminology, when compared with Western Oregon's damp, heavily wooded landscapes, much of the central and eastern parts of the state appears decidedly desertlike. Two completely different worlds coexist within Oregon: one of misty, balmy breezes, born of the wide sea and delicate, verdant growing things—the other of high, dry desert winds, bearing the tang of juniper and sage and the echoes of spacious solitude.

The moisture-trapping Cascade Range creates a pronounced rainshadow of dryness to the east. The volcanic crest of the Cascades, Three Sisters Wilderness, Central Oregon. Photo: George Wuerthner

Geological Underpinnings

I knew this now, through and through. I might not yet understand the explicit, absolute meaning of two hundred million years. But I had come to grips with the kind of geology I had hoped to find. I had begun at last to hear the rhythm of the rock.

COLIN FLETCHER
The Man Who Walked Through Time, 1967

To better understand why Oregon's various regions east of the Cascades differ so dramatically from the western parts of the state, we must look into the prehistoric past and trace the foundational history of the entire region.

It will help if we can radically alter our perspective for a few moments.

Imagine that you are hovering several miles above Oregon with a grand view of it all. Also imagine that you have gone back in time about 200 million years to the end of the Triassic period. One of the first things glaringly apparent from this ancient vantage point is that what we now call Oregon does not exist, except as the floor of a shallow sea. The western edge of the North American continent has not yet moved into its present position.

Plate tectonics

Although many theories regarding the origins of present-day landforms may differ and change, the hypothesis of plate tectonics has achieved wide and stable acceptance since it was

Pages 22–23: Classic semiarid "high desert" landscape: sagebrush-bunchgrass steppelands, basalt rimrock, and basin marshes, with western juniper on the uplands. Malheur National Wildlife Refuge below Steens Mountain, Southeastern Oregon. Inset: Western fence lizard. Deschutes River Canyon, Central Oregon

Opposite: The Cascade Range is the most recent chain of inland volcanic mountains to form in Oregon as a result of subduction. Pictured is Crater Creek flowing out of the caldera of Broken Top, a volcano that last erupted about 100,000 years ago.

first proposed in the mid 1960s. In a nutshell, the concept holds that our seemingly rock-solid continents are not as firmly fixed beneath our feet as they appear.

Like an egg with a badly cracked shell, the crust of the earth is divided into a number of gigantic pieces, called plates. Geologists subdivide these into two basic types: one, the oceanic plates, submerged underwater and built of densely hardened lava that wells up from cracks on the ocean floor; the other, thicker continental plates composed of less dense types of rock. Both oceanic and continental plates float slowly about the planet atop dense interior rocks so superheated by the earth's molten interior that they are like soft, malleable clay. This gradual plate movement (just an inch or two a year) is called continental drift. As can be imagined, when huge sections of the earth's crust collide and grind against each other, colossal events unfold.

Around 200 to 140 million years ago, the North American continent broke away from what is now Europe and northern Africa and started moving westward. Consequently, the geologic phenomenon known as subduction began to create the Oregon we see today.

It is the same ongoing process of subduction that is still taking place as you read these lines of text. Similar to other convulsing tectonic rift lines around the world, the western edge of the North American continental plate buckles upward as the oceanic Juan de Fuca plate, in its inch-by-inch eastward migration, slides under it. And as the plate disappears under North America and is absorbed into the bowels of the earth, sedimentary debris scrapes off the disappearing seafloor and accumulates along the seam. At this developing shoreline, over millions of years, the slow buildup will create a mountain range on the coast while concurrently a parallel volcanic chain of mountains will form some distance inland.

A volcanic range arises because of a somewhat unnerving fact: a mere sixty miles or so of the earth's crust separates us from a raging inferno below. Today, as the Juan de Fuca plate angles downward, it eventually reaches the hotter depths of the earth under the continent at a point about one hundred miles inland. Here, seawater carried down in the descending plate migrates up into the overlying mantle and partially melts it. Rising blobs of magma float upward and eventually make it to the surface, where they will erupt. This process has repeated itself whenever the subduction zone relocated, and over millions of years, new coastal extensions gradually become the interior ranges. Examples of coastal and inland ranges are the northeastern Blue Mountain complex, the currently active volcanic Cascade Range, and the Coast Range Mountains.

However, there are more complex influences that also contribute to the whole; but geological investigations into the transformations that have produced Oregon east of the Cascades are extremely difficult. This is because much of the evidence from the distant past has been covered and hidden by extensive lava flows. The challenges facing geologists could be compared to our attempting to assemble a puzzle while many of the puzzle's pieces are lost under the table we are working on.

One thing is reasonably certain: 200 million years ago, the region's coastline was more or less located in the vicinity of what is now the western border of Idaho. But that dramatically changed about 100 million years later.

Exotic terranes

Adding more pieces to the puzzle is the theory of "exotic terranes." This geological term refers to a grouping of related rock that via plate tectonics gradually moved from its original position and was incorporated into another landmass. This concept proposes that one such terrane—an ancient chain of tropical islands and coral reefs—existed in the middle of the Pacific Ocean (as postulated by some geologists, possibly around the same latitude as the present-day Hawaiian Islands). Beginning about 400 million years ago in the early Devonian period and evolving through several incarnations, these bits of land gradually accumulated within them mongrel pedigrees consisting of parts of volcanic islands, coral reef limestones, sandstones, granites, and other materials. When these built-up island groups collided with the inexorably westward-moving North American continent, they were scraped off the oceanic plate and subsequently incorporated into the larger American landmass.

Two of these roving archipelago terranes are referred to by geologists as the Blue Mountain island arc and the Klamath island arc, and they "docked" on the prehistoric coast and created the first dry lands of Oregon. Their dawning origins can be traced back 400 million years, bestowing upon them the honor of containing the oldest rocks in the state. After several million years as offshore islands, these terranes finally slammed into the creeping continental plate. Combined with the westward-building process of subduction, the wandering islands became part of the West Coast of North America.

This merging took place about 135 million years ago in the general vicinity of northwestern California, extending northward sufficiently to create a good portion of the southwestern section of Oregon. Close on its tectonic heels, around 100 million years ago, the Blue Mountain island arc moved into the neighborhood and much of Northeastern Oregon was born.

Later, during this middle Cretaceous period, waves washed upon the warm, tropical shores of a neonacent Oregon coast that meandered from the Blue Mountains to the Siskiyou Mountains. As geologist Ellen Morris Bishop writes in her fascinating book, *In Search of Ancient Oregon*, "The primeval, palm-fringed shoreline ran from Mitchell southwest to Medford, curving into flat-bottomed bays and broad beaches with a shallow sea offshore. Dayville and Grants Pass might have been seaports."

Thus, the westward-building process of subduction had help from these wandering exotic islands in creating the West Coast. Oregon appears to be a patched-together conglomeration of original seabeds, rock from distant locations, and lava flows.

To further add to the geologist's daunting task of making sense of the landscape's long history, terrestrial chaos has usually reigned along the subduction zones where the exotic island terranes arrive. It is as though a monumental train wreck of disparate kinds of stone careened off the tracks into a gaping chasm. Some varieties are left strewn about the brink of the precipice in clear view, while others have been swallowed up and secreted in its depths. Add to this other forces such as monstrous pressures that transform rocks into entirely different substances, liquefying heat, and all manner of formidable convulsions that whirlpool everything in all directions, and you have a sleuthing task worthy of

Columnar basalt in John Day Fossil Beds National Monument, Sheep Rock Unit. This site reveals a layered history of regional lava eruptions, the Picture Gorge flows in the foreground dating from 16 million years ago, to the more recent 5 million-year-old Rattlesnake tuff layer on the far skyline. Northeastern Oregon

Basalt rimrocks are a signature feature of the landscapes of Oregon's dry side. Fort Rock Valley area, Central Oregon

Sherlock Holmes. Fortunately for geologists, this jumbled geologic layer cake has gradually undergone warping uplifts and eroding canyon slicings to expose bits and pieces as visual clues.

Lava mega-floods

Reaching from the Eocene into the Oligocene, 50 to 28 million years ago, a series of volcanoes spewed lava and ash in Northeastern Oregon and the Mutton Mountains–Powell Buttes areas of Central Oregon. But this was merely a small prelude compared to the coming conflagration. During the Miocene, a span of time from 24 to 5 million years ago, an incredibly active volcanic period set the stage for what would eventually become the present-day visual signature of Oregon's

Autumn storm over Steens Mountain and Mann Lake. Sixteen million years ago, this area in Southeastern Oregon was ground zero for an explosive eruption of lava flows that spread as far as Idaho, Washington, and the Pacific Ocean.

dry side—lava formations. Nearly everywhere the eye may wander, far or near, one's gaze will ultimately come to rest upon brooding, dark basalt, whether in the form of rimrock, stolid buttes, cinder cones, or lava beds. Less extensively, other Miocene volcanic rock can be seen as pale cliffs of rhyolite, gray andesite layers, and eroded spires of golden to brick-red tuffs.

Initially, a combination of lava eruptions and blanketing ash in Southeastern Oregon opened the dawn of the Miocene. Following this, about 16 to 15 million years ago, even larger flows of lava issued from several locations in the Columbia Plateau and Southeastern Oregon. Nothing in Oregon's long geological history matches the magnitude of this fiery era when volcanoes and huge cracks disgorged a series of lava mega-floods.

Various reasons for this Miocene meltdown have been put forth. One of the more compelling proposals, dubbed the Yellowstone hot spot theory, is supported by several authorities. The idea contends that, like a festering boil just under the continental plate surface, this stationary, sizzling thin spot traces the creeping westward movement of North America above it with explosive eruptions. Glowering a mere five miles beneath earth's surface, the crustal weak site of percolating magma is presently under northwestern Wyoming, creating Yellowstone National Park's spouting geysers and other volcanic wonders. But around 16 million years ago, the continental plate had not progressed as far west, positioning the hot spot below what is now Steens Mountain in Southeastern Oregon.

The Steens ground-zero explosive force

Leslie Gulch contains many picturesque examples of the eroded tuff formations that are common throughout the Owyhee River Canyon of Southeastern Oregon. These colorful tuff deposits were formed by compacted collections of volcanic ash, pumice, and other debris.

Hot springs are fairly common in the geologically faulted basin and range country of Southeastern Oregon. Mickey Hot Spring, Alvord Basin

sent a crust-shattering network of deep, lava-belching fissures outward. This holocaust of fast-moving basalt flows spread its molten tentacles into adjacent Idaho, north to Washington, and even westward to the distant shores of the Pacific Ocean. Some experts believe that 80 percent of the lava poured out in a 2-million-year period—the mere blink of an eye relative to the earth's geologic time scale. When it ceased, half of Oregon east of the Cascades had become a vast, rolling plain of basalt that was nearly three miles thick in some places.

In the final twilight of the Miocene, some 12 to 5 million years ago, the ever-westerly inching movement of the continental plate had caused a tectonic repositioning that situated the Yellowstone hot spot under southern Idaho. This shift resulted in a lessening of volcanic activity in the eastern portions of Oregon. However, there was one final Miocene volcanic hurrah. After several comparatively small to moderate eruptions in Southeastern Oregon, a devastatingly large outpouring from a vent occurred about 7 million years ago near present-day Burns. The resulting eruptive cloud buried a good portion of the eastern parts of the state in a deep layer of welded ash called the Rattlesnake tuff. Around this same time, to the west, the Cascade chain moved into an active phase of volcanism.

AT ABOUT 6 million years ago, Northeastern Oregon began to undergo slow, wrenching changes. Like the crowns of sprouting mushrooms breaking through soil crust, uplifts caused the long-hidden exotic terranes of the Blue Mountain island arc to push through the covering basalt and expose their ancient rocks. This was the birthing of the Elkhorns, Wallowas, and other adjacent ranges.

Big Sand Gap along the low, eastern escarpment of the Alvord Desert. With its soaring opposite western escarpment of Steens Mountain, the Alvord Basin is a good example of a fault-produced, sunken graben valley. Southeastern Oregon

By the late Miocene, Oregon had more or less assumed the same general form that we see today. The climate shifted away from warm–temperate to a somewhat cooler environment with well-defined seasons.

Next came the Pliocene period (spanning 5 to 1.8 million years ago), during which the climate in the Northwest region became generally wetter. The run-off from heavy precipitation made a significant contribution to sculpting Oregon's landscapes and greatly accelerated the erosion of river valleys and canyons. The state's major river systems—such as the Columbia, Snake, Owyhee, John Day, and Deschutes drainages—carved their way through the layered lava, creating the basis for the valleys, canyons, and gorges we see today. More volcanic activity in the Cascades continued to lay the groundwork for the later higher crest of peaks and their moisture-blocking rainshadow.

Throughout the Pliocene, other forces were at work to refine and shape the country east of the Cascades into the modern-day geologic landforms. In Southeastern Oregon, tectonic spreading caused huge sections of the basalt lava plain to rise and tilt along north-south fracture zones. Classic examples of these fault block mountains include Steens Mountain, Hart Mountain, and Abert Rim. In some situations, where two faults ran closely parallel, the land between dropped, forming a graben—a basin valley bordered on each side by rock escarpments. The Alvord Basin below Steens Mountain's eastern face and the Warner Valley along the western side of Hart Mountain are good examples of the graben landform. These distinctive landscapes of enormous, alternating humps and depressions are seen throughout the interior North American West, from Oregon to Mexico. In geological parlance, this vast region is referred to as the basin and range physiographic province.

Wallowa Lake in Northeastern Oregon is an excellent example of a glacially excavated reservoir. Photo: David Jensen

Kiger Gorge on Steens Mountain, a typical glacial canyon. Southeastern Oregon

Glacially polished granite—the grinding "tracks" of ancient ice sheets that scoured the bedrock. Wallowa Mountains, Northeastern Oregon

The Ice Age

An even more dramatic shift in climate sculpted the landscape during the Pleistocene, 1.8 million to 10,000 years ago, when global cooling prevailed. Glacial ice sheets covered much of the northern regions of the continent and slowly gouged and sandpapered their way across the land. Overall during the Pleistocene, geologists speculate that ice sheets may have advanced and retreated as many as thirty times as the climate alternately warmed and cooled.

In the Northwest, this ice-locked world extended into the northerly portions of Washington, Idaho, and Montana. Spokane would have been situated near the southern terminus of the enlarged Pleistocene polar cap, with breathtaking views of towering walls of ice that may have been a half-mile thick. In Oregon, large, isolated glaciers formed in the Cascade, Blue, and Wallowa ranges and extended from the higher elevations down to the foothills. Farther south, even Steens Mountain in Southeastern Oregon had its own glaciers.

These glaciers scoured out their hallmark signatures in the form of U-shaped canyons. By the end of this frozen era, when temperatures had begun to climb, the ice receded and sometimes created lakes behind the bulldozed earth that glaciers deposited—a terminal moraine. In Northeastern Oregon, Wallowa Lake provides a textbook perfect example of this type of glacially dammed reservoir; and Kiger Gorge on Steens Mountain exemplifies a typical glacial canyon.

During the last 800,000 years, various eruptions along the Cascade Range caused an alternating clash between fire and ice. This marked the creation of most of the familiar, snowcapped western skyline of Central Oregon. Additionally, the latter part of the Pleistocene hosted some limited volcanic activity in Southeastern Oregon during a span of about 25,000 to 17,000 years ago. These relatively small volcanoes created the basalt lava beds of Diamond Craters and Jordan Craters.

During the frigid grasp of each Ice Age, large lakes formed in the landlocked basins of Southeastern Oregon. Today, we see only the remnants of these extensive bodies of water: Malheur, Harney, Abert, Summer, Warner, Goose, and Klamath lakes. In extremely arid sections, only parched alkali flats, sand dunes, and ancient, wave-cut terraces bear stark testimony to these prehistoric lakes.

Toward the end of the Pleistocene, giant dams of glacial ice formed to the northeast of Oregon in western Montana, impounding an enormous reservoir—3,000-square-mile Lake Missoula, with depths of nine hundred feet. Repeatedly, during a period from 19,000 to 13,000 years ago, these blockages broke free. Floods of mind-boggling proportions swept down the Columbia River drainage through what is now northern Idaho, then westward into Washington and Oregon.

These deluges, known as the Missoula floods, carried immense icebergs containing rocks and other glacial debris that acted like titanic battering rams, devastating everything in their paths. Whole forests, along with the soils they grew in, were stripped from the earth and carried away. Rocks known as glacial erratics, rafted by ice from distant Montana, remain visible today as far west as the Willamette Valley. Additionally, a similar gargantuan flood was caused by Lake Bonneville 14,500 years ago. Ranked among the largest of Pleistocene lakes, Bonneville covered much of the northern Great Basin. Great Salt Lake in northwestern Utah is one of its remnant puddles. Glacial meltwaters caused

A hiker approaches the summit of South Sister in the Three Sisters Wilderness of Central Oregon. Scientists are monitoring a nearby, gradual swelling caused by underground magma buildup.

the lake to rise and erode a spillway north into Idaho. Geologists estimate that a flow of one million cubic yards of water per second submerged the Snake River Valley and roared westward through the narrow portal of Hells Canyon into the Columbia Basin of Washington and Oregon.

Recent eruptions

In the current Holocene epoch, which began 10,000 years ago at the end of the Pleistocene Ice Age, there have been some relatively recent eruptions with lava flows. Mount Mazama, which originally topped out at over twelve thousand feet in elevation, had its most recent explosion 7,600 years ago, creating Crater Lake. Still closer to the present, there was a series of eruptions within the last 7,000 years in Central Oregon at Newberry Crater, Lava Butte, Lava Cast Forest, the Three Sisters peaks area, Belknap Crater, and

Sand Mountain. Of these, many geologists believe that the youngest lava flow was probably at Newberry Crater, southeast of Bend. This 1,300-year-old eruption produced a lava flow of pumice and obsidian, commonly called volcanic glass.

Newberry's sparkling obsidian beds may not continue to hold the record of being Oregon's most youthful rocks. In 2001, a U.S. Geological Survey geologist discovered a broad swelling in the Three Sisters area west of Bend. Further study revealed that the swelling began in 1997 and continues to this day over an area of more than a hundred square miles. Larry Chitwood, geologist for the Deschutes National Forest, graphically described what is happening: "The center of the Sisters Bulge rises the thickness of a nickel every twenty days (that's 1.5 inches per year). This swelling is due to magma slowly filling a chamber four miles down. Groups of small earthquakes shake the local USGS seismographs as deep rocks break and adjust to the swelling. No one knows when or if the bulge will erupt. Stay tuned."

Newberry National Volcanic Monument

The majority of Oregon's dry side is of volcanic origin, and nowhere is this more evident than in the central region. A good place to see examples of this is in Newberry National Volcanic Monument, which gathers an amazing array of geologic features within its 55,000 acres. Included are some of the youngest lava flows within the continental United States (other than at Mount St. Helens in Washington).

The monument's Lava Lands Visitor Center is located 10 miles south of Bend, just off the west side of Highway 97. Its excellent interpretive exhibits not only tell the fascinating story of the area's geology, but also inform about the archaeology and native flora and fauna. Brochures about the monument are available, along with a shop selling books and maps pertaining to the local region. Staff and volunteers are available to answer questions, and nature walks and presentations are offered as well.

Outside, the most eye-catching formation is Lava Butte, rising five hundred feet above surrounding lava beds. This open, reddish-colored promontory is a typical cinder cone located along a fissure that channeled molten lava to the surface. From the visitor center a road winds to the top of this butte, where there are interpretive displays and a Forest Service fire lookout tower (parking is tight, so no large vehicles are allowed). A quarter-mile viewing trail follows the rim of the 180-foot-deep crater and provides 360-degree views of the surrounding country, including the snowy volcanic peaks of the Cascade Range to the west.

Spreading immediately below are approximately ten square miles of dark, twisted lava that flowed from Lava Butte when it erupted about 7,000 years ago. Behind the visitor center, the paved, wheelchair-friendly Trail of the Molten Lands meanders through the lava beds for a three-quarter-mile loop. Scattered along the path are informational signs that bring the geological history to life. Don't forget your camera, as there are a number of photogenically twisted pines growing zenlike from the lava. You also may want to visit Benham Falls on the Deschutes River, a 4-mile drive from the Lava Lands entrance, west on Forest Service Road 9702. A path leads across a bridge, tracing the river's edge through shady pines for three-quarters of a mile to the site. Not a typical vertical falls, it is a series

Late evening on Paulina Peak. Below is Paulina Lake in Newberry Crater, with the peaks of the Cascade Range on the far western skyline.

of surging rapids that plunge down through a narrow, rocky channel. When lava flowed westward from the ancient Lava Butte eruption, it blocked the river and created a naturally dammed lake that extended south to present-day Sunriver. Eventually, this reservoir disappeared when water gradually cut the outlet that is now Benham Falls.

On the east side of Highway 97 and one mile south of the Lava Lands Visitor Center is Lava River Cave. This one-mile-long lava tube features stairs that provide access to a brochure-guided, sandy trail that penetrates the entire length. Lava River Cave is one of the longest uncollapsed lava tubes in the Northwest region. It's also a great place to explore during the hot summer because the cave's constant air temperature is a nippy 42 degrees. Even on a stifling August day, bring a warm coat, along with a dependable flashlight. After progressing for 1,500 feet inside the tube, you'll be eighty feet directly below Highway 97.

To the southeast, rising to nearly eight thousand feet, the forested heights of Newberry Volcano form the focal point of the monument. The varying peaks of this collapsed volcano, also called the Paulina Mountains, rise above slopes scattered with many interesting volcanic features. Nearly four hundred cinder cones on the volcano's flanks give the mountain a bumpy, uneven appearance.

During a period dating back approximately 7,000 years, several lava flows spilled down the mountainside, engulfing and burning forests in their paths. One such flow on the north slope enveloped trees, cooling and hardening around them. The charred wood eventually rotted away, leaving molds of the vanished trees. This is the Lava Cast Forest, accessed by a 9-mile length of gravel road (Forest Service 9720) that turns to the east off Highway 97 by the Sunriver exit. A mile-long paved trail loops through the area and gives visitors a glimpse into a fiery past era. In contrast, present-day ponderosa pines and bitterbrush are gradually reclaiming the lava-covered environment.

Some of the most scenically dramatic sections of the monument are found within the huge crater of the volcano itself. Drive 23.5 miles south of Bend on Highway 97, or 7 miles north of La Pine, if you're traveling from that direction. Then turn east on paved County Road 21, and it's a gradual 12.3-mile climb to where Paulina Creek flows out of the interior of the bowl-shaped mountaintop. At the bowl's rim, the creek spills sixty feet down an andesite cliff as a double waterfall. Paulina Creek Falls is quite beautiful and well worth a stop to enjoy one of the overlooks, or take a quarter-mile hike down a trail to the mist-drenched rocks at the foot of the cascading water.

Just upstream from the falls, the road enters the volcano's spectacular, five-mile-wide caldera, which cradles two large lakes. To obtain an initial overview of Newberry Crater, continue a quarter mile and turn right (south) on a gravel road that leads 4 miles to the summit of Paulina Peak. This 7,985-foot viewpoint (the highest elevation in the monument) provides sweeping vistas of East Lake and Paulina Lake in the seventeen-square-mile caldera, the Cascade Range far to the west, and the desert country to the southeast. Clearly evident is Central Pumice Cone rising between the lakes, with the adjacent Interlake Obsidian Flow. On the southern side of the caldera is the Big Obsidian Flow—at 1,300 years old, the most recent lava flow in Oregon. Archaeological investigations inside Newberry Crater have disclosed that Native Americans have come to these huge beds of "volcanic glass" for more than 10,000 years. They used obsidian for the making of arrowheads and cutting tools because it is capable of producing a fractured edge sharper than a modern surgeon's metal scalpel. This valuable commodity was traded with other tribes throughout the entire Northwest region.

There are more than 60 miles of hiking trails in the monument, with the longest and most panoramic being the 21-mile Crater Rim Trail around the entire perimeter of the volcano's crest. There are seven Forest Service campgrounds (one with a lakeside hot spring) that provide an opportunity to sleep inside a dormant volcano. Two old-fashioned rustic resorts, one at each lake, provide rental cabins, groceries, cafés, boat rentals, and fishing supplies. The Paulina Lake Resort is open through the winter, being snowbound three miles beyond the end of the cleared highway. Access is via their Sno-Cat shuttle, or on your own snowmobile, cross-country skis, or snowshoes. ■

Shifting environments and fossil records

The vast spans of time we have been examining with their dramatic geological and climatic changes gave rise to totally different ecosystems in Oregon, each with its own flora and fauna. Cataclysmic transformations such as moving continents, lava inundations, freezing Ice Ages, and apocalyptic floods exterminated entire plant and animal communities while successive new life forms adapted. Relative to these expansive epochs, human life spans seem but mere seconds in duration. This myopic snapshot of our current familiar environment with its modern species can foster an inaccurate perception of unchanging surroundings. But the fossil record tells us otherwise. The stone pages of this paleontological book of life give evidence of prehistoric realms when Oregon's botany and zoology were vastly different from today.

Returning to our initial imaginary 200-million-year-old viewpoint, a session of late-Triassic wildlife watching would be limited to marine creatures. Probably one of the most noticeable animals inhabiting the warm, shallow sea that covered the entire region would have been a reptile—the sleek ichthyosaur. Resembling a large dolphin equipped with a long, narrow, sharp-toothed snout, this fast-swimming predator fed on fish, squids, and other sea life. Pterosaurs, flying reptiles that foreshadowed birds, may have launched outward from the primordial coastline of western Idaho and soared salty breezes above Oregon's ancient sea. So far, there are no verifying fossils of these winged creatures from the area during the Triassic.

Oregon's first terrestrial life

By the middle of the Cretaceous period, around 100 million years ago, dry land existed in Oregon. Scant evidence has been found to reveal what sorts of animal life were native to this ancient terrain. There is a single 1927 record of some Cretaceous fossil fragments found near Mitchell, in Central Oregon, confirming that pterosaurs had definitely spread to Oregon by this period. Some

The colorful ash beds of the John Day country are considered to be among the finest fossil areas in the world. John Day Fossil Beds National Monument, Painted Hills Unit, Central Oregon

species in this group had wingspans of nearly forty feet; they are the largest-known flying animals of all time. Apparently, the Oregon pterosaur was a smaller, raven-sized variety.

The same Mitchell sediments also tell us that sharks swam the offshore seawaters of the Cretaceous. Recent finds show that other creatures inhabited these prehistoric Oregon waters. In the summer of 2004, two amateur paleontologists, Greg Kovalchuk and Mike Kelly, discovered fossil fragments of a plesiosaur near Prineville—the first ever recorded in the Pacific Northwest. These long-necked, flippered marine reptiles with rotund bodies and conical tails were the largest predators in their aquatic environment, some species reaching total lengths of nearly fifty feet. A 2005 Bureau of Land Management paleontological excavation of the site turned up still more plesiosaur fossils. The entire collection of specimens is currently being studied by scientists, and their delvings may shed new light on the dim Cretaceous past in Oregon.

Although it is well documented that during this period dinosaurs of many species and sizes were plentiful to the east in nearby Montana, no fossil proof of their occurrence in the interior parts of Oregon has ever been discovered. Some experts theorize that mountainous barriers may have kept dinosaurs from ranging into the Pacific Northwest.

Nevertheless, considering the warm, life-supporting climate that prevailed throughout the Cretaceous, it is highly probable that a variety of animals pioneered Oregon's relatively new landscapes. The period's plant fossil record is more extensive, clearly showing that palms and huge tree ferns grew along the coast, and the uplands supported forests of ginkgo, pine, oak, maple, and alder. It may seem odd when contemplated from our modern viewpoint, but grass species had not yet come into existence, and the newly evolved flowering plants had only recently spread to Oregon.

Despite the lack of concrete evidence that numerous animal species inhabited Oregon during the Cretaceous, we know that elsewhere around the planet the period was marked by an explosion of life in an astonishing multitude of forms. But this extravagance abruptly ended.

Global catastrophe favors the first mammals

Around 65 million years ago, a dead zone appears in the fossil record. It distinctly marks the culmination of the Cretaceous and the beginning of the Paleocene. Scientists estimate that a planet-wide catastrophe snuffed out 70 percent of all animal life on land and sea, including total extinction of dinosaurs. Plant life was greatly decimated as well.

What was the cause?

Most authorities now agree that all clues point to the probability that the earth sustained multiple impacts from a group of meteorites. At least one of them was quite large, perhaps as much as ten miles across. Like telltale fingerprints at the scene of a crime, a narrow layer of pulverized clay bears witness to the conflagration's resulting dust cloud, which settled over our planet's surface. Not only does this slim ribbon of clay reside exactly at the expected strata level of 65 million years ago, it also contains iridium—extremely rare on the earth's surface, but a major component of meteorites.

Like a spreading fog of death, the dust clouds thrown into the atmosphere from the exploding meteorites not only obliterated the sun, they also contained sulfuric components that created toxic acid rain. Additionally, the incinerating collisions undoubtedly ignited huge, smoky forest fires that increased the density of the sun-shroud, while the shock of the impacts caused coastal regions to be swept by immense tsunami waves.

The planet was plunged into a lethal frozen gloom. Conjecture proposes scenarios of anywhere from months to many years of this stifling, prolonged winter. But life is tenacious. In protected nooks and crannies, various small species of hardy animals and plants managed to survive.

Among this struggling remnant, a group of relative newcomers stirred in the ashes. These were tiny, primitive mammals, which may seem insignificant when compared to the extirpated dinosaurs. But warm-blooded crea-

The Painted Hills, John Day Fossil Beds National Monument

tures with insulating coats of fur had the advantage in the new, frigid environment. The mousy meek were poised to inherit the earth.

Staggered by the blow, global life faltered for nearly 10 million years through the Paleocene. Slowly, conditions warmed and flora and fauna began to thrive and diversify. By 45 million years ago in the mid Eocene, things were toasty-warm and the Pacific Northwest was covered with lush, subtropical forests. Although originating from humble beginnings, ancestors of the small furred survivors of this meteorite-induced Cretaceous holocaust prospered. Branching into an astonishing multitude of forms, the mammals came into ascendancy.

This mild, balmy era prevailed until the beginning of the Oligocene, some 34 million years ago, when conditions suddenly shifted toward a cooler and drier temperate climate. Some scientists speculate that this was possibly caused by atmospheric dust from another meteorite-related collision, in tandem with volcanic-spewed ash. Again, life on the planet diminished, though less severely than with the previous cosmic cataclysm. The global cooling trend continued on through the Miocene and Pliocene, culminating in the Pleistocene's Ice Age.

The John Day fossil archives

Layer by layer, paleontologists have traced these climatic transitions and their subsequent life-forms in Oregon's various geologic strata—most notably in the John Day coun-

Oreodont skull imbedded in strata of the John Day formation. John Day Fossil Beds National Monument, Sheep Rock Unit, Northeastern Oregon

Giraffe-like deer, peccaries, large rhinoceroses, and massive mastodon elephants moved through the prairies and scattered woodlands of oak, walnut, maple, cherry, elm, and sequoia. Higher elevations supported coniferous forests of pine, fir, spruce, and hemlock. Oreodonts of several species, resembling furred, oversized hogs with prominently sharp teeth, were particularly common in the region. Predators of a number of varieties also prowled this long-ago land, such as saber-toothed cats, early forms of dogs, bears, weasels, and martens.

Ice Age flora and fauna

The frozen era of the Pleistocene is well represented in Oregon's fossil record, particularly in the ancient lakebeds of Southeastern Oregon. Towering woolly mammoths, twelve-foot-tall ground sloths, shaggy rhinoceroses, giant-sized bison, bears, wolves, beaver, and other oversized, cold-adapted megafauna dwelled in the chilled environment of this epoch. Forests of fir, spruce, cedar, and pine, mixed with groves of quaking aspen, adjoined open, grassy savannas where horses of several species grazed, along with camels and giant bighorn sheep. Large numbers of bird bones of many species have been retrieved from the shifting sands of Fossil Lake's parched basin in the high desert of northwestern Lake County. These finds are indicative of the rich avian fauna that were attracted to the waters of the region's abundant Pleistocene lakes.

By the close of the Ice Age, 12,000 to 10,000 years ago, conditions in the Pacific Northwest began to trend toward a temperate climate. This resulted in familiar ecosystems, with their typical flora and fauna, which we see today east of the Cascades in Oregon.

try, an area considered to be one of the world's most important fossil-bearing archives. Here, in the multicolored bands of the Clarno, John Day, Mascall, and Rattlesnake formations, is plentiful evidence marking the region's botanical and zoological past.

The fossil beds of these sediments tell us of the Eocene's hot, subtropical forests of palm, banana, fig, avocado, kiwi, cashew, magnolia, sycamore, cinnamon, and coffee trees. Roaming these verdant landscapes were such exotic creatures as tigerlike saber-toothed predators, miniature forest horses with toed feet, tapirs, small rhinoceroses, lemurs, crocodiles, alligators, and enormous lumbering tortoises.

Fossils from the Oligocene, Miocene, and Pliocene layers reveal the dramatic shift from a subtropical world to progressively more temperate climates with extensive areas of dry, open grasslands. Animals suited to grazing became dominant: an ancestral form of the pronghorn (often confused with the antelope, which we will discuss a bit later), camels, and larger, more advanced types of horses.

Thomas Condon, frontier paleontologist

While chasing a band of warring Indians through the upper reaches of the Crooked River drainage in July of 1864, U.S. cavalrymen made an interesting discovery: fossilized seashells embedded in an outcrop of gravelly sedimentary rock.

Intrigued by the discovery of marine shells in this high, semiarid region of sagebrush and juniper, Captain John M. Drake sent specimens to Fort Dalles on the Columbia River. He knew the missionary pastor at The Dalles Congregational Church would be interested in these fossils. This unusual man of God, Thomas Condon, often roamed the hills behind the frontier town, carrying both a Bible and a geology pick, seeking inspiration for his sermons and studying rock formations. Along with a deep commitment to spread the Christian gospel, he also had an intense fascination with geology and ancient fossils.

Condon's scientific zeal was so contagious that Drake's entire unit of hardened soldiers combed the hills that day for more specimens. In the letter that accompanied the fossils, Drake told Condon, "I found our camp converted into a vast geological cabinet: everybody had been gathering rocks."

During autumn of the following year, the pastor was allowed to accompany the next army detail traveling into the then largely unexplored interior of Oregon. The cavalry was acting as a protective escort for a caravan bringing supplies to the Harney Basin in Southeastern Oregon.

On the return trip to The Dalles, the group passed through the John Day Basin. Condon

Thomas Condon, circa 1895. Courtesy of the Division of Special Collections and University Archives, University of Oregon Libraries

was captivated by the picturesque, brightly colored hillsides eroded into fascinating columns and rounded domes. Before long, he had found several excellent fossil specimens. His discerning eye could plainly see where the river had cut down through the topmost layer of basalt lava and then, below that, into the soft, ashy deposits with their bands of red, yellow, green, and buff. It was apparent that these strata represented vast periods of time from long-gone ages past.

The pastor soon returned to the area and began unlocking the secrets contained within these sun-baked hillsides. Throughout several subsequent trips, Condon discovered numerous fossilized remains of animals and plants no longer native to the region. Proof unfolded of a past age of lush, subtropical forests inhabited by giant cats, rhinoceroses, immense bear-dog creatures, ancestral tapirs and pigs,

Ashbeds in The Nature Conservancy's Juniper Hills Preserve, near the site where Captain John M. Drake discovered fossils in 1864. Central Oregon

tortoises, and a primitive horse with claws. Painstakingly, over a period of several years, Condon cataloged species of flora and fauna contained within the various strata. His findings indicated that the region had once been submerged under a shallow sea. Then, as the land eventually rose from beneath the waters, successive forested periods, each characterized by its own animals, developed over spans of millions of years, finally evolving into open grasslands.

When Dr. John S. Newberry of Columbia College in New York received several of Pastor Condon's fossils, the famed paleontologist was so interested that he immediately requested shipment of an entire series of speci-

mens. However, return trips to the John Day country at that time were dangerously risky because of hostile Indians. In a letter to Newberry dated May 31, 1869, Condon wrote of his study area, "I am hungry for a sight of that hill again, when no fear of prowling Indians shall compel me to hold a rifle in one hand and my pick in the other."

By 1870, threatening conditions in the area diminished and the pastor-scientist was free to continue his work on what was once Native American land. Before long, news of Condon's discoveries circulated throughout the world's scientific community. Dr. Joseph Leidy of the University of Pennsylvania, the nation's leading paleontologist, requested specimens, as did other noted scientists and their respective museums and colleges, such as the Smithsonian Institution and Yale. Eventually, several authorities—O. C. Marsh, Edward D. Cope, and Joseph LeConte—brought colleagues and students to visit the now world-famous John Day fossil beds. A highlight of Condon's fieldwork was his discovery of a series of primitive horse fossils that constituted several new species and genera. One, *Miohippus condoni*, was named by Dr. Leidy to honor its finder.

Thomas Condon, who migrated to America from Ireland with his family at the age of eleven, was a gifted, natural teacher. As a young man he devoted several years to teaching grammar school before entering theological seminary. He employed this talent again, beginning in 1873, as lecturer in Geology at Pacific University in Forest Grove. He also served as Oregon's first state geologist, but resigned from that post in 1876 when the University of Oregon opened its doors in Eugene and Condon was asked to chair its Natural Science Department. He held this position for the remainder of his life and was a highly regarded, inspiring, and beloved professor. During his tenure there, he continued doing fieldwork throughout the state and made significant paleontological discoveries among the shifting dunes of Fossil Lake in the high desert of Lake County. In later years he was often referred to as Oregon's Grand Old Man of Science. Condon's landmark book narrative about the state's geology, *The Two Islands*, was published in 1902 and represented a summation of his life's work.

In 1907, after a long, full career, Thomas Condon passed away, following a severe bout of influenza. His life ended just a month prior to what would have been his eighty-fifth birthday.

Condon's legacy endures. The visitor center at John Day Fossil Beds National Monument near Dayville bears his name, as does the Condon Museum of Geology at the University of Oregon in Eugene; and when students read a modern college textbook on paleontology, they indirectly benefit from the foundational research of this pioneer scientist. ■

Dry Side Flora

These bushes shade the ground and hold the snow, build up humus, bind the soil, conceal the sage grouse and young antelope, and provide choice fuel for the camp fire. Their pleasant odor is one of the charms of the desert, and the smell of a dried spray brings back the memory of broad valleys and clean wholesome air. The sagebrush has no direct commercial value, but without it or an equivalent, the desert would be poor indeed.

VERNON BAILEY
The Mammals and Life Zones of Oregon, 1936

No less than geological landforms and climate, plants are a prime contributor to the appearance, aroma, and "personality" of the three regions east of the Cascades. Each has its own floristic essence: Central Oregon seems synonymous with ponderosa pine and western juniper; the southeastern corner of the state brings to mind sprawling sagebrush-bunchgrass steppelands, saltscrub deserts, and basin marshes; Northeastern Oregon is the dramatic contrast of valley and canyon grasslands that sweep upward to dense mountain forests of mixed pine, fir, spruce and larch.

As the accompanying vegetation zones map illustrates, the varied terrain of Oregon's dry side makes understanding its rather complex, interlaced vegetational areas somewhat challenging. Nevertheless, even a modest amount of knowledge about these zones and some of their distinctive plant species will greatly enrich your explorations. Let's take a streamlined botanical ramble through these landscapes to gain a greater familiarity with the native flora.

Springtime lupines and sagebrush in the eastern foothills of the Pueblo Mountains, Southeastern Oregon

Vegetation Zones
of Oregon's Dry Side

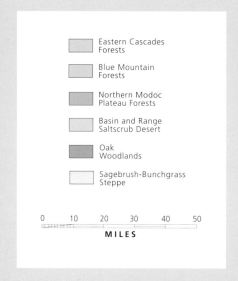

Eastern Cascades
Forests

Blue Mountain
Forests

Northern Modoc
Plateau Forests

Basin and Range
Saltscrub Desert

Oak
Woodlands

Sagebrush-Bunchgrass
Steppe

0   10   20   30   40   50

MILES

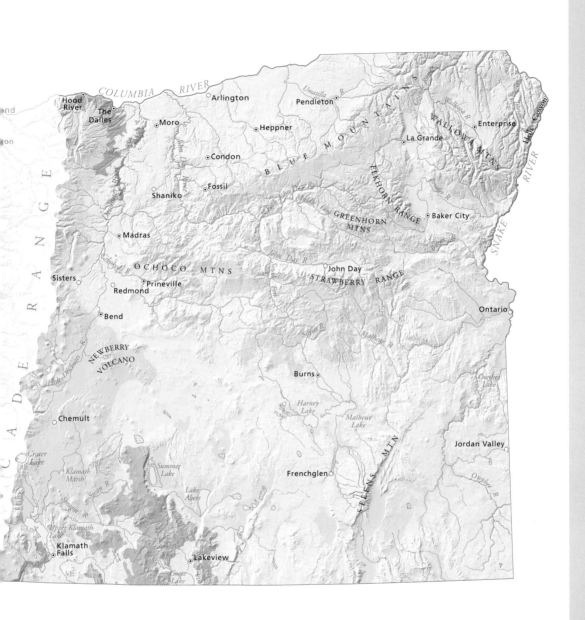

The sagebrush-bunchgrass association is the most distinctive, widespread vegetation zone east of the Cascades, so we'll begin with this type of classic "high desert" environment. Broad stretches of these open, semiarid plains extend for mile after mile, culminating at the base of a rimrock plateau, or being curtailed at the forest-line of higher, more moist mountain ranges. Initially, a cursory viewing presents a seemingly desolate land, covered with only one kind of plant—sagebrush (actually, there are several sagebursh species). But closer examination will reveal many other types of vegetation adapted to this parched landscape.

Dry side vegetation zones

Because of Oregon's diverse terrain east of the Cascades, plant communities are equally varied according to elevation, localized precipitation, soils, and a host of other factors. Placing a categorical framework upon this vegetational complexity is difficult. Although the accompanying vegetation zones map indicates clear-cut borders for each zone, in reality plant communities are generally discontinuous, spotty, and interlaced, forming an intricate mosaic across broad landscapes. Therefore, these divisions are necessarily somewhat of an oversimplification. However, for the purposes of this book, they should convey a generalized picture of the botanical lay of the land.

Eastern Cascades forests

This lofty volcanic range is rich in diversity of plant species. Notably, one of the most extensive ponderosa pine forests in the world stretches along the lower- to mid-elevation eastward flanks of the Cascade Range. Intermixed are lodgepole pine, grand fir, and western larch in the northern sections, along with sugar pine, incense cedar, white fir, and red fir to the south. An often thick understory of bitterbrush, green manzanita, kinnikinnick, pinemat manzanita, serviceberry, common snowberry, grouse huckleberry, creeping Oregon grape, wax currant, nootka rose, and bracken fern is typical. Here and there, quaking aspen groves occur in moist places. Pacific yew grows in shady, cool locations, along with occasional stands of typically Western Oregon trees, such as red cedar and bigleaf maple, sometimes in accompaniment with western swordfern. At slightly higher elevations, Douglas fir, western white pine, and western mountain maple comprise the forests; and approaching the treeline level, a different mix occurs—subalpine fir, Pacific silver fir, noble fir, Engelmann spruce, mountain hemlock, and Alaska cedar. The margins of the harsh, nearly barren alpine zones usually support only one tree species: stunted, twisted whitebark pines.

Blue Mountain forests

Composed of several Northeastern Oregon subranges—the Ochoco, Aldrich, Strawberry, Elkhorn, Greenhorn, and Wallowa—these mountains have many of the same species seen on the eastern slopes of the Cascades. Conifers include, depending upon elevation, ponderosa pine, lodgepole pine, western white pine, whitebark pine, Douglas fir, grand fir, subalpine fir, western larch, mountain hemlock, Engelmann spruce, and Pacific yew. Broadleaf trees, such as black cottonwood and quaking aspen grow primarily in riparian areas, along with Pacific willow, Scouler willow, Sitka alder, thinleaf

Sagebrush-bunchgrass steppelands along Highway 20, west of Burns, Southeastern Oregon

alder, western mountain maple, black hawthorn, and water birch. Again, much as in the Cascade Range, there is a forest understory consisting of serviceberry, creeping Oregon grape, common snowberry, pinemat manzanita, kinnikinnick, bitterbrush, wax currant, nootka rose, grouse huckleberry, and bracken fern. Patches of curl-leaf mountain mahogany are common on dry, rocky ridges. The Blue Mountains, however, differ from other Oregon ranges in having a Northern Rocky Mountain floral component. Examples are wildflowers that reach the western extent of their ranges in Northeastern Oregon, such as the yellow columbine, alpine paintbrush, and alpine forget-me-not. So, too, the state's only stands of Rocky Mountain juniper and

paper birch grow in the Wallowa Valley area, and limber pine occurs in the high-elevation zones of the Wallowa Mountains.

Northern Modoc Plateau forests

Bordering desert country at the northwestern edge of the Great Basin, these timberlands take in the Warner Mountains, Winter Rim, Gearhart Mountain, and the various small ranges at the headwaters of the Sprague River drainage. The area is biogeographically complex, with a blending of vegetative influences. From the west, much the same mix of plant species that cloak the eastern slopes of the southern Cascade Range occur here—ponderosa pine, lodgepole pine, western white pine, whitebark pine, and Douglas fir, with an understory of bitterbrush, grouse huckleberry, kinnikinnick, pinemat manzanita, wax currant, creeping Oregon grape, and common snowberry. Groves of quaking aspen are common in moist places, and dry, open ridges have an association of western juniper, curl-leaf mountain mahogany, common rabbitbrush, green rabbitbrush, and several kinds of sagebrush. Adding a southern component are a number of Sierran species characteristic of California, such as sugar pine, incense cedar, white fir, Klamath plum, birchleaf mountain mahogany, and wide-stemmed onion. Contributing botanical diversity from the east are some Rocky Mountain species at the westernmost extent of their distributions, examples being alpine lily, snowline spring parsley, and dwarf lousewort.

Basin and range saltscrub desert

This zone marks the northernmost limits of the Great Basin and is the primary vegetative cover of Oregon's only true deserts. Limited to the parched basins and eroded canyon "badlands" of the southeastern corner of the state, this treeless environment is characterized by resilient shrubs that have adapted to the alkali-encrusted, sandy soils—predominantly, black greasewood, shadscale, four-winged saltbush, and spiny hopsage. Other associated plants may include salt sage, winterfat, spiny horsebrush, bud sage, and at the fringes where less alkaline soils prevail, an intermixing of big sagebrush, silver sagebrush, black sagebrush, common rabbitbrush, and green rabbitbrush. The Alvord Basin contains Oregon's most extensive, pure examples of saltscrub ecosystems and several Great Basin species reach their northern limits here, including iodine bush, green ephedra, Nevada ephedra, and prickly poppy. Scattered small pockets of saltscrub communities also occur

in the upper John Day River drainage at the edges of barren ashbeds, and in a few dry spots in the Columbia Basin.

Oak woodlands

Although primarily found west of the Cascade Range, the Oregon white oak ranges into the north-central portion of the state via the Columbia River Gorge. These sturdy trees intermingle with ponderosa pines and western junipers, often with a thick understory of western poison oak. Relatively limited in Oregon's dry side, this plant association stretches south from The Dalles area along the eastern slope of the Cascades to the vicinity of Warm Springs. Similarly, in south Central Oregon, these oaks trace the Klamath River drainage through the Cascades to the southwestern shore of Upper Klamath Lake. A second species, California black oak, also occurs in the Klamath River Canyon.

Sagebrush-bunchgrass steppe

The primary plant cover of this zone consists of big sagebrush and common rabbitbrush, interlaced with bunchgrass species—bluebunch wheatgrass, Idaho fescue, Sandberg's bluegrass, Indian ricegrass, and others. In some areas, sections of pure grasslands occur. To a slightly lesser degree, depending upon the location, other shrub species add to the botanical complexity. Examples are green rabbitbrush, threetip sagebrush, silver sagebrush, and on higher, exposed ridges the "dwarf sagebrush communities"—low sagebrush, stiff sagebrush, and black sagebrush. Western juniper woodlands are also a prominent component of the steppelands, and because of the lack of periodic range fires, they are more widespread than a century ago. Where moisture allows, small stands of ponderosa pine with a bitterbrush understory manage to grow, along with infrequent groves of quaking aspen. ▪

Two common shrubs

Let's venture out into the waist-high sea of bushes and focus on details within the overall broad brushstrokes of gray-green. It will quickly become apparent that there are actually two shrub species brushing against your legs as you walk. In some locations they may not be intermixed, but generally are in proximity to each other.

One has a more subdued, grayish appearance with gnarled, stiff stems. This is big sagebrush. The other is silvery-green with more delicate, straight stems that flare outward from the plant's base and give it a broom-like shape. Now you are looking at common rabbitbrush.

You can use a simple test—your sense of smell—to differentiate the two species. Alternately crush the leaves from both shrubs between your fingers and sniff their aroma. Big sagebrush exudes the pleasantly aromatic, herby aroma that most people associate with the high desert. Conversely, common rabbitbrush has an unpleasant, pungent smell, reflected by its scientific name, *Ericameria nauseosa*.

Despite its disagreeable odor, common rabbitbrush adds great beauty to the open rangelands when in bloom with masses of small, bright yellow flowers in late summer through autumn, creating a sweeping, golden blanket of vegetation. The concurrent, tiny blooms of big sagebrush are muted yellow and rather drab by comparison. As the crisp, sunny days of October wane into winter, the sulphur yellow display of common rabbitbrush bleaches to creamy white, and the desiccated blooms of big sagebrush darken to rusty brown.

By late autumn, the blooms of big sagebrush turn rusty brown.

Common rabbitbrush in bloom

It should be noted that another species of rabbitbrush is nearly as abundant east of the Cascades. Called green rabbitbrush, it is similar in appearance, though differences become apparent upon closer inspection. As the common name indicates, it has a greener appearance than its pale, silvery relative, and also differs in feeling syrupy-sticky when touched.

Sagebrush

The distinctive, herby fragrance of sagebrush signifies Oregon's high desert country to most people. Seas of the gray-green shrubs seem to spread endlessly toward dry horizons. Although sagebrush is associated with deserts, the most common, widespread species, big sagebrush, cannot grow in the extremely arid, alkaline soils of true desert basins. Much of our so-called high desert is actually semiarid steppelands where sagebrush is plentiful.

This plant, typical of the untamed places of the earth, derives its genus name, *Artemisia*, from the Greek goddess of wild nature, Artemis. Sometimes known as wormwood, approximately 250 species occur around the world. Most grow in high-plateau, low-rainfall environments similar to Southeastern Oregon. An American hiker visiting Eurasian steppelands would be pleasantly surprised by whiffs of a familiar pungent scent from other forms of sagebrush. None are the same thing as the culinary herb sage. Instead, sagebrush (a member of the aster family) is related to another spice used in cooking—tarragon.

Big sagebrush, which has been divided into several sometimes difficult-to-distinguish subspecies, ranges in size from less than a foot tall in dry, rocky areas, to treelike, eight-foot-high bushes in deeper, moister soils. It occurs at nearly all elevations where there is appropriate habitat, from barely above sea level along the Columbia River to the subalpine zones of Steens Mountain at more than seven thousand feet.

Superbly adapted to a dry climate, the small leaves of big sagebrush limit surface loss of precious moisture. A covering of fine hair reflects sunlight and further retards moisture loss. The root system employs a twofold method of extracting maximum moisture from the plant's environment. A shallow network of roots spreads out horizontally just below the soil's surface to collect rainwater quickly before it evaporates, while robust penetrating roots grow deeply into the earth to tap underground reserves. In some areas, big sagebrush comprises 80 percent of the local plant community, with as many as seven thousand individual shrubs per acre.

Each year, in late summer and early fall, big sagebrush produces small, yellowish blossoms. Allergy sufferers who move to the high desert to avoid the pollen-rich air of more lushly vegetated places discover the pollen of these shrubs, along with that of rabbitbrush and juniper. Nevertheless, sagebrush is a popular symbol of the American West and Nevada has designated its blossoms as the state flower.

The Paiute people used sagebrush in ingenious ways to survive in this harsh environment. They were a nomadic people who

Big sagebrush, the most common, widespread *Artemisia* species east of the Cascades

moved from one area to another to utilize various food sources, and their temporary shelters often incorporated sagebrush. During cold winter months, men wore leggings made of sagebrush bark and women often dressed in sagebrush skirts. Footwear consisted of well-crafted, durable sandals made of the all-purpose sagebrush bark.

There are a number of other *Artemisia* species native to Oregon. Some are inconspicuous, herblike plants, but the shrubby kinds covered here fit the usual sagebrush image. Threetip sagebrush with its deeply cleft leaves, is nearly as common as big sagebrush in some places. Stiff sagebrush, low sagebrush, and black sagebrush are found in what is often referred to as dwarf sagebrush communities on exposed ridges and bench tops with shallow, rocky soils. Silver sagebrush, so named because of its pale, almost white appearance, generally grows in moist soils along stream terraces or around the margins of lakeside meadows. Conversely, the spiny, small bud sage is adapted to the dry, alkaline soils of basin and range saltscrub desert habitats. The Owyhee River drainage of far Southeastern Oregon has two other species: the rather unusual Packard's sagebrush, which is confined to rock ledges, and the Owyhee sagebrush of the open uplands.

A century ago, before cattle grazing and fire suppression, sagebrush was less dominant than grasses in many areas east of the Cascades. Artemisia shrubs, with their flammable, dead, woody stems, were thinned out by periodic prairie fires, leaving the more flame-resistant, widely spaced bunchgrasses. The twin factors of many past decades of overgrazing native grasses throughout large sections of the Intermountain West and lack of sagebrush-inhibiting fires have reversed this ancient biotic balance. ■

Native grasses and exotic interlopers

The other major vegetative component of Oregon's steppelands is bunchgrass. This term collectively includes a number of native species, primarily bluebunch wheatgrass, along with Idaho fescue, Sandberg's bluegrass, Indian ricegrass, and others. They all have one thing in common: the highly successful adaptation of growing in widely spaced clumps. This allows them to spread their roots outward and absorb the maximum moisture from the dry soils of the Intermountain West. A more specialized species, giant wild rye, is visually notable as its often six-foot-high clumps sway in breezes. It occurs in slightly moist, alkaline soils, helping to stabilize the banks of desert washes.

Commingling with the sagebrush-rabbitbrush combo, and in other places coalescing into clumpy cadres of their own, bunchgrasses are not nearly as widespread as they were a century ago. Originally, pure bunchgrass communities swept from horizon to horizon throughout enormous sections of Oregon's dry side. However, long-term human influences have greatly altered these biotic communities, and only limited native grasslands still survive here and there. It's probable that if a Native American Paiute of two hundred years ago was magically transported forward to our present day, he or she might not initially recognize this homeland.

Besides long-term livestock overgrazing of native grasses, which encourages sagebrush to increase, one of the prime culprits in this rangeland degradation is cheatgrass, an exotic, accidentally introduced European plant species. Thriving on overgrazed land and other disturbed areas, this tenacious plant carpets the ground and has encroached upon

November's first snowfall whitens a bunchgrass prairie of the Owyhee uplands, Southeastern Oregon.

the drylands of the entire American West. Fires, whether natural or human-prescribed for range management, unfortunately cause cheatgrass to proliferate. Additionally, because native bunchgrasses spread slowly, the more rapidly reproducing cheatgrass easily dominates its surroundings. With the arrival of summer, this tinder-dry, heavy fuel-load results in wildfires of such intense heat that soil quality is degraded. This in turn discourages or entirely eliminates the native grasses, shrubs, and other plants—and the downward-spiraling cycle continues. Prior to the cheat invasion, natural fires were less frequent and more subdued. They progressed slowly in irregular, patchy patterns because of the broad spaces of open soil between the native steppe shrubs and bunchgrasses.

Other exotic grasses have been introduced

intentionally. The U.S. Bureau of Land Management, in an attempt to improve grazing conditions for cattle, uses mechanical clearing and herbicides to exterminate sagebrush, reseeding with Asian crested wheatgrass in some parts of their districts. Although the plantings provide more forage for cows, these artificial monocultures preclude suitable habitat for many native animals that require more complex natural plant communities. Examples are the greater sage grouse, pygmy rabbit and, several kinds of lizards.

Ironically, the famous "tumbleweed" of American cowboy song and lore is also an introduced foreigner: Russian thistle. This prickly, shrublike weed with its drab green to pinkish-red coloration is another indicator of unhealthy rangelands. When dead and dry, the vegetative carcasses blow for miles across the plains, piling up in the thousands along fencerows and in roadside ditches. Often sharing quarters with Russian thistle and the pervasive cheatgrass is the familiar common rabbitbrush, one of our few native plants that thrives on disturbed ground.

Damage control

Workable solutions to gradually return the sagebrush-bunchgrass biotic zones to their original integrity are proving to be frustratingly difficult. Complicating things is the fact that the science of ecology is a relatively recent innovation. No researchers were around two hundred years ago to pass on detailed observations of the pristine conditions that existed at that time in the Intermountain West; and today there is no exacting recipe with the proper proportions of plants, animals, fire, and other components that would assure a positive outcome.

One little-known component is the interdependent collections of microscopic fragments of lichens, fungi, mosses, algae, and nitrogen-fixing bacteria that congeal in the soil surface between shrubs and bunchgrasses. The degree of importance that this complex "cryptobiotic crust" contributes to the health of sagebrush-bunchgrass ecosystems is only now beginning to be understood. Opinions vary among ecologists and range management scientists as to whether livestock grazing causes long-lasting detrimental effects to these crusted soils. Some experts speculate that once damaged, whether by cow hooves or hikers' boots, cryptobiotic crusts might take a century or more to reform. Others argue that the crusts are resilient, having adapted to countless millennia of periodic disruption from naturally occurring range fires. Consensus awaits further research results.

High desert color: A wildflower sampler

A special springtime beauty of Oregon's dry side is the sudden proliferation of delicate, brightly colored wildflowers amid the comparatively muted tones of this rugged land. If there has been ample precipitation throughout the winter, the steppelands and deserts can magically burst alive at this season with the blooms of a myriad of species.

Arrowleaf balsamroot

Large and showy, this member of the sunflower family could arguably be ranked as the most familiar wildflower of Oregon's dry side. In the early spring, after a long, cold winter, its welcome April blooms seem to blanket every sunny slope with yellow cheer. By late June, the display is largely over, but arrowleaf balsamroot is still easily identified by its namesake triangular-shaped, wooly leaves that are often over 12 inches in length and 6 inches wide. Summer to autumn, it creates green swaths across the sagebrush-bunchgrass plains and upward to open mountain ridges below six thousand feet. This species springs up in abundance after a fire, and provides important forage for deer, elk, and bighorn sheep. Native Americans used all parts of the plant as a food source. Some tribes combined the roasted ground seeds with animal fat to form nourishing lumps from the mixture—the forerunner of our popular energy bars.

Blazing star

There's no missing this one! Growing to 3 feet tall, with spectacular, lemon yellow flowers that can measure 4 inches across, the blazing star is appropriately named. It blooms throughout most of the summer on the dry, rocky slopes of sagebrush country. Particularly prevalent on road banks, this wildflower captures the eye of even the most uninterested driver. The flowers close during the heat of midday and open again by early evening. This plant's star-shaped blooms can be seen in abundance on Pilot Butte in Bend, from late June through August.

Bitterroot

Bitterroot lacks stems and is ground-hugging. The fleshy, succulent leaves first appear in early spring, but vanish before its compact cluster of bright pink (sometimes white) flowers appear in May and June. It occurs on gravelly soils of slopes and ridgetops, from sagebrush steppelands into the ponderosa forest zones of mountain ranges. The cooked roots were an important dietary component for the intermountain Native American tribes. When the Lewis and Clark expedition passed through the Northwest region in 1806, this food item was tried but deemed unsuitably bitter in flavor, along with causing diarrhea. Its genus name, *Lewisia*, honors Captain Meriwether Lewis, who first described the bitterroot in his journal.

Cusick's monkeyflower

Although somewhat diminutive in size (averaging only 3 to 6 inches in height), this monkey flower definitely makes its presence known by its hot-pink flowers. A wildflower of the pumice sands and cinder grit, when there have been sufficient spring rains, this plant blooms in colorful profusion from late May through August. It is native to volcanic country from northeastern California, through the central and southeastern portions of Oregon, to southwestern Idaho. Enjoy a hike in the Badlands east of Bend during early summer when Cusick's monkeyflower is sprinkled everywhere beneath the gnarled western junipers.

Desert evening primrose

Stemless and growing close to the ground, the delicate white flowers of this well known primrose open when the desert sun sinks below the horizon. The fragrant blooms attract flying nocturnal insects, such as the white-lined sphinx moth, which visit the plant to sip nectar and consequently contribute to its pollination. As the blooming period wanes, the petals turn pink. Look for flowering evening primrose during May to July in sandy-soiled places, from basin deserts to open ponderosa forests.

Desert paintbrush

This is one of the most eye-catching of the many Indian paintbrush species. From April through July, its DayGlo shades of red, orange, or yellow can be seen throughout the basin and range country of Southeastern Oregon. These color variations often all occur together on the same hillside, or only a single hue may prevail. What appears to be flowers are actually the brightly colored upper leaves and bracts. Besides utilizing photosynthesis, paintbrush is also semiparasitic. This is why they can commonly be observed growing upward through shrubs and bunchgrasses, their roots intertwined with those of the host plant to filch nutrients and water—an adaptation that allows them to survive in dry habitats.

Long-leaved phlox

This flower is the most common phlox of the sagebrush steppelands. Unlike most kinds of phlox, which grow tight to the ground in small-leaved mats, this species with its namesake elongated leaves is a nonconformist. It is a relatively upright plant that often uses neighboring shrubs and bunchgrasses as support to attain more height. The accompanying photograph of long-leaved phlox intertwined with stiff sagebrush illustrates this clambering strategy. Although often occurring in low canyons, it seems to favor the rock-strewn ridges of sagebrush-bunchgrass uplands. The pink, pale purple, or white flowers appear from April to July, according to elevation. View long-leaved phlox in bloom during June on the open slopes of Glass Buttes, just south of Highway 20.

Orange globemallow

Anyone who has spent time in the northern Great Basin has probably encountered this wide-ranging mallow of arid places. It is difficult to ignore because the gaudy red-orange flowers sharply contrast with the subdued tones of its typical sandy, rocky habitat. During an especially wet spring season, masses of these plants impart desert basins with a rich sprinkling the color of ripe apricots. The blooms resemble those of the domestic hollyhock, a close relative of orange globemallow. Expect to see flowering displays of this species from May into early summer.

Prickly poppy

Resembling a thistle, this unusual poppy's northernmost limit is in the vicinity of Southeastern Oregon's Alvord Desert. Its large flowers (3 to 5 inches across) have snow-white petals arranged around a center of bright yellow stamens. Every gust of wind causes these pale petals to flutter as though they are made of delicate white paper. Growing to over 3 feet in height, this conspicuous species blooms from June through most of August, but occurs at only a few scattered localities in the Alvord Basin. A reliable place to see the prickly poppy's flower display is along road margins near the little community of Andrews.

Purple sage

This flowering low shrub is not a true sagebrush. Crushing its leaves between your fingers will release a pleasantly familiar fragrance that reveals it is a member of the mint family. The title of Zane Grey's famous novel *Riders of the Purple Sage* actually refers to this species. The intensely bluish-purple blooms appear during May and June, often dominating entire slopes of rocky-soiled desert ridges. A spring drive over Domingo Pass in the Pueblo Mountains provides the experience of being a rider of the purple sage—the dirt road winds through several miles of intermittent patches of these colorful little bushes.

Sagebrush mariposa lily

This elegant flower, perched atop its 14-inch-tall stem, resembles a lovely botanical butterfly. Indeed, in the Spanish language, "mariposa" means butterfly. Its pinkish purple flower has three extremely elongated, green sepals that flare outward. Look inside the "cup" formed by the broad, sharp-tipped petals and you'll see that the bottom has a bright yellow pattern, edged in dark maroon. By July, blooming mariposa lilies can be seen swaying in the high desert breezes throughout the sagebrush and bunchgrass prairies. Native American Indians ate the bulbs of this plant, both raw and boiled.

Sand penstemon

Of the many penstemons occurring in Oregon east of the Cascades, this species is particularly associated with deserts and plains. It is easily differentiated from other penstemons by its distinctive gray-green leaves, which are large, thick, and rather leathery. The sand penstemon grows to 24 inches in height and produces bluish-purple flowers during the warm days of May and June, but enjoy it while you can because its blooming period is somewhat brief. As the name suggests, sand penstemons are most often found near sand dunes and along dry, sandy washes, sometimes growing in surprising profusion.

Silky lupine

This is the common lupine of the Intermountain West. A tall plant (to 24 inches), it adds splashes of lavender-blue across the sagebrush-bunchgrass steppelands and in sunny openings of ponderosa forests. Depending upon the elevation, silky lupine blooms May through July, ranging from basin flats to the upper foothills of mountain ranges. All of the various kinds of lupines are members of the pea family (legumes), which are noted for enriching soils with nitrogen, to the benefit of neighboring vegetation. Following a trail through thick carpets of these wildflowers immediately after a rain shower is a visual treat—the center of each green lupine leaf captures a droplet of water and they collectively sparkle when reappearing sunshine bathes the landscape.

Skyrocket

Equally well known by the name scarlet gilia, this plant's clusters of bright red (sometimes pale pink), trumpetlike corollas are hummingbird magnets. In contrast to its beautiful flowers, the smell of its crushed leaves is decidedly like skunk musk. This species is common throughout the sagebrush slopes and open pine forests of Oregon's dry side. Watch for its blooms along roadsides from May through July. Skyrocket seems to celebrate its name by always being in bloom on Independence Day. The seeds are easily grown in a home flower garden and add a bit of brilliant local color.

Sulphur buckwheat

Hike through just about any drylands east of the Cascades and you'll encounter buckwheats of one species or another. These hardy members of the genus *Eriogonum* grow in harsh environments from near sea level in the Columbia Basin, to the alpine zones of Steens Mountain. The sulphur buckwheat is one of the most distinctive and widespread species in this group. Rising from a base clump of spade-shaped green leaves are numerous 4- to 12-inch stems that branch outward at the top and support ball-like clusters of tiny flowers. This blooming canopy gives rise to its other common name, umbrella buckwheat. Depending upon elevation, the sulphur yellow flowers (sometimes creamy white) appear in May or June, and by the end of summer take on a pinkish tinge.

Western prairie clover

Superficially resembling alfalfa, this legume's 1- to 2-foot–high stems terminate in a dense, conical spike. Beginning in May, a fringe of tiny, rose-pink to purple blossoms appears at the bottom of each spike. The colorful blooms keep sprouting ever upward on the spikes until all are fully flowered by June and July. Patches of western prairie clover occur here and there in sandy-rocky spots of sagebrush country, bunchgrass prairies, and openings in juniper woodlands.

Wooly sunflower

This flower is named for the fuzzy coating of fine, white hairs on the stems and leaves, which give the plant a frosted-green appearance. This is an adaptation to its dry environment—the wool reduces evaporation of vital water. The bouquetlike clumps often grow to 24 inches in height and appear to absorb every sunray into the glowing, yellow blooms. This attractive visual quality has earned the plant its other common name, Oregon sunshine. From April to July these flowers seem to be everywhere in the sagebrush steppelands and sunny openings among juniper woods and pine forests. ▪

Northern Great Basin botany

The next destination on this botanical tour is the basin and range landscapes of Southeastern Oregon. Sunken between dramatic upthrusts of fault block mountains are the immense, sun-scorched troughs of the Alvord Basin, Catlow Valley, Harney Basin, Warner Valley, Lake Abert, Alkali Lake, and Summer Lake. Though limited in extent, compared to the sagebrush-bunchgrass steppe vegetation zone, these ancient, desiccated lakebeds with their alkaline, sandy soils comprise the only true deserts of Oregon. Scattered pockets of saltscrub communities typical of the northern Great Basin grow here—resilient shrubs adapted to alkali-encrusted desert soils, such as black greasewood, shadscale, four-winged saltbush, and spiny hopsage. The same shrub mix also occurs in the eroded badlands of the Owyhee, Malheur, and Snake river drainages, although these areas are technically not part of the true, internally drained Great Basin.

The arid Alvord Basin contains Oregon's purest examples of basin and range saltscrub desert. It lies within double rainshadows, located not only far to the east of the Cascade Range, but also leeward of the moisture-sapping bulk of 9,733-foot Steens Mountain. In

Saltscrub ecosystem in the Alvord Basin

Iodine bush, near Borax Lake, Alvord Basin,
Southeastern Oregon

Spiny hopsage in bloom, foothills of the Pueblo
Mountains, Southeastern Oregon

the harsh environment of this rain-starved basin, several interesting desert-adapted plants have the northern limits of their distributions in North America. A short hike along the edges of alkali flats near Borax Lake will disclose the iodine bush, so named for its inky-dark juices exuded from smashed stems. This low-growing plant has an amazing tolerance for salt-poisoned soils. When the sparse rains of spring bless these flats with a temporary inch or two of water, the iodine bush soaks up and stores the moisture, bloating its segmented stems like a succulent cactus. This effectively dilutes the salts in its cells to a tolerable degree. At this time, it resembles strings of tiny, green pickles, giving rise to its other common name, pickleweed. Surviving the dry summer on its water reserves, by autumn it turns bright orange-red, like gaudy, plastic pop-beads.

A bit farther south in the Alvord Basin, along the eastern foothills of the Pueblo Mountains, scan the shrubby slopes for relatively large, broomy-shaped bushes of conspicuous yellowish green that have jointed, course stems. This is the green ephedra, named for the fact that this plant contains traces of the alkaloid drug ephedrine, a stimulant and anticongestant. Used as a medicinal tea by Native Americans and pioneers, it is sometimes called Mormon tea. A second species of the same genus, very similar in appearance, occurs in these foothills—the pale gray-green Nevada ephedra. The Alvord Basin also marks the northernmost extent of the thistlelike prickly poppy, its lovely white blooms fluttering in late-spring breezes.

A number of regionally endemic, uniquely localized plants are native to Southeastern Oregon. The summit of Steens Mountain alone boasts several varieties—the most notable being the Steens Mountain thistle. The

Malheur wire lettuce, a federally protected species, occurs only in the Harney Basin, where its entire range is confined to several acres on a sagebrush-covered hillside. By 1984 the plant was extinct in the wild, but thanks to this species being included in a seed bank, it was successfully reintroduced to its habitat. Another botanically endemic-rich area is in the Owyhee Canyonlands at Leslie Gulch. Adapted to the unique soils found in this geologically scenic place, a number of plants new to science have come to light there. Among others are the Packard's mentzelia and Packard's sagebrush—both named for their discoverer, botanist Pat Packard.

High-elevation endemics of the desert ranges

Small-leaved lupine

The dwarf lupine populations that are isolated on Oregon's Steens Mountain and the White Mountains of northeastern California are recognized as a separate subspecies, unique to the summits of these ranges. It grows in a low, 5- to 12-inch–wide mat with bright purplish-blue flowers from July to September. Numerous scattered groupings of this plant can be seen along the highest sections of the Steens Mountain Loop Road, above 7,500 feet. Watch for it around alpine snowmelt areas where the soil is gravelly-stony.

Steens Mountain penstemon

A subspecies of the alpine penstemon, this endemic variation is confined to Oregon's Steens and Pueblo mountains, and some of the desert ranges of northern Nevada. Growing in shrubby, low mats on rocky places above 6,500 feet, it has intensely bluish-purple flowers from late June to August. A good place to see it on Steens Mountain is along rocky ridges where the Loop Road traces the head of Big Indian Gorge.

Steens Mountain paintbrush

This is a highly localized Steens subspecies of the hairy yellow paintbrush. Growing to a maximum height of about a foot, the Steens Mountain paintbrush has dark reddish stems and leaves, with the upper leaves and bracts (the "flower") being a yellowish creamy white. To date, this unique variation has only been found on the summit of Steens Mountain, above 6,500 feet elevation. During July and early August, look for its pale blooms on rocky, grassy tundra ridges along the highest reaches of the Steens Mountain Loop Road. (Photo: Mark Turner)

Steens Mountain thistle

This is generally considered to be the signature endemic plant of Steens Mountain, although it also occurs in the adjacent Pueblo Mountains. Its overall distribution is small, being limited to elevations above six thousand feet in these ranges. Within these narrow altitude zones, however, it is quite com-

Wetlands at Malheur National Wildlife Refuge, Southeastern Oregon

mon. Anyone driving the upper sections of the Steens Mountain Loop Road during July and August will notice this conspicuously tall (to 5 feet), prickly plant, with its clusters of bright purple flowers. The Steens Mountain thistle grows abundantly along the rims of gorges and throughout the stony, gravelly soiled meadows and slopes of the two mountain ranges. ▪

The desert's wet side

Although it may seem incongruous to include marshes and lakes in a discussion of deserts and sagebrush steppe, in reality many such wetlands cover portions of Southeastern Oregon's basins. Most are remnants of formerly much larger Pleistocene lakes that existed during the last Ice Age when the climate was cooler and more moist. The most extensive

example, Malheur Lake, is actually a huge, shallow marsh. Lush growths of cattail, bulrush, burreed, and Baltic rush provide nesting cover for thousands of migratory waterfowl and other wetland birds. Similar habitats exist at Warner, Goose, and Summer lakes.

High desert trees

One obvious characteristic of deserts and grasslands is their lack of trees. A few varieties do grow in Southeastern Oregon, but they are scarce. The tree most successfully adapted to Oregon's dry climates is the western juniper. It usually occupies a belt just above the arid, alkaline basins, often in association with mountain mahogany.

Where higher elevations trap sufficient precipitation, groves of ponderosa pine manage to survive. Small, isolated stands of white

Western juniper at sunset

Autumn quaking aspen leaves. Hart Mountain, Southeastern Oregon

fir grow in two canyons high on the western slope of Steens Mountain, and there are other disjunct groves of these trees to the west on Hart Mountain. Otherwise, conifers are a rarity in this arid land, as most require 15 to 30 inches of yearly precipitation.

Still, as with most things, there are exceptions: an unusual 9,000-acre stand of ponder-osa pine grows in the open sagebrush country of northeastern Lake County where the yearly rainfall averages less than ten inches. Located almost fifty miles from the nearest timberlands, these isolated trees have been dubbed the Lost Forest—a remnant of widespread Pleistocene woodlands of 10,000 years ago, when conditions were less arid. The adjacent Fossil Lake shifting dunes, with a moisture-trapping, impervious lakebed buried below, create the unique conditions that have allowed the pines to survive.

At the margins of basin and range streams and springs, several species of deciduous trees snaking along the watercourses stand out sharply against the muted, gray-green sagebrush surroundings—narrow-leaved willow (coyote willow), arroyo willow, black cottonwood, mountain alder, and water birch collectively green these riparian zones. But it is the beautiful quaking aspens, with their white bark and shimmering leaves, that capture the eye, especially in September and October when they blaze with the autumn colors of golden-yellow and red-orange.

Northern Modoc Plateau forests

Westward, the open sagebrush steppelands and saltscrub deserts give way to the forested heights of the Warner Mountains, Winter Rim, Gearhart Mountain, and the various small ranges that birth the Sprague River drainage. Perched on the northwestern rim of the vast Great Basin region, these desert-bordering timberlands have a complex botanical mix that reflects the influences of three different regions.

Most of the plant species are typical of other Oregon dry side forests, with a pronounced similarity to the Cascade Range west beyond the Klamath Basin. Second-

Ponderosa pines. Black Butte, eastern slope of the Cascade Range, Central Oregon

arily, there is a Sierran component from the south, characterized by sugar pine, incense cedar, white fir, Klamath plum, and birchleaf mountain mahogany. Another example is the wide-stemmed onion (pink star onion), which has the northern limits of its range in Oregon's Lake County. It can be seen in the Warner Mountains during May and June when its ball-shaped blooms frequently carpet rocky openings with splashes of pink. Because of this noticeable Sierran element, most botanists consider the area to be primarily a northern extension of California's Modoc Plateau forests. However, a third influence comes from the east to contribute more vegetative diversity. Several species of the Northern Rocky Mountains reach the western extent of their distributions in Lake County—the alpine lily, dwarf lousewort, and snowline spring parsley.

Eastern Cascades forests

As you progress still farther west from the basin and range country, the tree density increases. One of the most extensive ponderosa pine timberlands in the world stretches along the lower and mid-elevation flanks of the Cascades in Central Oregon. Intermixed are lodgepole pine, grand fir, and western larch in the northern sections of the range, along with sugar pine, incense cedar, white fir, and red fir to the south. However, the towering ponderosas dominate. Scattered groves of quaking aspen occur in moist places throughout the eastern Cascades, and bitterbrush, green manzanita, kinnikinnik, pinemat manzanita, wax currant, nootka rose, serviceberry, common snowberry, grouse huckleberry, creeping Oregon-grape, and bracken fern create an often thick understory. Pacific yew, one of the few conifers that lacks cones, grows in shady, cool places. The wood of this small evergreen is prized for making quality archery bows, but its red, cuplike fruit should be avoided—they are dangerously poisonous. The gray, scaly bark of the Pacific yew produces a chemical called taxol that protects it from insects and diseases. Research on this substance has disclosed that it can help humans resist cancer.

The ponderosa pine

Along with sagebrush and juniper, the ponderosa pine is a signature plant species of Oregon's dry side. Although widespread east of the Cascades, in areas where the rainfall is fourteen inches or more, ponderosa forests are most prevalent in Central Oregon. Espe-

An old fire-scarred ponderosa

cially eye-catching are the stands of huge old-growth trees with their cinnamon-orange bark.

Originally, before human fire suppression, there was a natural cycle of low-intensity burns (about every 10 to 20 years) that would gradually move along below these pines and consume the undergrowth of smaller trees and brush, along with the buildup on the forest floor of dead branches, logs, needles, cones, and other debris. Primarily, only the largest trees with fire-resistant, thick bark and high branches survive these repeated flame cleansings. Consequently, prior to the early 1900s ponderosa pine forests were open and parklike with large spaces between trees. The journals of pioneers describe how a horse-drawn wagon could travel for unimpeded miles beneath the lofty canopy of pines. The U.S. Forest Service is now using prescribed burns in an attempt to simulate nature's ways of keeping the forests thinned and cleared of fuel overload that leads to catastrophic wildfires.

Venturing out into an old-growth stand of ponderosas can not only inspire awe but also cause a painful cramp in your neck. This affliction comes from the irresistible temptation to tilt the head far backward and gaze up into the heights of these venerable giants, which often top out at more than 175 feet. Forest explorers should also not miss the experience of poking their noses into the cracks of the jigsaw-puzzle-piece textured bark. Pick a sun-warmed spot on the trunk and you will sniff the unmistakable scent of vanilla. Children love this and often exclaim it causes them to have a mouthwatering urge for a vanilla ice cream cone. Sometimes, on a hot summer day, this delicious scent can be detected twenty feet or more away from one of these trees. And there is no more relaxing experience than reclining against the sturdy trunk of an ancient yellow pine, as they are sometimes called, and listening to the peaceful song of the ponderosa—the wind sighing gently through the shroud of enormous branches far overhead. ■

AT SLIGHTLY higher elevations, Douglas fir, western white pine, and western mountain maple comprise the forests. Along some shady, moist canyons, typically Western Oregon trees such as western red cedar, bigleaf maple, and vine maple also grow, sometimes in accompaniment with western swordfern. Climbing farther upward toward the treelines of these mountains brings you into stands of subalpine fir, Pacific silver fir, noble fir, Engelmann spruce, mountain hemlock, and Alaska cedar. Thick carpets of Cascades blueberry occur at these elevations, providing both tasty snacks for hikers and breathtaking red leaves in autumn. Still higher, whitebark pine manages to grow at the harsh edges of the nearly barren alpine zones, frequently as twisted, weather-beaten trees of no more than six feet in height. Surprisingly, some of these stunted, hardy pines are nearly five hundred years old.

The rare pumice grape fern is unique to the Oregon Cascades, and occurs only on the pumice sand of high-elevation volcanic peaks. Remotely related to the true ferns, this small (to 3 inches), state-protected endemic is known only from the Mount Bachelor, Broken Top, Newberry Volcano area, south to Crater Lake. From July to early September, a frond of yellow, rounded, grapelike sporangia appear at the top of the gray-green, rubbery leaves.

More widespread in the eastern Cascades are scores of typical mountain wildflowers, blooming at successive times in their re-spective elevational zones—western trillium (wake robin), glacier lily, tiger lily, Cascades lily, bear grass, western iris, mountain lady's slipper, pinedrops, pearly everlasting, fireweed, red columbine, scarlet (Indian) paintbrush, bluebell, shooting star, skyrocket (scarlet gilia), pink spiraea (hardhack), spreading phlox, orange honeysuckle, alpine laurel, and the list goes on and on.

One Cascades wildflower species has a limited range, occurring only in the Metolius River drainage and the Black Butte–Sisters area. Called Peck's penstemon, this endemic is adapted to grow on the volcanic pumice soils of sunny openings among old-growth ponderosa pines. Look for its pale pink to purplish blue blooms during June to August. Originally, periodic, low-intensity fires kept these forests free of shading tangles of small trees and brush, creating this plant's required habitat. Human fire suppression over the

Old-growth Douglas fir and vine maple. Santiam Pass, Cascade Range, Central Oregon

past century, however, has caused a decline in the Peck's penstemon, and it is now federally listed as a species of concern. The modern management methods of the U.S. Forest Service are attempting to mimic nature by thinning small trees and utilizing prescribed burns. Resultantly, this plant may become a more common sight in the future.

Western junipers

Not only do the gnarled shapes of juniper trees add a scenic touch to Oregon's dry side, they also contribute fragrance. After a drenching summer thunderstorm, the strongly aromatic combination of sagebrush and juniper is particularly pungent. To anyone who has spent time exploring east of the Cascades, the smell of western juniper triggers pleasant memories of hikes in open vistas and favorite camping places. This same olfactory enjoyment is savored through the cold winter months by numerous dry-sider households when a crackling fire of juniper wood provides both warmth and its pleasant incense.

Another quality of this tree is its lack of a distinctive shape that immediately communicates to an observer, "This is a western juniper." A walk through a stand of junipers quickly demonstrates that no two are alike. They have an endless variety of forms, resembling the shape of oaks, maples, pines, cedars, manicured ornamental shrubs, and even cultured Japanese bonsai trees.

The scratchy, gray-green foliage, thin, shredded bark, and the blue, hard berries of the female trees make this evergreen easy to identify. The "berries" are actually tiny cones that do not open like other conifer cones. Native American Indians used the juniper berry as an herb for cooking and medicinal purposes.

The western juniper is well adapted to successfully grow in very dry habitats where other trees would perish. The world's most extensive forests of this species grow in the Deschutes Basin of Central Oregon. Anyone driving east of Bend on Highway 20 is treated to good views of these woodlands, especially in the Badlands area where contorted old-growth junipers grow from jumbled lava beds. On rocky ridges the western juniper will be the size of a twisted, large shrub, and in other areas with more moisture, it may grow to heights of fifty feet or more. The largest known example, located in the Sierra Nevada Range of northern California, towers almost eighty-six feet, with a massive trunk of nearly thirteen feet in circumference.

A venerable western juniper post, the Pillars of Rome formations, Owyhee River Canyon, Southeastern Oregon

Typical western juniper and sagebrush association. Eldorado Pass, near Unity, Northeastern Oregon

Western juniper forests have expanded greatly in the last one hundred years, probably due in large part to modern fire suppression. Easily killed by flames, they were very vulnerable to the natural thinning processes of low-intensity burns that regularly moved through sagebrush-bunchgrass prairies. Consequently, junipers were originally limited primarily to thin-soiled, rocky places that were free of combustible shrubs and grasses.

Counted among the oldest growing trees, 1,600-year-old specimens have been documented. Some experts maintain that these junipers may achieve greater ages than this. Even the dead, weathered snags survive decade after decade in their dry environments. The hard, durable wood of these trees inspires a joke common among high desert ranchers: "Yessir, it's a fact. A juniper post will wear out three sets of post holes!"

EAST of the Cascades, the surroundings change dramatically. The dense pine forests end abruptly and the comparatively sparse western juniper woodlands begin, punctuated with openings of big sagebrush and common rabbitbrush. Hurtling at sixty miles per hour out of the shadowy forests into the nearly blinding sunlight of the sagebrush expanses can be momentarily disorienting. In the northern and southern portions of Central Oregon, oak groves intermingle with pines and junipers in some places. Although found primarily west of the Cascades, the Oregon white oak ranges through the Columbia River Gorge into The Dalles area and then southward along the eastern slope of the Cascades to the vicinity of Warm Springs. Likewise, these sturdy trees also spread through the southern end of Oregon's Cascades via the Klamath River Canyon.

Grove of Oregon white oak in Tygh Valley, Central Oregon

The Blue Mountain forests

Steering the field trip through Northeastern Oregon now takes you into the Blue Mountain complex with its various subranges—the Ochoco, Aldrich, Strawberry, Elkhorn, Greenhorn, and Wallowa mountains. These ranges have a mix of vegetation similar to that found on the eastern slope of the Cascades, with the addition of several species typical of the Northern Rocky Mountains that occur nowhere else in Oregon. Examples are wildflowers familiar to anyone who hikes mountain trails in Idaho and Montana—yellow columbine, alpine paintbrush, and alpine forget-me-not. Likewise, Oregon's only stands of Rocky Mountain juniper and paper birch are to be seen in the Wallowa Valley, and limber pines grow in the high Wallowa Mountains.

Along with the Rocky Mountain species, there are unique Blue Mountain endemics we should watch for—Wallowa penstemon, Blue Mountain penstemon, Wallowa lewisia, Oregon twinpod, dwarf golden daisy, Blue Mountain lomatium, Wallowa primrose, Cusick's camas, fraternal paintbrush, and purple alpine paintbrush.

Northeastern Oregon grasslands

This region has another similarity to the nearby Rocky Mountains—open grasslands are extensive. Compared to other regions east of the Cascades, sagebrush is somewhat uncommon or entirely lacking. Dominating the valleys, foothills, and canyons are bunchgrass prairies that sweep upward to meet the forest borders. This type of biotic landscape is especially prevalent along the steep canyon sides and broad bench summits of the lower Grande Ronde, Imnaha, and Snake river

Western larch in autumn color. Larch Summit, Greenhorn Mountains, Northeastern Oregon

Bunchgrass slopes of the Imnaha River Canyon, Northeastern Oregon

drainages. Just north of the Wallowa Valley, on the rolling, bisected breaks above Hells Canyon, Zumwalt Prairie is the heart of this vast realm of grass. It encompasses more than two hundred square miles of lonesome highlands and is the largest remaining native bunchgrass prairie in North America.

The canyons of the Snake River drainage are recognized as a significant area of regional endemism with several unique native plant species, such as Snake River phlox, Hazel's prickly phlox, Cusic's milkvetch, large-flowered tonella, and bartonberry. Notable is MacFarlane's four-o'clock, found only

Dry Side Flora **75**

in Hells Canyon and the adjoining Imnaha River Canyon. This nearly extinct, federally protected wildflower is one of Oregon's rarest plants. Consider yourself blessed if you witness the late-spring blooming of its vivid magenta flowers.

By late summer and fall, the grasses of Northeastern Oregon's canyon country have ripened and mellowed to a warm yellow, accented by vertical slashes of autumn red where smooth sumac follow deeply etched ravines. At this time, the rounded, steep-sided benches, narrowly separated by creek drainages, resemble giant rows of golden bread loaves. The gilded, dividing gulches plunge ever downward by twists and turns into the impossibly deep main chasm of the Snake River. If you peer over the rim's edge, the bright yellow leaves of black cottonwood and the orangish yellow foliage of several willow species will be seen far, far below along the river's edge. Here and there, small stands of ponderosa pine can be spotted as well, contributing contrasting splotches of green among the surrounding autumn colors.

Our botanical tour of Oregon's dry side ends at an overlook along Interstate 84, east of Pendleton. High on the northwestern verge of the Blue Mountains, this pullout affords a spectacular view of the Columbia Basin below. It is also situated on the original route of the Oregon Trail. As you gaze west down the Columbia River and north toward Washington, realize that what you are seeing is quite different from what the pioneers witnessed during the 1840s. Before the Columbia Basin lands were converted to agricultural use, nearly all of this vast country was covered with bunchgrasses. The 200-square-mile bunchgrass ecosystem at Zumwalt Prairie is but a postage-stamp-sized remnant of what once existed in the Columbia Basin. This sea of grass stretched north from the foothills of the Blue Mountains in Oregon all the way to Canada.

Nourished on deep silt soils (loess) deposited by wind and ancient glacial megafloods at the end of the Ice Age, the grasslands now exist only as relict fragments. This immensity of grass was called the Palouse Prairies, and we'll never see the likes of it again in the Northwest.

Where are the cacti?

Although usually associated with deserts and plains, cacti are uncommon on the drylands of the Northwest. Three species occur in Oregon, possibly four, depending upon the authority consulted. All have wider ranges beyond the state's boundaries.

Plains prickly pear
This is the classic cactus of the American West, here shown growing on Cactus Mountain in the Imnaha River drainage. It ranges into the northeastern portions of Oregon and

is especially abundant in the Hells Canyon area. Formidably spined, it grows in clumps that are 4 to 12 inches in height and has large, flattened stem segments. From May to early July, this species sports attractive yellow or reddish yellow blooms.

Brittle prickly pear

So named because sections of this plant easily break free and stick to passing animals and careless people, facilitating its dispersal. Brittle prickly pear differs from the plains prickly pear in being low growing, with a maximum height of only 2 inches, with rounded stem segments. Additionally, the yellow blooms lack a reddish tinge. Brittle prickly pear has a spotty distribution in Oregon. It has been recorded at a number of dry locations along the Columbia River and in the vicinity of the Painted Hills as well as at a few sites in the Baker Valley and in Southeastern Oregon. Recent studies have led some botanists to believe that hybrids with characteristics of both species of prickly pear are widespread in the Columbia drainage. (Photo: Glenn & Barbara Halliday)

Hedgehog cactus

One of the West's many barrel type cacti, it occurs at scattered locations east of the Cascades but is rarely seen because it usually grows on the high, exposed summits of rocky ridgetops and buttes. The hedgehog, seen here in the John Day River drainage, is small (to 5 inches high) and often grows in clusters, displaying rose pink to purplish pink flowers during April and May. The species native to Oregon is presently considered by most botanists to be the black-spined hedgehog cactus. Hedgehog cacti from the southeastern sections of the state have differing characteristics, however, and may be either the closely related Simpson's hedgehog cactus or an entirely new species. ■

Dry Side Fauna

I was thinking of these things as I last stood on the top of Hart Mountain, watching the lengthening shadows streak across the plateau far below me. It struck me that man sometimes seems to try to crowd everything but himself out of the universe. Yet he cannot live a full life from the products of his own creation. He needs a measure of the wilderness, so that he may relax in the environment that God made for him. He needs life around him in order to experience the true measure of living. Then only can he get a sense of the full glory of the universe. There is a place in man's life for the antelope, just as there is for the whir of sage grouse and the song of the thrush. There would be a great emptiness in the land if there were no pelicans wheeling in great circles over Hart Mountain, no antelope fawn in its aspen groves, no red-shafted flickers in its willow. I say the same for the coyote and golden eagle.

JUSTICE WILLIAM O. DOUGLAS
My Wilderness: The Pacific West, 1960

With a range of habitats that include sagebrush-bunchgrass steppelands, saltscrub deserts, basin marshes, juniper woodlands, pine forests, watercourses, lakes, meadows, and alpine zones, Oregon's dry side has a corresponding broad array of animal species inhabiting these ecosystems. Grab your binoculars and we'll take a fauna-watching trip, progressively exploring all of these various areas.

Let's begin with the sagebrush country, one of the most dominant habitats east of the Cascades. It's common for vis-

Mule deer buck. Malheur National Wildlife Refuge, Southeastern Oregon

itors to mistakenly regard these vast shrublands as being rather lifeless. A good example is Highway 20 between Bend and Burns. Many motorists crossing this stretch of high desert think it's a boring distance to be covered as quickly as possible—and wildlife watching at sixty miles per hour is usually unproductive, conveying an impression of sterility. In actuality, an abundance of creatures, exquisitely adapted to this harsh environment, inhabit the sagebrush off the edge of the pavement. Unfortunately, this wealth of native animal life remains largely unnoticed. Nevertheless, even from a fast-moving car, an interested observer will be rewarded with signs of life.

Life (and death) on the road

Most often, seemingly suicidal black-tailed jackrabbits attempt to cross the road directly in front of your wheels, particularly at night during the hot summer. These lanky, large-eared animals are not true rabbits but belong to the hare family—rabbits are born nakedly furless and remain shut-eyed and nursing

Black-tailed jackrabbit. Hart Mountain National Antelope Refuge, Southeastern Oregon

for nearly two weeks; hares enter the world furred and open-eyed, prepared to run and eat vegetation. A second species, the white-tailed jackrabbit, also occurs east of the Cascades. It has become somewhat rare in recent years, as its preferred bunchgrass habitat continues to disappear. Population densities of both of these hares fluctuate up and down in cycles. Studies have linked their proliferation with extended years of above-average rainfall and the resultant luxuriant growth of food plants. By day, jackrabbits usually crouch in the shade of a bush (hares do not live in burrows), but when startled from hiding they spring into action with hops that may measure twenty feet in distance. Every fifth bound is higher so they can peer back over shrubs to see if danger is gaining behind them.

Despite the fleetness of these animals, however, car headlights befuddle jackrabbits and large numbers die each night on highways. Mule deer are also common on the sagebrush steppelands and are frequently hit by cars as they cross roads. The following morning, these road kills attract nature's cleanup crews. Turkey vultures patrol in languid, spiraling flights and use vision and an acute sense of smell to detect their grisly meals. Alighting in the middle of a highway, they risk becoming casualties themselves while precariously feeding in the path of approaching cars. Raucous flocks of shiny-black common ravens and iridescent black-billed magpies frequently vie with the vultures over roadkills. And don't be surprised if you see a golden eagle lifting off the road with its impressive adult wingspan of nearly seven feet. Despite their regal bearing, these large raptors are not above opportunistically feasting at these carrion smorgasbords as well.

While driving, watch the tops of roadside fence posts and utility poles. In summer, turkey vultures, with their distinctive, naked red heads, can often be sighted on chilly mornings spreading their wings to soak up the sun's warmth like basking reptiles. Birds of prey, such as red-tailed hawks, Swainson's hawks, ferruginous hawks, rough-legged hawks, and American kestrels (sparrow hawks) will also be seen on these perches along the highway, or passing overhead in search of small animals for food. Where wetlands and grasslands are in proximity to the road, be alert for the sight of a low-cruising raptor with a conspicuous white rump patch—a foraging northern harrier, sometimes known as a marsh hawk. Occasionally, a Merriam's ground squirrel will scuttle across the highway. Resembling pint-sized prairie dogs, they constitute a major dietary component of the aforementioned hawks and eagles. And rare is the length of roadside fencing that doesn't boast a western kingbird perched on the top strand of barbed wire, its lemon-yellow breast on display.

Mule deer bucks

A wildlife walk in the sagebrush steppelands

Oregon's sagebrush wildlife, however, goes far beyond the few species of birds and mammals seen on or immediately adjacent to the highway. A leg-stretching walk away from the road reveals the subtle richness of life-forms found in this open land. Preferably, rather than a pullout at the edge of the busy highway, find a little-used side road and drive down it a short distance where things are quiet.

On a warm, sunny day at the height of spring, the first signs of life are usually audible ones. Birds call from the surrounding sea of sagebrush: the tinkling twitterings of the sage sparrow, a green-tailed towhee's meowing trill beneath a bitterbrush, the flutelike

Golden eagle

A horned lark greets a cold March dawn on the high desert.

Western tiger swallowtail on a Steens Mountain thistle, Southeastern Oregon

melody of a western meadowlark on a weathered fence post, a series of warblings from a sage thrasher perched atop a bush, and the delicate, high-pitched song of the horned lark. Insects add a busy undertone of sound: the murmuring drone of bees, the intensely loud buzz of a cicada, and the sudden, clicking flight of startled grasshoppers.

Watch for eye-catching butterflies that flutter among the spring wildflowers: the desert marble with its green and white, squiggley-patterned wings can be seen sheltering from breezes among phlox blooms, or the sagebrush checkerspot will be moving from one rabbitbrush to another (its larval host plant), showing its orange and black markings. If you see a small, whirring winged form zipping from flower to flower, don't mistake it for a hummingbird; it's actually a white-lined sphinx moth, sometimes called a hummingbird moth because of the uncanny similarity. These moths, with their attractive pink-and-black hind wings, can be seen visiting flowers for their nectar both night and day, especially after rain. While investigating the wildflowers, should you encounter a plump, grass green caterpillar with an orange horn on its rear end, realize that you're looking at the larva of the white-lined sphinx moth.

Be careful not to place a knee in an anthill while crouching low to watch the moths—especially if it happens to be a nest of harvester ants. Reflecting their body color, they have red hot, defensive temperaments and can deliver painful bites and stings. Legions of these industrious little insects radiate from their swarming, pebbled mounds, which are commonly underfoot throughout the sagebrush steppelands. While remaining vigilant to keep ants out of your socks, closely inspect the surrounding ground for small pits. Each of these contains a larval ant lion buried at the bottom. Until it transforms into a winged adult, the larva utilizes the tiny sand trap to capture ants and other insects for food. The ant lion will often flick sand at a victim and tumble the would-be meal to the formidable, pincerlike mandibles waiting below.

The observant hiker who searches open

sandy areas between sagebrush may be rewarded with a glimpse of the small, darting sagebrush lizard or the rotund, 3-inch-long pigmy short-horned lizard, a member of the misnamed "horned toad" group. In sun-warmed, rocky places, watch for the western fence lizard, a larger relative of the sagebrush lizard. This prickly scaled reptile is sometimes referred to as the blue-bellied lizard, because of the bright, turquoise-blue coloration on its abdomen. Western fence lizards can often be seen bobbing up and down on adjoining rocks, having territorial disputes among themselves, during which they tilt their bodies sideways and display the blue undersides. The posturing communicates to other lizards, "Scram! This is my rock!"

And where there are lizards, snakes are usually in the vicinity hunting a meal. Be alert for the gray-tan, 2- to 4-foot-long racer. This sleek, nonvenomous reptile is a visually oriented predator that keenly focuses on movement to locate potential food or swiftly escape enemies. Therefore, if you encounter one, observe the snake for a few minutes. You may witness it capturing and swallowing a lizard—nature's everyday predator-prey drama.

Remaining quiet might allow you to hear a faint rustling beneath nearby sagebrush. Presently, a shy least chipmunk appears as it scurries from one hiding place to the next while foraging for seeds, insects, and other items in its varied diet. Common in open shrub steppelands, it is more grayish in dorsal coloration than the darker chipmunks of forested regions. At the opposite end of the squirrel spectrum is the large, bulky (up to 23 pounds) yellow-bellied marmot. Popularly known as the rockchuck, it boldly gives a shrill "chirr" warning from the top of a rock outcrop as you approach. Family colonies of several individuals inhabit stony dens, and one is always posted as a lookout for possible danger.

True rabbits are represented by two species east of the Cascades in Oregon. The mountain cottontail is commonly encountered, but is generally not an animal of open country. It favors the transition between juniper-pine woods and steppe shrublands with plenty of vegetation and rock jumbles for cover, especially along riparian zones. The pygmy rabbit, however, is adapted to sagebrush flats. This short-eared, little mammal (the smallest rabbit in North America) requires deep-soiled areas with dense growths of big sagebrush, where it excavates extensive burrow systems. Because it is largely nocturnal and the sage-enshrouded burrow openings are less than four inches in diameter, pygmy rabbits are seldom seen. Additionally, populations seem to be declining, so if you are fortunate enough to see one, report the sighting to a wildlife management agency. Though similar in appearance to a cottontail, it can be differentiated by the lack of a conspicuous white tail.

The Great Basin spadefoot

The Great Basin spadefoot is the Northwest's most desert-adapted amphibian. Ranging in size from 1.5 to 2.5 inches, this little toad's common name is derived from a dark, sharp-edged nubbin that protrudes from the heel of each rear foot. These "spades" are used to burrow rapidly backward into soil. It manages to survive in arid environments by remaining underground during dry periods—possibly two years or more when extended droughts occur.

Great Basin spadefoot emerging from rain-soaked sand, near Bend, Central Oregon

A prairie falcon feeds a ground squirrel to its young. Photo: Tom and Pat Leeson

With the arrival of spring and early summer rains, spadefoots emerge to breed in any available shallow water—rain pools, lake and stream edges, irrigation ditches, stock tanks and ponds, and even the warm, muddy water in a cow hoof print. The males quickly attract large aggregations of both sexes with their loud, monotone choruses of "whaaa, whaaa, whaaa." After hatching, the larvae develop rapidly and can transform from aquatic tadpoles to terrestrial adults in as little as two weeks or less. This allows them to be ready for existence on land before their often temporary pools of water have evaporated under the summer sun.

The Great Basin spadefoot inhabits sagebrush steppelands, saltscrub deserts, and dry juniper-pine associations east of the Cascades. It is primarily active at night, with a diet consisting largely of insects. The next time you're driving during a spring cloudburst on the high desert, watch the wet pavement ahead. Chances are, you'll see one or more of these hardy toads hopping purposefully across the road. ■

Wary wildlife of the steppelands

If time permits, venture deeper into this fragrant sagebrush world. Walking farther from the road, you'll be treated to the sight of wildlife that are more wary; but quiet, slow movements, patience, and binoculars are required.

If you spot a group of golden-tan, white-rumped pronghorn—often incorrectly called the American antelope—appreciate the fact that this would have been a rare sight in the early 1900s, when their numbers dwindled dangerously low because of overhunting and restrictive rangeland fencing. Now, after hunting controls and redesigned fences, they are a relatively common sight. Not a true antelope, these alert animals rely on speed as their defense. Pronghorn are curious, however, and will invariably stop to look back at you after an initial spooked run.

Don't forget to lift your eyes above the gray-green horizon from time to time. If a high-flying speck suddenly turns into an earth-seeking, feathered missile, you've spotted a prairie falcon. Just as the pronghorn rep-

Burrowing owl, near Halfway, Northeastern Oregon

American badger. Photo: Tom and Pat Leeson

resents freedom on the run, this streamlined bird of prey symbolizes the unrestrained liberty of the vaulted desert skies. Breathtakingly designed for speed, it may plunge at nearly two hundred miles per hour to capture other flying birds for food. Prairie falcons hunt the open rangelands as well as rocky canyons and mountain cliffs, where they lay their eggs on high, bare clefts of precipices.

While watching the falcon's daring swoops, don't stumble into an American badger's twelve-inch-wide burrow opening. This stout, short-legged member of the weasel clan is equipped with powerfully clawed forelimbs that allow it to dig at amazing speeds. Abandoned badger homes supply subterranean retreats for several species of other animals, ranging in size from snakes to coyotes. Burrowing owl pairs often appropriate these empty lairs for nesting. By late spring and early summer, the owlets can be seen gathered at the entrance of their burrow, resembling little knock-kneed gnomes conducting serious discussions. Should you chance upon such a congregation, listen carefully—distressed young burrowing owls use an excellent imitation of a rattlesnake's buzz to scare enemies away from the nest.

The pronghorn

Journals of the first trappers and explorers who crossed the expansive prairies of the American West tell of the many herds of pronghorn they encountered. Unfortunately, this soon changed.

With the growth of more and more white settlements, unrestricted hunting began to take its collective toll on the pronghorn. Discovering that these fleet tan-and-white-patterned animals are very inquisitive, clever hunters learned to tie a strip of brightly colored cloth on a bush, and wait nearby in concealment. Attracted by the fluttering banner, curious pronghorn would approach within shooting distance. In this way, meat was easily procured. Later, ranchers added their bul-

Pronghorn. Summit of Steens Mountain, Southeastern Oregon

lets to the killing spree, believing that prong-horn competed with cattle and sheep for food and water. Additionally, miles and miles of stockmen's fencing hampered the seasonal movements of pronghorn and blocked escape from predators. Unlike deer, pronghorn will not bound over a fence.

It is estimated that approximately 35 million pronghorn inhabited North America in the early 1800s. By the beginning of the twentieth century, the sustained overhunting and habitat loss had reduced the total population to about fifteen thousand. As with the thoughtless slaughtering of the vast bison herds on the Great Plains, extinction loomed on the horizon. In 1936, famed Oregon mammalogist Vernon Bailey wrote in defense of the pronghorn:

> For ages past they furnished food to native tribes, and during the exploration and settlement of the country, they played an important part in supplying food to explorers, pioneers and settlers. Their destruction, however, has been unnecessarily rapid and wasteful—a part of the national disgrace that characterizes our treatment of so many of our best game animals. It would seem now a national duty, as well as an honor, to protect in a few scattered areas remnants of the species for the pleasure and admiration of future generations.

Others joined Bailey in voicing concern and 1936 marked the establishment by President Franklin D. Roosevelt of the Hart Mountain National Antelope Refuge in Southeastern Oregon along with its sister sanctuary in adjoining Nevada, the Sheldon National Wildlife Refuge. With federal protection and strict hunting regulations, pronghorn numbers have successfully rebounded and their herds are now a frequent sight across the open country of Oregon's dry side. Original avenues of dispersion are again unimpeded due to redesigned wire fences that have an elevated bottom strand, allowing pronghorn to scramble beneath.

Pronghorn are most common on the plateaulands, feeding on shrubs, grasses, and herbaceous forbs. These unfettered vistas allow its large, telescopic-vision eyes to detect the movement of possible enemies as far away as four miles. During summer, pronghorn may also range upward into the unforested sections of mountain ranges. They are sometimes seen as high as 7,000-feet elevation in the Cascades at Crater Lake, and at over 9,000 feet on the summit of Steens Mountain.

The pronghorn is actually the only surviving member of the uniquely North American family Antilocapridae, which boasted a number of species during the Miocene through the Pleistocene. (The antelope, with which the pronghorn is often confused, is in the same family as cattle, goats, and sheep, the Bovidae.) Second only to the African cheetah for the animal world speed record, the pronghorn is capable of sustaining 30 to 40 miles per hour for distances of fifteen miles, with short bursts to more than 60 miles per hour. Even week-old fawns (born in May, often as twins) can easily outrun a human. Newborns, largely odorless for the first several days, lie hidden in sagebrush and grass, avoiding hungry coyotes. When the animal is alarmed, its distinctive white rump hairs become erect and flash a warning to other herd members. The horns of both sexes have a bone core with an external keratin covering; unlike the true antelopes of Asia and Africa, the outer sheaths are shed yearly. Male's have larger horns, each equipped with the namesake, short prong.

The next time you hike in the high desert and enjoy the sight of a pronghorn herd racing across the sagebrush plains, be grateful to the foresight of people like Vernon Bailey and President Franklin D. Roosevelt. Because of their successful efforts, this magnificent animal is still with us in the twenty-first century. As Justice William O. Douglas wrote in 1960, "Those who visit Hart Mountain next century will know that we were faithful life tenants, that we did not entirely despoil the earth which we left them. We will make the tradition of conservation as much a part of their inheritance as the land itself." ▪

Creatures of the Great Basin true desert

Continuing your drive east on Highway 20, past Burns and southeastward into the vast "backside of beyond," you'll eventually enter the true deserts of the northern Great Basin—places such as the Alvord Desert and the eroded badlands of the Owyhee River Canyon. In the saltscrub communities that occur here, a variety of animals adapted to extreme aridity reach the northern limits of

Male Great Basin collared lizard. Eastern foothills of the Pueblo Mountains, Southeastern Oregon

Desert horned lizard. Eastern foothills of the Pueblo Mountains, Southeastern Oregon

Pigmy short-horned lizard. Fort Rock State Park, Central Oregon

their ranges in western North America.

Reptiles are especially suited to these sunny, dry habitats. Here, if you're lucky, you might find the state's rarest reptile—the ground snake, a small, secretive burrower with a variable dorsal pattern that often consists of alternating orange and black crossbars. Also found, moving about on sandy areas between black greasewood, shadscale, and other shrubs, are large desert lizards: the long-nosed leopard lizard, western whiptail, and desert horned lizard. Exploring loose-soiled hillsides among scattered boulders will often turn up the Great Basin collared lizard with its distinctive black and white "collar" markings on its neck. This lizard sometimes attains a total length of thirteen inches, has a big head, bulky body, large hind legs, and a long tail like a miniature *Tyrannosaurus rex*. This impression is enhanced when it is startled into fleeing, as it often runs on its hind legs in bipedal dinosaur fashion.

Horned lizards

With their bizarre, spiny appearance and odd body shape, the well-known horned lizards resemble tiny dinosaurs or dragons. If astronauts exploring Mars discovered small creatures adapted to the red planet's barren surface, this is the sort of thing that would be expected. Often mistakenly called horned toads, they are not an amphibian like true toads. These interesting animals are actually reptiles that are well adapted to harsh, dry environments.

Of the two species native to Oregon, the desert horned lizard is a classic example of this group. It sports large crownlike spines at the back of the head and a scattering of smaller spines on the body, legs, and tail. Adults may reach nearly six inches in total length. Conversely, the pigmy short-horned lizard's characteristics are completely opposite. Its spines are much smaller, being reduced to mere nubbins at the rear of the head. And as its name suggests, the overall size is diminutive with a maximum length of no more than 3.5

inches. If any reptile could be called cute, it is the pigmy short-horned lizard. Both species may range from brown or pale tan to grayish, along with some darker markings, and their undersides are always a uniform white or cream. Coloration varies greatly from one geographic place to another, as they match their habitats remarkably well. Desert horned lizards generally exhibit brighter colors, often having an attractive rusty-orange speckling dorsally.

All horned lizards (there are fifteen species in North and Central America) have wide, flat bodies and short tails. This low profile allows them to quickly burrow into sand when seeking escape, and the spines discourage hungry predators.

Horned lizards prefer open, sandy-gravelly areas with scattered shrubs, but both species rarely share the same location. The desert horned lizard is a Great Basin reptile that reaches the northern limits of its distribution in the arid saltscrub ecosystems of Southeastern Oregon. The pigmy short-horned lizard is unique to the lava plains of the Northwest region and is more tolerant of cold at higher elevations. It occurs throughout much of the sagebrush-bunchgrass steppelands and open juniper woodlands of Oregon's dry side. Surprisingly, this little lizard even ranges upward to near timberline at seven thousand feet along the crest of the Cascade Range in exposed pumice sand areas.

The favored food of all horned lizards is ants, although they feed on other insects and spiders as well. Reproduction differs in the two species: the desert horned lizard lays eggs, whereas the pigmy short-horned lizard is live-bearing.

Although these reptiles are popular as pets, do not be tempted to take one home. Horned

White-tailed antelope squirrel. Owyhee River Canyon, Southeastern Oregon

lizards usually do not live long in captivity and are best left in the wild. ■

OTHER animals that are restricted to these deserts in Oregon include the attractively marked black-throated sparrow, white-tailed antelope squirrel, and the small kit fox with its large, alert ears. Hiding under rocks are a host of invertebrates that range from scorpions and centipedes to spiders and insects. Most impressive among these creepy-crawly critters is the yellowish colored giant desert hairy scorpion. It grows to nearly six inches in length and is the largest scorpion in the United States. Despite its horrific appearance, the sting of this species is only mildly poisonous to humans. Another unusual secretive creature is the two-inch-long Jerusalem cricket. Reddish brown in color, with a bulbous head and humped back, it gives many people the shivers, but is a harmless nocturnal scavenger.

When in rocky desert terrain, you can expect to encounter two species of wrens. The pale tan rock wren is seen on boulder-strewn

Giant desert hairy scorpion. Alvord Basin, Southeastern Oregon

Borax Lake chub

slopes, voicing its buzzing "zeee" call. Entering a cliff-hemmed gulch brings us into the habitat of the canyon wren, with its reddish brown coloration. Its distinctive, downward-spiraling song echoes from the stone walls, sounding as though the bird has plummeted downward from a precipice.

UNLIKELY as it may seem, fish are native to these arid landscapes—even trout. Here and there, draining from the higher ranges, are watercourses of varying sizes, and some basins contain spring-fed pools and salty lakes. Several species and subspecific forms of fish that swim these desert waters are endemics that exist as relict, isolated populations. Examples are the Warner sucker, Foskett speckled dace, Catlow tui chub, Summer Basin tui chub, and Alvord chub. The tiny Borax Lake chub is particularly interesting. Found nowhere else in the world, it has evolved the ability to inhabit the slightly alkaline hot-spring-heated, 93-degree aquatic environment of Borax Lake in the Alvord Basin. Because of habitat deterioration and a subsequent lowering of population numbers, the Borax Lake chub is a federally protected, endangered species.

While hiking the parched shorelines of these desert lakes, watch for the uncommon snowy plover. Listed by the state as a threatened species, this small grayish- tan and white shorebird nests on barren sand and the margins of alkali flats, spring through summer. The color pattern of the eggs and young blend with the habitat, so take care not to accidentally trample them. The little chicks leave the nest within hours after hatching, and the parents can be seen guiding their offspring to good foraging areas where they peck about for various small invertebrates.

Desert trout

During the chilly climate of the last Ice Age, enormous pluvial lakes existed throughout the Great Basin and fish abounded. When the climate warmed and became drier about 10,000 years ago, these reservoirs dwindled over the millennia to shallow, alkaline lakes with adjacent feeder streams. Resultantly, fish populations were trapped in scattered, land-locked desert basins. Isolated for great spans of time, many of these evolved into unique endemics.

Lahontan cutthroat trout

For anyone traveling through the baking aridity of a summer day in Southeastern Oregon, the first thought that springs to mind isn't, "This sure looks like good trout country." Nevertheless, they're there, tucked away in canyon streams that are shaded by flimsy ribbons of riparian cottonwoods—watercourses that empty onto shimmering alkali flats and evaporate into nothingness. In a few basins, semipermanent lakes temporarily welcome trout, but these fish must retreat back up the streams during drought years when the ephemeral bodies of water disappear.

Although most trout require cool streams, the desert populations have adapted to survive the inhospitably hot months of July and August in the basin and range country. Two kinds occur there. One is the northern Great Basin redband trout, a subspecies of the well-known rainbow trout. The other is the Lahontan form of the cutthroat trout, named after Lake Lahontan, which once inundated much of the region during the Pleistocene.

Because the various basins are inward draining, there has been no genetic inter-change between fish populations for many thousands of years. Often, a narrow ridge might be the only barrier dividing two groups of trout, but the gap may as well be a million miles. All of this parochial divergence offers fascinating lessons in endemism.

Intersubspecies diversity among northern Great Basin redband trout and Lahontan cutthroat trout in each watershed has long been noted. Distinctly differing populations of redbands occur in Southeastern Oregon's Harney Basin, Catlow Basin, Goose Lake Basin, Warner Basin, and Chewaucan Basin. Likewise, divergent cutthroat populations inhabit the Alvord Basin, Whitehorse Basin, and Quinn River drainage. Among ichthyologists, those tending to be "lumpers" view these merely as interesting, extremely localized forms of two highly variable subspecies. Conversely, the "splitters" regard them as significant enough to warrant recognizing each population as a separate subspecies. No matter how they are taxonomically categorized, these endemic trout contribute a unique component to the biodiversity of Oregon's dry side.

Unfortunately, the waters have been genet-

Gopher snake swallowing a rat

were altered and stream health improved there. A 1999 census showed that Whitehorse Basin cutthroat numbers had dramatically increased. With more enlightened management, similar success stories are unfolding for other relatively pure populations of native cutthroat and redband trout. ■

Desert nightlife

When the desert sun sinks low, a number of animals become active, often through the entire night. Daytime temperatures are usually too high during the summer for many species to be out and about. Snakes, such as the gopher snake (also called the bullsnake) and western rattlesnake, will remain sheltered in the cool of deep rock crevices and rodent burrows. Emerging from their diurnal retreats during the more moderate temperatures of evening, these reptiles begin hunting for food.

And what prey are these snakes seeking? Rodents. After sunset, the desert comes alive with the hurry-scurry of countless mice and rats. Deer mice, canyon mice, Great Basin pocket mice, little pocket mice, sagebrush voles, western harvest mice, and dark kangaroo mice comprise this miniature midnight army. Their ranks include the rather unusual northern grasshopper mouse that has a diet composed of more than 80 percent animal food—insects, scorpions, lizards, and other species of mice. This little predator is the wolf of the mouse world. While on the hunt, it throws back its head and howls at the dark desert sky with a drawn-out, whistling call, and kills prey with its slashing incisors. Two species of gentle-natured kangaroo rats— Ord's and chisel-toothed—hop through the sagebrush as they forage in the darkness,

ically muddied by nearly a century of hatchery trout introductions (primarily a coastal rainbow subspecies), which hybridized with nearly all of the native varieties. In the 1990s, the trend began shifting away from hatchery stocking to an emphasis on promoting native trout and their habitats, but it was too late for most of these endemics: the Alvord cutthroat is now extinct, having been hybridized out of existence; and except for the Whitehorse Basin cutthroat, which escaped introductions of nonnative fish into its drainage, all the other redband and cutthroat populations have been genetically diluted to varying degrees.

But there is reason for optimism. Because the Lahontan cutthroat is federally protected over its entire range, the Whitehorse variation is afforded the same status. However, Whitehorse Basin riparian zones were badly degraded by many decades of intense grazing, resulting in a decline of these remnant fish. During the early 1990s, Bureau of Land Management grazing policies for the basin

stuffing their cheek pouches with seeds. Another nighttime prowler, the desert wood rat, continues to earn an infamous place in desert lore as the thieving "pack rat." These rodents have a strong attraction for small, shiny objects in human camps and cabins, hoarding the pilfered loot in their large nests of jumbled sticks.

Ord's kangaroo rat, the Badlands near Bend, Central Oregon.

Kangaroo rats

On a dark, moonless night, drive almost any stretch of desert road and your headlights will probably reveal what appear to be miniature kangaroos hopping about. No, you're not having Australian hallucinations. The little mammals are real, but they're actually rodents.

The sandy-soiled drylands of the American West are inhabited by seventeen species of kangaroo rats, which, to be taxonomically correct, are not true rats. These fascinating creatures are more closely related to pocket mice. With their tiny forelimbs, enormous hind legs and feet, long tail, and predominantly bipedal stance, they do somewhat resemble kangaroos. Most kinds average three inches in body length, with seven inches of tail, and are generally tan-colored above and white below. Their powerful rear legs allow them to escape predators with impressive hops of up to several feet, utilizing the elongated, tufted tail to maintain balance.

Besides athletic agility, these rodents possess another remarkable adaptation for survival. They never have to drink water—a handy ability for a creature that lives in parched environments where the annual precipitation may dip below ten inches. This is possible because the minuscule amounts of moisture contained in seeds they eat (their primary food source), along with plant leaves and the occasional insect, are metabolically processed in marvelously economical ways. Kangaroo rats have superefficient kidneys, their bodies retaining vital fluids so well that uric acid wastes are excreted as thick, pasty urine. Additional liquids are saved because they do not sweat. Instead, they have a respiratory cooling system. The temperature of their nasal passages is lower than that of the body, resulting in each breath being chilled and moisture retained through condensation. Other strategies to avoid dehydration involve retreating into their extensive burrow systems during daytime hours and plugging the entrances with sand to retain coolness and humidity. After sunset, they emerge to forage for food, stuffing their fur-lined external cheek pouches with seeds. Kangaroo rats are solitary, with each individual caching collected food in its own burrow. They are

Coyote. Malheur National Wildlife Refuge, Southeastern Oregon

very gentle, rarely attempting to bite when handled, but have lively territorial disputes among themselves. Morning in vegetated dunes will reveal the many foot and tail prints from their nocturnal activities. Also, look for small depressions in the sand where they take dust baths to keep their fur from becoming matted with oils.

Three species are native to Oregon, all similar in appearance. Ord's kangaroo rat is the most common, occurring nearly everywhere east of the Cascades in sagebrush areas and open juniper woodlands. The chisel-toothed kangaroo rat is a resident of Southeastern Oregon's saltscrub deserts, and the California kangaroo rat is found in the chaparral habitats of the Klamath Basin and west of the Cascades in the Rogue Valley. ■

NEARLY as abundant as the rodents, legions of bats take wing and begin their nightly pursuit of flying insects. These unique little mammals utilize sonar (echolocation) to efficiently locate food by emitting ultrasonic sound pulses. It has been estimated that a sin-

gle bat may eat approximately six hundred mosquitos in an hour. Although little brown bats, western small-footed bats, and Yuma bats are generally common in the open sagebrush country, three species are particularly drawn to desert river canyons where water attracts insects. One of them, the western pipistrelle (our smallest bat), is sometimes called the canyon bat because of this predilection. Likewise, the aptly named pale golden-tan pallid bat hunts stony habitats, and typical of this species, often alights on the ground to include centipedes and scorpions in its diet. The third is the little-known spotted bat, which is unusual in having a high-pitched, squeaking call that falls within the range of human hearing. Additionally, this species is highly distinctive within the predominantly brownish bat family because of its bold, black-and-white patterned body.

While watching the night sky, be alert for a white form with a forty-inch wingspan. As it momentarily glides into your field of vision and then vanishes into the darkness, you may hear a bansheelike, raspy shriek. This ghostly apparition betrays the silent flight of a barn owl in search of rodents.

Of all the nocturnal sounds, however, no animal gives a voice to the loneliness and expanse of the desert better than the coyote. Anyone who has sat by a sagebrush campfire at night and listened to its yipping howl has sensed something of the soul of this land. The coyote personifies the myth, the very essence of the arid American West. Both loved and hated by mankind, the coyote's adaptability and resourcefulness earn it the respect of friend and foe alike. These wily canines prowl throughout Oregon, but they seem most at home on the sagebrush plains.

Rattlesnake! Is it dangerous?

The rattlesnake is one of the classic wildlife icons of the American West. Although commonly feared and hated, these unique reptiles are ecologically important in keeping mice, rats, and ground squirrels from overpopulating and should not be needlessly killed in areas away from human habitation. If you are hesitant to hike in the desert because of the apprehension of coming upon a "rattler," relax. Rattlesnakes are not nearly as dangerous as is popularly believed. Few animals have generated so many misconceptions, fables, and just plain tall tales and lies.

A rattlesnake will never advance toward you to attack. If you leave it alone, it will leave you alone. They are actually rarely seen and will merely try to escape if encountered. A rattlesnake can strike outward with only about a third to a half of its body length. If you remain six feet or more away, you are well beyond striking range. On outings, just be sure to wear boots that cover your ankles and avoid placing your feet or hands near crevices, thick grass, and brush that may conceal a snake.

Despite the common belief that diamondbacks, sidewinders, and timber rattlesnakes occur in Oregon, only one species is native to the Northwest region—the western rattlesnake. It is rather mild-mannered in temperament when compared to the high-strung diamondback of more southerly climes. However, as with all kinds of animals, there is some individual variation in personality. Occasionally, a western rattlesnake will be found that is a bit scrappy and will immediately throw itself into a defensive coil and give a warning "buzz" with its tail. Given the chance, though, it will soon retreat into the nearest hiding place.

Western rattlesnake (Northern Pacific subspecies). John Day Fossil Beds National Monument, Sheep Rock Unit, Northeastern Oregon

Another erroneous belief is that a rattlesnake's age can be computed by counting its rattles. Actually, a new segment is added to the base of the rattle each time the skin is shed, but a rattlesnake may cast its old skin more than once a year. Also, as the rattle becomes longer and more fragile, several segments may break off at the end and be missing.

Adult western rattlesnakes average from 15 to 36 inches in length, occasionally reaching 48 inches, and rarely to 60 inches. Matching their surrounding habitat remarkably well, they exhibit considerable geographic variation in color and pattern. Consequently, herpetologists recognize several subspecies over this snake's broad distribution in western North America. Some authorities even consider these races distinct enough to be classified as full species. Suffice it to say, though,

Canada geese at dawn

western rattlesnakes from the predominantly more forested central and northeastern portions of the state will be darker with large dorsal blotches (referred to as the Northern Pacific subspecies); those from the open landscapes of Southeastern Oregon are lighter with smaller blotches (the Great Basin form). Where the ranges of the two subspecies meet (roughly, a 50-mile-wide zone that arcs northeastward from Klamath Falls to Baker City), intergrades that have blended characteristics of both varieties will be seen. ▪

Marshland multitudes

In this parched land, the marshes that occur in some basins act like magnets to draw waterfowl. Lushly vegetated aquatic areas such as Malheur, Warner, Summer, and Klamath lakes are rich, life-supporting ecosystems with incredible concentrations of wildlife. As you drive downward from the rimming, arid heights into one of these marshy basins, open the car windows and savor the commingling sensations of increasing air moisture and botanical aromas.

Located on the Pacific Flyway, these desert oases attract large numbers of migratory birds during spring and autumn. Many species will have traveled thousands of miles, and it is well worth your effort to visit one of these area's wildlife refuges to greet their arrival and witness the ornithological spectacle. At such times, the familiar clanging call of Canada geese can be heard everywhere as wedge-shaped squadrons of "honkers" circle the sky. Their multitudes are greatly magnified by other members of the goose clan. If you can manage to be in the right place at the right time, it's possible to experience the

Snow geese flock lifting off. Photo: Tom and Pat Leeson

Male red-winged blackbird. Sycan Marsh,
Central Oregon

Male mallard

A male ring-necked pheasant, creeps through grass in the Malheur National Wildlife Refuge. Introduced from Asia in the 1800s, these birds inhabit farmlands and grassy-brushy areas.

cacophonous liftoff of more than five thousand snow geese, usually mixed with Ross's geese—the combined white-feathered flock is like an avian blizzard. Keep your binoculars handy for encounters with greater white-fronted geese, tundra swans, mallards, ruddy ducks, cinnamon teals, Wilson's snipes, Wilson's phalarope, white-faced ibis, great blue herons, black-crowned night herons, American bitterns, black-necked stilts, snowy egrets, American avocets, western grebes, double-crested cormorants, and others too numerous to list. Also expect to see American white pelicans, along with gulls and terns of several species, that impart an oceanic coastal flavor to the surroundings. Another possible sighting for the alert birdwatcher is the impressively large trumpeter swan (to nearly 30 pounds with a wingspan of 80 inches). It was nearly extinct in the United States by the 1930s, but thanks to protection and reintroduction programs, this species is making a gradual comeback.

Even if you don't see the birds, you'll hear them—marsh wrens busily trilling, ducks placidly quacking and red-winged blackbirds exuberantly singing "bomp-ah-lee." Occasionally, seeming like a discordant note, a yellow-headed blackbird contributes its brash song, which has been likened to the noise of a strangled chainsaw. Another idiosyncratic sound is made by the gangly, 42-inch-tall sandhill crane, which produces a rattling effect reminiscent of stones being rolled down a length of pipe. But somehow, with Pacific treefrogs singing chorus, it all harmonizes into the symphony of the marsh.

Inhabitants of the junipers

Ascending out of the lake basin to slightly higher elevations, you enter the western juniper belt and its distinctive variety of wildlife. Although these open, semiarid woodlands are rather austere, several animal species are specialized to prosper here. The most noticeable will be flocks of audacious black-billed magpies moving through the trees. With their black-and-white bodies, beautiful iridescent green long tails, and noisy chattering, it's easy to know when these birds are in the vicinity. Less apparent will be the soft, high "weep" call of the Townsend's solitaire, repeated at intervals, or its prolonged, fluty song. Commonly seen perched at the very top of a juniper, this gray, robin-sized bird can be distinguished by a distinctive white ring that encircles each eye. Intimately tied to these fragrant groves, the favored food of the Townsend's solitaire is juniper berries, and it can often be seen vigorously chasing competing American robins and other birds from its territory. Also be alert for the visual treat of the mountain bluebird, which matches the clear high desert sky in color intensity, and uses juniper snag cavities for its nests.

The black-billed magpie

If you take a hike through juniper woodlands and peer upward into the branches as you meander, chances are you'll eventually see a large bundle of sticks stuffed between some limbs. This is the nest of the black-billed magpie. Effectively barricading the eggs or young birds ensconced within from predators, this magpie fortress may be nearly three feet in diameter. If it is during the breeding season (March through June), even before seeing the nest, you'll know it's there: the adult magpies will begin screaming warnings while frantically circling the specific tree. The black-billed magpie will also utilize riparian trees and large, thorny bushes in which to construct its nest, but nearly always in proximity to stands of juniper where dead limbs can be scavenged for nesting material. The dedicated pair may work as long as forty days to complete their nest, sometimes incorporating shiny, human-made objects pilfered from campgrounds and ranch sites. Magpies are very intelligent birds with complex social interactions within their groupings, and a male and female pairing may last for a lifetime.

The black-billed magpie is one of the signature species of Oregon's dry side, their brash, "mag, mag, mag,"or short "jeeck" calls being heard nearly everywhere. These large (to about 20 inches in length) birds are boldly patterned with black and white, and when they fly in conspicuous groups, their long black tails flash iridescent blue-green. With their elegant plumage and flamboyant manner, magpies convey the impression of a tropical bird of Central and South American jungles, rather than a resident of the semiarid steppelands.

Black-billed magpie, Cabin Lake, Central Oregon. Photo: Frank Cleland

When not flying high above the juniper forests, magpie gangs will be seen foraging on the ground for just about anything edible—insects, mice, fruit, seeds, carrion, and the eggs and nestlings of other bird species. Sometimes magpies will alight on the backs of cattle, deer, and elk to pick ticks from their hides.

Many farmers and ranchers dislike magpies because these opportunistic birds will occasionally break chicken eggs and slurp the contents, kill barnyard chicks, and pick unmercifully at sores on livestock. However, without the bombastic black-billed magpie, the country east of the Cascades would certainly be less lively and interesting. ▪

ANOTHER species, the pinyon jay, is most often encountered at the blending zone of western juniper and ponderosa forests, where it feeds on pine seeds. These grayish-blue birds usually fly in large flocks, their calls sounding as though they are collectively chuckling at a shared joke. The loggerhead shrike, with its distinctive black mask markings across the eyes, also frequents open juni-

California quail. Malheur National Wildlife Refuge, Southeastern Oregon

Yellow pine chipmunk. Bend, Central Oregon

per country. It is a formidable predator that pounces upon insects, lizards, small rodents, and birds, and then impales its dead prey on a sharp thorn or a barbed wire fence as a food cache.

The golden evening hours will be graced by the sweet-sad, peaceful cooing of mourning doves. When these common birds are startled into flight, you'll hear the whistling sound produced by their wings. In all probability, the mellow twilight sounds will also include the soft "but-we-doo" calls of a covey of California quail scuttling through the brushy understory. As its name suggests, this species is native to California, along with the valleys of Southwestern Oregon, but has been widely introduced east of the Cascades. When dusk further deepens, a new sound appears: a rather startling "bruuup," produced by the wings of a common nighthawk as it pulls out of a swooping dive. Not really a hawk, it is a member of the nightjar family, which includes its relative, the common poorwill. Later, if you prowl the juniper zone after dark and poke about in rock outcrops, your flashlight beam may disclose a foraging little rodent with noticeably large ears. This is the pinyon mouse, which feeds primarily on juniper seeds and makes its nest from the shredded bark of these trees.

Forest squirrels

Advancing upward in elevation, just above the juniper belt, brings you into stands of towering ponderosa pines, with a subsequent change in fauna. To observe these native residents, you can choose just about any place where the sun streams down through the trees onto the needle-and-cone-littered forest floor. This is prime squirrel habitat, so pick a comfortable seat on an old, fallen log and quietly watch and listen. More than likely, a diminutive yellow pine chipmunk will appear first. This species is usually darker than the grayish least chipmunk we saw earlier in the open sagebrush steppe country. Its golden-cinnamon tinges match the ponderosa bark of the surrounding environment. Equally common is the golden-mantled ground squirrel, which is often misidentified as an oversized chipmunk. It can be easily differentiated, however, because it lacks the chipmunk's distinctive light stripes along each side of the head. Chubby, well-fed golden-mantled ground squirrels are often seen begging for handouts in picnic and camping areas, where they quickly lose their fear of humans. Although these small mammals look like cute escapees from a Disney animated movie, resist the temptation to feed them—the resultant obesity is not healthful for the squirrels. It is also advisable to avoid touching and cuddling these overly friendly creatures; they sometimes harbor fleas that can transmit bubonic plague bacterium.

Golden-mantled ground squirrel. Bend, Central Oregon

Tree squirrels are represented by three diurnal species in Oregon's dry side. The industrious red squirrel (or pine squirrel) occurs in the mountains of Northeastern Oregon. Its darker, close relative, the Douglas' squirrel—often descriptively called the chickaree for its sassy, chattering call—is found in the Cascade Range and eastward into the Ochoco and Warner ranges. The larger western gray squirrel primarily inhabits oak woods west of the Cascades, but ranges along the eastern slopes of these mountains in Central Oregon, trading its usual acorn-dominated diet for one composed mostly of pine seeds.

There is another tree-dwelling squirrel in Oregon's mountain forests, but finding it will necessitate staying out after sunset. This is when the small northern flying squirrel ap-

Red squirrel. Wallowa Lake, Northeastern Oregon

pears, but it doesn't actually fly with flapping wings in the manner of a bird or bat. Instead, there is a fur-covered fold of skin along each side of the body that enables it to glide from tree to tree—sometimes soaring for nearly three hundred feet. Unfortunately, because of its nocturnal habits, few people ever have the enjoyment of witnessing the aerial acrobatics of this fascinating animal. Although occurring in ponderosa pinewoods, it often seems to favor areas a little higher in eleva-

The great horned owl is found nearly everywhere east of the Cascades, in both forests and open country. Malheur National Wildlife Refuge, Southeastern Oregon

hear the bass hooting of the great horned owl, a long-eared owl's soft barking, or the trilling whistle of the little screech owl. A soft "booot" sound reveals the presence of the flammulated owl, and a raspy screech, likened to a saw being sharpened on a whetstone, discloses the northern saw-whet owl. And if we are lucky, the uncommon great gray owl, North America's largest member in this bird group, might be heard sending its low, booming "whoos" into densely timbered sections.

The famed (or infamous, depending upon your point of view) spotted owl ranges beyond the Cascade crest along the east slope of these mountains. Caught in the crossfire between the timber industry and environmental groups, it has become an iconic species that is synonymous with its preferred dwindling old-growth forest habitat. Spotted owls have had added stress from competing barred owls, which have been expanding their range southward into Oregon. Likewise, the rare northern hawk owl seems to be venturing out of its usual Canadian haunts, with recent sightings causing a stir among Oregon bird watchers.

tion where there are stands of Douglas fir, grand fir, western larch, and lodgepole pine. The thicker canopies of these conifers create a more shaded, moist forest floor where truffles (a subsurface fungi) can grow beneath rotting wood duff—the primary food of the northern flying squirrel.

Forest owls

The night shift also brings forth owls of several species to ambush the cavorting northern flying squirrels and other small mammals. These highly specialized predators approach their quarry in complete silence because of soft-edged, muffling primary wing feathers. This, teamed with incredible hearing provided by their wide, sound-gathering faces and large-eyed night vision, makes owls formidable hunters.

Quietly listening in the dark forest, we may

Nocturnal mammals and frogs

Other animals abroad at night are the striped skunk and its smaller cousin, the western spotted skunk. These odoriferously armed omnivores snuffle about in the forest undergrowth in search of foods that may range from insects and mice to berries. Porcupines are often out trundling around after dark as well. Other forest creatures stay at a prudent distance from both the musk-spraying skunks and the formidably quilled porky.

Anyone taking a moonlight stroll by a stream or lake will probably encounter a family of northern raccoons. Looking like bandits with their black-mask eye markings, these familiar animals will be poking about in the water. Their sensitively dexterous front feet, which resemble human hands, allow them to feel for food in the dark. "Coons" are highly omnivorous and most of their diet reflects a foraging preference for aquatic habitats—fish, frogs, mollusks, crayfish, and the eggs and nestlings of waterfowl, with riparian berries and nuts for hors d'oeuvres.

If you are by higher elevation waters, be sure to shine a flashlight along the shoreline. You might see a mouse with a short tail that resembles a miniature muskrat. This is the water vole, colonies of which live in burrow systems at the water's edge. Or if you catch a fleeting glimpse of a small, furry creature literally running on the water for a moment before it vanishes beneath the surface, you've witnessed a fleeing water shrew. This feat is made possible by elongated, stiff hairs that flare from the shrew's large hind feet and act as paddles. Like all of the shrew family, its hyperactive metabolism necessitates eating its own weight in food each day to avoid perishing from starvation. Consequently, this tiny, fierce predator attacks and eats nearly every kind of suitable prey it encounters, including diving under water and capturing small fish.

Aiming your flashlight upward might disclose long-legged bats skimming above the water in pursuit of insects. A forest dweller, this species is more adapted than most bats for flying in the chilly night air of mountain climates. The cold, rocky streams of the Blue Mountain complex and the eastern Cascade Range are inhabited by a diminutive amphibian unique to the Northwest region. Known as the tailed frog, its "tail" is actually a reproductive appendage found only on the males of this species. Again using your flashlight, you can observe these little animals perched atop protruding boulders in midstream as they wait to gulp down passing insects.

Diurnal forest birds and riparian mammals

Morning along streams and rivers is greeted by the ringing, bubbling song of the American dipper, or as it is sometimes called, the water ouzel. Anyone who spends time exploring a mountain brook may be surprised to see this gray wrenlike bird hop from a rock into the rushing waters and walk about on the stream bottom to eat aquatic insect larvae. Dippers are the constant, cheery companions of the forest watercourses in any season, bobbing up and down on spray-soaked rocks. They never leave these riparian corridors, rearing their young in a moss-and-twig-woven nest that is tucked into an inaccessible rock cleft, often within the torrent-mist shroud of a waterfall. It's also quite likely that a belted kingfisher's rattling call will resound above the roar of flowing water, and then living up to its name, the bird will fold its wings and dive into the stream after a fish. American mink and common muskrats are typical wildlife along these watercourses, and northern river otters are occasionally seen as well. Follow a stream far enough, and you will probably come across signs of the American beaver: stumps of gnawed-off trees and a broad pond created by its stick-and-mud dam.

Moving away from the rushing stream into the hushed environment of a mixed conifer forest, you will soon encounter other diurnal birds; brash blue-black Steller's jays usually scold trespassers and sometimes a large pileated woodpecker's loud "tap-tap-tap" resounds as it pummels a dead pine to extract insects for food. Scanning the surrounding trees will often disclose other members of the woodpecker clan, such as the red-naped sapsucker, downy woodpecker, northern flicker, and if you are fortunate, the uncommon black-backed woodpecker. Closer scrutiny might bring into focus small gray-backed, light-breasted birds that are walking up and down the tree trunks, busily eating insects. These will be any of three species of nuthatches—the white-breasted, red-breasted, or pygmy. In the branches above, the similarly sized and patterned mountain chickadee will be voicing its namesake "chick-a-dee-dee-dee" call, and a brilliant color splash of yellow and orangish-red plumage marks the arrival of a western tanager. Where these assortments of small birds abound, the sleek Cooper's and sharp-shinned hawks will be hunting them, rocketing between the trees with high-speed precision to make a capture.

Mountain quail, with their tall, black head-plumes, move through brushy places, and during the spring mating season, the deep drumming sound of ruffed grouse and the bass hoot of blue grouse are heard as males perform their respective courtship displays. Around forest-bordered lakes, use your binoculars to spot the fish-catching osprey (fish hawk) and stately bald eagle, perched on snags at the water's edge. In campgrounds and picnic areas, you may be surprised when a gray jay fearlessly snatches food directly from the table, earning it the popular name of "camp robber." The larger, distinctively gray-and-black-patterned Clark's nutcracker also enjoys human-provided snacks (flocks of them panhandle tourists at Crater Lake National Park).

Small fauna of the meadows and forests

If the trail breaks out of the forest into a sunny meadow filled with summer wildflowers, you can expect to be treated to the sight of those buzzy little jewels of the ornithological world, the hummingbirds—usually the rufous hummingbird but sometimes calliope and black-chinned hummers, along with the occasional Anna's hummingbird on the eastern flanks of the Cascades. More than likely, this grassy glade will also contain a colony of Belding's ground squirrels, sounding their whistled warning calls. These orangish-brown animals are common in forest openings east of the Cascades, from the lower western juniper–ponderosa pine transition areas to quite high elevations. They can be seen scurrying about at nearly nine thousand feet on the crest of Steens Mountain, where much of their life is spent in hibernation. A larger species, the Columbian ground squirrel, occurs in the mountains of Northeastern Oregon. Having a distinctive red coloration on the face and undersides of the body, it inhabits meadows in coniferous forests and ranges upward into the subalpine zones. This squirrel is very common in the Wallowa Mountains, and backpackers who hike the high country of the Eagle Cap Wilderness are familiar with it.

Small, secretive creatures live under moist, rotting logs on the shadowy forest floor. Among these is the long-toed salamander, with its greenish-yellow marbled dorsal pattern. Another seldom-seen inhabitant of Oregon's dry side forests is an unusual stubby little snake called the rubber boa, named for its pliable rubbery skin. The most northerly ranging boa in the world, it is sometimes called the two-headed snake because it often displays its blunt tail as a decoy "head" to draw an attacking predator away from the snake's more vulnerable body and true head.

Predator and prey

Larger animals inhabit these forests as well, such as the commonly seen mule deer, or the more dainty white-tailed deer of the Columbia Basin and Snake River drainages. Other species, however, are more wary of humans and less often encountered. Nevertheless, anyone who spends time exploring the backcountry of Oregon's dry side will eventually have the thrill of sighting some of the more elusive wildlife. While you are driving a far-flung stretch of Forest Service road, a small herd of Rocky Mountain elk will cross your path. As they seemingly melt away into a thick stand of lodgepole pine, you'll shake your head in amazement as to how the huge bulls, with antlers that may spread six feet across, manage to negotiate the close-growing trees. Or it might be a female black bear scooting across the road, a pair of teddybear-cute cubs in tow. It is also not uncommon for a motorist or hiker to spot a coyote intently hunting mice in a meadow, or a red fox or gray fox darting into the undergrowth.

Two native members of the cat family—the bobcat and cougar—are widely distributed east of the Cascades in Oregon, both in forests and open sagebrush country. Sightings, though, are definitely not everyday occurrences. Occasionally, a bobcat will appear, but encounters with its phantomlike, larger relative, the cougar (also called a mountain lion or puma) are even more infrequent. People who have devoted their entire lives to roaming the mountains and deserts can usually tally on the fingers of one hand the number

Gray jay. Sparks Lake, Cascade Range, Central Oregon

Belding's ground squirrel. Steens Mountain, Southeastern Oregon

Long-toed salamander. John Day River drainage, Northeastern Oregon

Always alert, a cougar warily drinks from a canyon stream. Photo: Cathy and Gordon Illg

of times they have glimpsed these big cats, if ever. Cougar populations are on the increase in Oregon, however, because of tightened hunting restrictions, so the chances of seeing this lithe predator are improving.

Interestingly, recent studies indicate that when it comes to dining, male cougars prefer elk, while females have more of a taste for deer. Because males have huge home ranges (often more than 100 square miles), these gender-specific food choices possibly allow both sexes to hunt their separate prey species in the same area without competition. Although a male cougar often tolerates several females in his territory, an intruding male will be chased away or even killed. Another cat species, the Canadian lynx, is even rarer and is known in Oregon by only twelve confirmed specimens, the most recent being in 1993 near Drewsey in Harney County. As reflected

by its name, this is a cat of the north woods that moves through the snowy landscapes on its large, snowshoe-like paws and preys primarily upon rabbits and hares. Studies have shown that when snowshoe hare populations drop in these northern forests, lynxes will often range far southward in search of food, probably accounting for the occasional Oregon occurrence.

If an elongated, 10- to 15-inch mammal with short legs and a thin tail flashes across the forest trail, it is probably a long-tailed weasel, or its slightly smaller cousin, the short-tailed weasel (also known as the ermine). Both of these fierce, little hunters have brown fur during the summer but transform to pure white in winter, except for a black tail tip. Two larger members of the weasel family, the American marten and fisher, have declined considerably in Oregon because they require remote old-growth forest wilderness, a rapidly disappearing habitat. The misnamed fisher actually doesn't eat fish; it prefers small mammals, birds, and berries, and is one of the few carnivores that preys upon porcupines. The extremely rare wolverine is another weasel that requires pristine wilderness, where it roams enormous distances in its search for food. The size of a small bear and aggressively powerful, wolverines will often kill and eat animals much larger than themselves, including deer. Most biologists doubt that breeding populations of wolverines exist in Oregon; field studies have indicated that the few sightings probably represent far-traveling, transient individuals from out-of-state.

Wildlife of the alpine zones

Choosing a steeper trail that takes you to higher elevations provides the chance to observe an interesting animal. Where the route passes a rockslide, stop and quietly listen. Soon a "peeek-peeek" call will probably emanate from the boulder jumbles above. Scanning with binoculars will disclose a chubby, tailless, guinea pig–like creature scampering about between the rock crevices—the American pika (pronounced "peeka" for its distinctive call), sometimes referred to as a cony. These small relatives of rabbits do not hibernate through the long, brutal mountain winters; instead, pikas remain active in their rock retreats and construct elaborate snow tunnels to move about. They literally make "hay" while the summer sun shines by cutting and drying green plants, surviving on these stored food caches until spring arrives.

Trekking ever upward, you breathlessly reach the alpine zone. If the hike is in the Wallowa Mountains, be sure to watch for a

American pika. Photo: Tom and Pat Leeson

small bird with pinkish wings and sides, usually seen foraging around patches of snow on the open tundra summits. This is a geographic variation of the gray-crowned rosy finch that is unique to this range. In the same class is a brassy, reddish-orange butterfly flitting among alpine flowers in these rarefied Wallowa heights. This endemic race of the American copper represents the only populations of this species in Oregon. Also be alert for the snowy-white mountain goats that live among the lofty crags. These surefooted mountaineers are not native Oregonians (at least within the past century), having been introduced into the Wallowa and Elkhorn ranges several decades ago.

Bighorn sheep also share these high-elevation Wallowa haunts with the mountain goats. Originally, the bighorn occurred throughout most of the steep, rocky terrain east of the Cascades in Oregon's mountains and deserts. However, it was totally extirpated from the state by the early 1940s because of overhunting and competing domestic sheep that introduced lethal diseases. Starting in 1955 on Hart Mountain, bighorn sheep

Bighorn sheep ram. Photo: Tom and Pat Leeson

have been reintroduced into mountain ranges and canyons at scattered localities throughout Oregon's dry side. Once again, during the autumn rutting season, the loud "craaack" of rams butting heads with their magnificent, spiraled horns echoes through the region's stony chasms.

Struggling to survive

Unfortunately, the bighorn sheep isn't the only animal species of Oregon's dry side that has struggled for survival. After the coming of white settlements, the mighty grizzly bear eventually lost this battle in 1931 when the last known individual in the state was killed in Wallowa County. The gray wolf was exterminated in Oregon by the mid-1940s, but appears to be attempting a return. During 1999 and 2000, it was confirmed that a total of three wolves crossed the Snake River into Oregon. The trio came from Idaho, where

the U.S. Fish and Wildlife Department has a wolf reintroduction program that is managed by the Nez Perce Tribe. One animal was captured and returned to Idaho, another was hit by a car, and the third was shot. Oregon ranchers are wary of these developments, envisioning future losses of cows and sheep to wolf predation. The Oregon Department of Fish and Wildlife has developed a wolf management plan that attempts to address both the concerns of ranchers and wildlife advocates who welcome these canids back to Oregon. Undoubtedly, this program will need continued fine-tuning over time as a wolf population grows in the state.

Oregon fish are in trouble, too. The famed native chinook salmon, sockeye salmon, and steelhead runs of the Northwest's interior rivers have declined greatly over the past century; some populations, to dangerously low levels, others vanishing entirely. In 1805, the Lewis and Clark expedition saw incredible numbers of these fish swarming up the Columbia and Snake river drainages, hurling themselves up surging waterfalls, with many fish ultimately reaching the most remote tributary streams and mountain lakes. Nevertheless, though greatly diminished, they are still here continuing the ancient anadromous migration—obeying genetically programmed urgings, the adults travel upstream from the sea to their natal streams to spawn. The following year, the juvenile smolt offspring swim downstream to the ancestral briny waters, completing the reproductive cycle.

Returning to our earlier hike in the Wallowa Mountains as an example, finding these fish will require descending from the alpine habitat of the mountain goats we were observing. Follow an Eagle Cap Wilderness trail from the headwaters of the Lostine River, down the gurgling brook to where it gathers size. In the wide, clear pools with gravelly bottoms, you will begin to see them —chinook salmon and steelhead (the seagoing form of the rainbow trout), battered after their long journey from the Pacific Ocean. The trip is an arduous one in these modern times with many hazards to navigate: exhaustingly steep fish ladders at manmade dams; overheated tributary streams that have been stripped of shading vegetation by bad cattle grazing practices; silted, oxygenstarved waters where the surrounding forests were improperly logged—it's a genuine miracle any of them survive! The little smolts face even worse obstacles as they find their way to the ocean: they must pass through the lethal turbines of huge dams along the Columbia. Thousands upon thousands perish in the attempt.

As for the sockeye salmon, don't expect to see this species in the Lostine River, or anywhere else in Oregon. All of its ocean-going runs are gone from the state. Originally, sockeye fought their way ever upward along riverine systems to mountain lakes, their favored spawning environment. Classic examples are Wallowa Lake, created by the Wallowa River in the northeastern corner of the state, and Suttle Lake in Central Oregon's Metolius drainage. However, localized dams have effectively made salmon barriers between these lakes and the Columbia River, disrupting their connection with the Pacific Ocean. Now only the landlocked kokanee form of the sockeye occurs in these localities. In adjacent Idaho, a remnant anadromous run of sockeye that breed in Idaho's Salmon River has managed to survive. Each year, they trace Oregon's northeastern borders in the Snake and Columbia rivers during their migrations, but their numbers appear to be dwindling.

Although extensive portions of the land-

A male Chinook salmon plows its way through the shallow waters of a spawning stream. Photo: Tom and Pat Leeson

The Columbia spotted frog seems to be declining in some parts of its range.

Biologists surveying frog and toad populations at Crane Prairie Reservoir, Cascade Range

scapes east of the Cascades may appear relatively wild and natural, unfortunately, this is not entirely the case. A number of long-term, adverse effects have taken their collective toll on our native wildlife during the past century. Most are related to habitat loss and degradation, such as overgrazing, improper logging practices, water pollution, abuse of riparian habitats, and encroachment of access roads into the last retreats of shy wildlife. Additionally, the introduction of competing non-native species has affected Oregon's wildlife. As mentioned earlier, the sage grouse, snowy plover, white-tailed jackrabbit, pygmy rabbit, American marten, and fisher are also in decline. And other species could probably be added to the list, such as the Columbia spotted frog, which seems to be disappearing in some places.

Alarmed by these problems, environmental organizations have become increasingly active in their efforts to protect and restore the remaining places that have relatively intact natural ecosystems. They argue that these areas provide critical habitat for several declining species of animals and associated flora. East of the Cascades in Oregon, this has resulted in ongoing clashes with the beef industry concerning grazing on public lands. These groups are also vociferously opposing the practice of harvesting the last stands of old-growth trees in our national forests. As to the issue of declining salmon and steelhead runs, environmentalists have been joined by both commercial and sports fishermen, along with several regional Native American Indian tribes. They are collectively calling for effective solutions to the problems dams create for anadromous fish; some are even demanding that the dams be removed entirely. Other conservation groups, such as Trout Unlimited and Oregon Trout, are questioning the stocking of streams with hatchery-raised fish and are calling for greater protection and enhancement of wild native trout and their habitats.

The greater sage grouse: Victim of habitat loss

Perhaps no other animal is so closely intertwined with the sagebrush steppe as the greater sage grouse. Nearly every aspect of this bird's life is dependent upon these fragrant shrubs; during winter, its entire diet is composed of sage. And large old-growth sagebrush provides shelter from the intense cold of snowy blizzards, gives refuge from predators, and shades nests in springtime.

A thick, unbroken sea of sagebrush, however, is not sufficient. Sage grouse require a mosaic of interrelated habitats that include a reliable water source, wet meadows for seasonal greens, and open spaces to use as strutting grounds (called a lek) for their annual mating rituals—essentially, an intact steppelands environment, rich in biodiversity.

During the blustery days of March and April, males of this species gather on their ancestral lek. In the chilly dawn hours they begin enacting a complicated courtship performance for an admiring audience of females, which are slightly smaller and drab by comparison. Standing up to their full 24-inch height, the strutting males fan out their long, pointy tail feathers and arch their wings. Simultaneously, they inflate naked yellow air sacks on their breasts and then bounce them up and down to produce loud blooping sounds as they rapidly deflate. Eventually, one or two dominant males that give the most impressive performances win the hearts of most of the females and mate with them. The females

Male sage grouse strutting on its snow-covered lek near Brothers, Central Oregon

then move away from the lek (often several miles) and each lays seven to nine eggs in a shallow, sage-leaf-lined depression, concealed beneath sagebrush. By summer, they can be seen shepherding their chicks into meadows, where herbaceous forbs and insects are eaten.

When Lewis and Clark first described the sage grouse in 1806, there were fantastic numbers of them throughout the interior plateau lands of the American West. Populations have dwindled greatly over the past century, largely due to habitat loss. Some biologists estimate that overall sage grouse populations have declined from 45 to 85 percent just since the 1980s. This has mostly resulted from improper grazing methods, conversion to agricultural crops, herbicides to eradicate sagebrush, poorly placed OHV (off-highway vehicle) trails and racetracks, and subdivi-

sion sprawl at town edges. Another pervasive problem is the invasion of nonnative cheatgrass, which fuels frequent wildfires of such intensity that sagebrush is reduced to smoldering ash. Experts who have studied the life history of the sage grouse claim there is probably no better indicator species of sagebrush ecosystem health. If these birds are prospering, then everything else is probably in harmony as well.

The greater sage grouse has vanished from Kansas, Oklahoma, Nebraska, New Mexico, Arizona, and British Columbia. In early 2005, a proposal to place it on the federal endangered species list was deemed unwarranted by the U.S. Fish and Wildlife Service. They concluded that the available data showed that although the bird had declined over much of its original range, the remain-

Red-winged blackbird nest. Goose
Lake, Southeastern Oregon

The human-wildlife interface

Conversely, difficulties have arisen with certain animal species that, instead of declining, have actually increased their numbers
and are now a nuisance. Raccoons and skunks
have prospered greatly in both urban areas
and backcountry camping and picnicking
grounds, where they pilfer discarded human
food and raid backyard gardens. It is now
common for city dwellers to be awakened in
the middle of the night by the loud clatter of
their garbage can lid being removed by a gang
of nimble-fingered raccoons. Coyotes, too,
have proliferated and expanded their range
from coast to coast, their nightly howls being
heard in even the largest of cities. Out on the
range, wild horses compete with native animals for food and water.

Cougars have become problematic as well.
During the 1960s, their numbers in Oregon
had sunk very low, estimated at a state total of
only about two hundred at that time. However, following a 1994 ban on using hounds to
hunt the cats, Oregon's cougar population has
skyrocketed. These large predators are more
frequently invading residential areas and
parks, often preying upon pet dogs and cats.
Each cougar requires a huge section of land
for its territory, and the citified individuals
are usually young males that have been chased
from prime wild habitat by older, dominant
males. Although attacks on humans by cougars are so rare as to be nearly nonexistent,
the close quarters of a fenced backyard provides the potential for a dangerous encounter.
Neighborhood deer should not be fed at the
edge of one's patio, which could inadvertently
entice a cougar.

Human-wildlife interface problems also
occur when homes are built at the base of a
rocky, south-facing hillside where rattle-

ing populations appeared relatively stable in
a number of locations. Immediately, some environmental groups vowed to fight this deci-
sion, predicting that the sage grouse will continue to decline without federal protection.
Other groups, such as the National Wildlife Federation, agreed with the federal pro-
nouncement, but with a caveat: their Northern Rockies representatives, Tom France and
Ben Deeble, wrote, "By deciding not to list
the species now, the Fish and Wildlife Service has, in effect, given states and local people a second chance to conserve this bird and
its habitats. This is an opportunity that should
not be squandered."

Time will tell. On your next hike through
a sagebrush expanse, if you are delightfully
startled by a flock of sage grouse bursting
forth nearby, savor the experience. ■

snakes spend the winter hibernating in denning sites. These venomous snakes invariably pass through yards as they disperse from their dens in spring, and the migration is repeated during their return in the autumn season. Again, as with the cougar situation, it is advisable to not make the area around a house attractive for the animals. Potential hiding places for rattlesnakes, such as boards laid flat on the ground or stone retaining walls with deep crevices, should be eliminated.

There are no easy answers for all these interrelated, complex problems. Management decisions based on sound science instead of emotion are required to wisely craft a sustainable balance between the needs of human society and that of the natural world. Occasionally, a wary, temporary truce has been established and disparate factions have sought common ground and more or less united their efforts. Some of these coalitions have successfully hammered out grazing strategies to restore damaged riparian zones, or created innovative timber thinning projects that reduce the potential for catastrophic forest fires. A good example of group cooperation happened in 2000. After many months of strained negotiations, environmentalists, ranchers, politicians, and governmental agencies developed a plan that led to congressional approval for the Steens Mountain Cooperative Management and Protection Act. When the vitriolic dust settled, the enormous conservation area had been divided into various designations. Included are 100,000 acres of cow-free, roadless wilderness, the withdrawal of 1.2 million acres from mineral and geothermal development (including most of the adjoining Alvord Basin), several water courses set aside as Wild and Scenic, a redband trout reserve in the Blitzen watershed, and more than 70,000 acres for grazing allotments.

Nevertheless, the situation is still far from sweetness and harmony. Contentious issues remain unresolved, and debates rage as the management saga of Oregon's dry side continues to evolve. Most environmental groups remain passionately devoted to their visions of vast stretches of public lands restored to their original biodiversity, with sagebrush-bunchgrass plains free of cows and old-growth ponderosa forests protected from clearcutting. With equal passion, traditional ranchers and loggers defend their lifestyles and maintain that their land stewardship methods successfully support the production of food and timber products, along with healthy wildlife habitat.

In the end, no matter our philosophical and political persuasions, we all must do what is best for the long-term health of the land and its fauna and flora. As famed conservationist Aldo Leopold wrote in his classic 1949 book, *A Sand County Almanac*, "When we see the land as a community to which we belong, we may begin to use it with love and respect."

PART II

Central
Oregon

Central Oregon

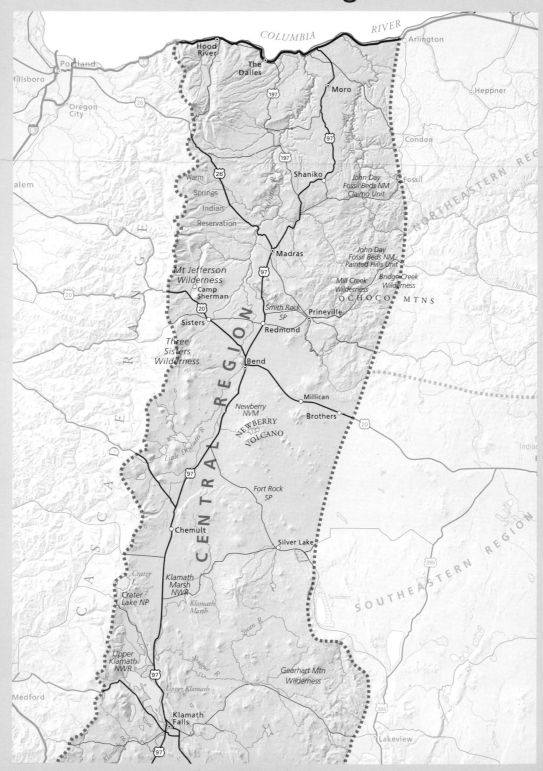

From Sagebrush Sandals to Ski Boots

It will be seen that the Deschutes Valley is mostly a barren region, furrowed by immense canyons, and offering very few inducements to settlers. Its few fertile spots, excepting those in the immediate vicinity of The Dalles, are separated from the rest of the world by almost impassable barriers and nature seems to have guaranteed it forever to the wandering savage and the lonely seeker after the wild and sublime in natural scenery.

LIEUTENANT HENRY L. ABBOT
Describing possible railroad routes into Central Oregon
Pacific Railroad Survey Reports, Volume 6, 1855

The overwhelming impact of the wild, rugged character of Central Oregon on early white explorers emerges in journal entries such as Lieutenant Abbot's. If such dramatic pronouncements seem humorous compared with the region's present-day highways, railroads, farmlands, and modern cities, we must reflect upon the times in which they were written.

In the early 1800s, the only way to reach Central Oregon's largely unexplored interior plateau was by lengthy, arduous travel, either by foot or horseback. No clearly marked trails or roads led the way into this frontier, and its breathtakingly deep canyons were without bridges. Away from river courses, locating water was a dangerous problem on the dry uplands, and much of the food on these long marches depended on the successful hunting of game along the way. Contributing further risk, some local Indian tribes were defensive toward invading, light-skinned explorers.

Pages 114–115: First snow at Sparks Lake, below South Sister. Inset: Gray jay, Sparks Lake, Cascade Range. Page 116: The Bridge Creek drainage, below Sutton Mountain.

Opposite: Mount Bachelor from Sparks Lake

Originally deemed impassable by early Euro-American explorers, the Crooked River Gorge in the Deschutes Valley is now spanned by a railroad line and major highway. Photo: Dave Z

Despite the civilizing influences of the past century, Central Oregon's scenery still has the power to inspire awe, and many sections of the region's backcountry continue to retain a comparatively wild, Old West flavor. Because of its geographical location at the very heart of the state, Central Oregon has a remarkable amalgamation of nearly all the features found east of the Cascades. Additionally, influences of Western Oregon spill over this mountain range and contribute to the mix.

Dominating Central Oregon, the imposing peaks of the high Cascade crest define the western skyline. The northern portion of the central region is hemmed on the east by the pine-clad Ochoco Mountains, a subrange of the Blue Mountains; the arid Great Basin forms the eastern boundary to the south. Within these perimeters, snow-fed rivers descend from mountain realms of lake-dotted ponderosa pine forests. The waters surge ever downward through basalt-rimmed canyons into an open, sun-drenched landscape fragrant with sagebrush and juniper.

The first Americans

Of course, early white explorers were not the first to gaze upon this alluring topography. Long, long before, predating more recent Native American tribes by unknown numbers of generations, Central Oregon's true first explorers encountered this land.

No one knows for certain just who these ancient ones were. Evidence indicates they were wandering, small bands of aboriginal, Ice Age hunter-gatherers, probably of Asian origin, who slowly drifted down from the far north. The 1996 discovery of the approximately 9,200-year-old skeletal remains of "Kennewick Man" along the Columbia River in Washington has added a new question mark to the Northwest's anthropological distant past. Though controversial, according to the scientists who made initial examinations, the skull's characteristics are not typical of most Native Americans, past or present. Rather than the usual traits of an ancient Mongolian descent, Kennewick Man evidences a lineage more akin to the prehistoric inhabitants of Southeast Asia, Polynesia, or Japan. Whatever their origins, these earliest ancestors of all North and South American native tribes apparently navigated the shores of a then-exposed land bridge (or walked its interior) between what are now Russia and Alaska. Unwittingly, they discovered a vast new continent.

Humans are thought to have arrived in

Cow Cave Butte in the Fort Rock Valley, where sagebrush sandals that are in excess of 9,000 years old have been unearthed.

Oregon some 14,000 to 15,000 years ago. Some of the oldest archaeological artifacts unearthed east of the Cascades in the state are those from Fort Rock Cave in northern Lake County. There, in what is now a dry, sandy high desert basin, archaeologists found woven sagebrush sandals that are dated to be somewhat more than 9,000 years old, along with basketry, matting, scrapers, knives, stone awls, and animal bones. Among these artifacts were stone weights, likely used by the aborigines on nets for capturing waterfowl. This suggests that Fort Rock Valley contained a lake or marshy wetlands at that time—remnants of the once huge Pleistocene Fort Rock Lake. Excavations in the general area have also disclosed projectile points carbon dated

at 13,500 years. Findings such as these continue to provide proof extending human occupancy in Oregon ever farther back in time.

As the climate east of the Cascades gradually became drier and the food-abundant lakes receded and vanished, the inhabitants shifted to a broader spectrum of resources. These bands of First Americans settled into various sections of the region and lived there generation after generation. Each tribe's culture eventually reflected its respective surrounding environments in intimate ways, the ebb and flow of seasons and cycles in the natural world. Food gathering, fishing, hunting, clothing, shelter, social customs, songs, ceremonies, religions, and myths all harmonized in ways that were both practical and deeply spiritual. Besides the interactions between interior plateau tribes, trading with coastal Indians was common as well.

Early white trappers and explorers

When the first white trappers arrived in Central Oregon in the early 1800s, they found groups of people with evocative names: Wasco, Wyam, Tygh, Tenino, Paiute, and Klamath. The meeting of entirely different cultures and races produced divergent reactions. Some tribes welcomed the pale-skinned explorers into their land; others resented the intrusion and tried to discourage the invaders. Beginning in the 1400s, when European explorers misnamed Native Americans as "Indians," racial stereotyping, discrimination, devastation of tribal cultures, and usurption of their lands have become a shameful part of our nation's history. Complex misunderstandings by whites continue to the present day.

At the beginning of the nineteenth century, the only white settlements in the Oregon Territory were fur company outposts; most established by the famed Hudson's Bay Company. These were located in what is now the Portland-Vancouver area and farther inland along the Columbia River. Interior Central Oregon was largely ignored until 1825 to 1827, when Peter Skene Ogden, representing the Hudson's Bay Company, led two exploratory expeditions up the Deschutes River into this high, wild country east of the Cascades. His parties, composed of hardy trappers and Indian guides, undertook harrowing treks that tested even these experienced woodsmen.

The first journey started out on a bad note when horses were lost while crossing the swollen Deschutes. Then the expedition spent a grim winter trapping and exploring the mountains, finally butchering some of the remaining horses to escape starvation. During the second trip, despite attacks by Indians and still more drowned horses, Ogden and his party accomplished much in the way of exploration. They were among the first whites to see and describe such Oregon features as the Paulina Mountains' huge crater containing two lakes, the Klamath Basin, and the Malheur-Harney region. The group even ventured into northern California, discovering and naming Mount Shasta.

Following Ogden's example, other explorers, such as John Work and Nathaniel J. Wyeth, investigated the Central Oregon area during the early 1830s. Wyeth, a trapper and trader, led the first probe by whites into what is now the Bend area before continuing on into the upper Deschutes drainage.

The best-known expedition through Central Oregon was led by the colorful John C. Fremont, accompanied by the equally colorful scout Kit Carson, and guided by Wasco Indian Billy Chinook. Fremont, then a young lieutenant with the Topographic Engineers of the U.S. Army, was rather ambitiously assigned to "explore the West." With a number of men under his command, and a cannon to assure protection from combative Indians, Fremont left The Dalles on November 25, 1843, and progressed south, up the Deschutes River, to the Klamath area of south Central Oregon. From there, the party moved eastward into the mountains, weathering a bitterly cold snowstorm. When the struggling group at last broke out of the trees onto the top of a high escarpment, they were astonished by the view that spread before them. Far below the vertical drop-off, sunshine bathed a large basin and its grass-edged lake. The dramatic contrast in this scene prompted Fre-

U.S. Army explorer John C. Fremont led an 1843 Topographic Engineers expedition through the entire length of Central Oregon. Courtesy of Deschutes County Historical Society

mont to christen the stormy prominence on which they stood Winter Rim and the attractive water below, Summer Lake. The Fremont expedition continued on through Southeastern Oregon, and then south into California.

High desert wagon trains

Most early settlers who crossed the continent in wagon trains on the Oregon Trail bypassed interior Central Oregon. They instead followed the Columbia River to their goal, the fertile Willamette Valley. Several adventurous caravans, however, abandoned the main route at the Snake River and crossed the middle of the state through the sagebrush-covered high desert and the open southern foothills of the Blue Mountains. These pioneer settlers often bisected the trails of those earlier pathfinders—Fremont, Work, and Wyeth.

Of these inland Oregon wagon trains, the first and most famous became known later as the Blue Bucket Train. Led by Stephen Meek, the band of eight hundred people and two hundred wagons ventured across the Oregon high desert in 1845, attempting to navigate this trailless, unknown expanse. The procession was soon lost, and casualties occurred, including a number of the immigrants dying of dehydration and from drinking alkali water. With Meek and another train member riding ahead to seek aid, the group eventually moved northwest to reach the Crooked River. In the area of present-day Prineville, the wagon train was met by a rescue group from The Dalles that Meek had alerted. The stricken caravan was then guided to the rescuing party's Columbia River town. Regardless of knowing the news about this group's hardships, other wagon trains soon followed the risky route through the desert on the "Meek Cutoff."

How the Blue Bucket appellation became attached to this group has become a venerable legend of the Old West. As one version of the story goes, while camped at a stream, children collected water in a blue bucket. Later, after the wagon train had moved some distance, someone noticed gold nuggets in the bottom of the bucket. After the rescued train members eventually reached their destinations, some of them unsuccessfully attempted to retrace the route and find the nugget-bearing stream. For more than a hundred years, other gold-seekers, too, have tried in vain to relocate the source of the famous blue-bucket nuggets.

The Blue Bucket Train's disastrous first crossing of interior Oregon did not deter other wagon trains following in their tracks across the desert sands, exposing their immigrant travelers to both known and unknown dan-

November fog in the Badlands east of Bend, an uncommon sight in the dry high desert country. Seeking a less mountainous route, some wagon trains risked crossing many miles of these waterless sagebrush-juniper expanses.

River Gorge to the Willamette Valley. Thus, the shortcut across Oregon's central plateau became even more attractive to weary travelers on the long Oregon Trail. Guided by the snow-capped beacons of the Cascade peaks in the heat-shimmering distance, the wagon trains kept coming from the east across the high desert.

The promised land west of the Cascades—Willamette Valley's mild climate and rich soils—was the goal for these settlers, but some remembered Central Oregon's grassy meadows along the Crooked River and ponderosa pine forests edging the rushing Deschutes and decided to return. These first white residents began settling the Central Oregon region, but not without initial risks. Some Native American tribes east of the Cascades proved friendly to white settlers, while others refused to give up their traditional homelands without a fight.

Loss of tribal lands

In 1855, the Wasco people and another large tribe consisting of four Sahaptin-speaking bands (the Tenino, Tygh, Wyam, and Tukspushes) were persuaded to give the U.S. government 10 million acres of their combined traditional lands along the mid–Columbia River and the lower portions of the Deschutes and John Day drainages. In return, they received the equivalent of $150,000 in goods and promised services. These tribes were moved to a 578,000-acre southerly section of their territory along the Deschutes River at Warm Springs. Later, the Northern Paiutes were also required to settle there, causing inner-reservation conflict because Wascos and Paiutes were long-time enemies. Thus, with this restricted containment of the Native Americans, most of north Central Ore-

gers. Paiute Indians massacred one party near the Snake River; another lost its way in the desert—a trail of discarded furniture and belongings marked this erratic, desperate journey as drivers lightened the wagons for their dehydrated beasts. Regardless of hardships and suffering, determined pioneers could not be dissuaded from this perilous trek. The 1846 opening of Barlow Pass over the Cascades near Mount Hood eliminated the need for a harrowing float trip through the Columbia

Warm Springs tribal members in traditional Native American dress dance at the Pi-Ume-Sha Days Pow Wow. Photo: Jason Mitchell

gon's finest lands were opened to white settlement. A Klamath reservation established in south Central Oregon at about the same time also made available more former Indian lands for Euro-American settlement.

For two years following this Indian relocation, the U.S. Army attempted to use the Cascade Range as a barrier to separate whites and Native Americans, hoping to prevent conflicts between the two races. In the interior areas of Oregon, east of the mountains and south of the already settled vicinity of The Dalles and the Columbia Basin, whites were forbidden to homestead. Soon, however, this edict became difficult to enforce and the order was revoked. Eventually the Homestead Act of 1862 was passed, offering lands for settlement in the West. Nevertheless, comparatively few Euro-Americans were entering the wild interior of Oregon.

Several U.S. Army forts had been established east of the Cascades by this time. In 1864, at Fort Klamath in south Central Oregon, a peace meeting gathered white officials and representatives of Oregon's dissatisfied Indian tribes. Chief Paulina and his Hunipuitokas band of the Northern Paiutes did not attend, foreshadowing one of Oregon's bloodiest chapters in Native American resistance against white intrusion.

Native American resistance

Throughout most of the 1860s, there were no white communities of any kind in Oregon's remote central region, and only one rough "road" ran south from The Dalles, crossing the Deschutes at Sherar's Bridge. Then it progressed easterly to the gold fields discovered in 1861 in the Blue Mountains of Northeastern Oregon. This gold rush necessitated the transport of supplies and passengers, prompting the establishment of a regularly running stagecoach line on this route by 1864. For several years, Chief Paulina burned and pillaged way stations and attacked travelers along this road. No settler in the area believed his home or livestock safe. On one notable occasion, Paiutes attacked Henry Wheeler, owner of the stage lines, near the present site of Mitchell. His one passenger kept the attackers at bay with rifle shots while Wheeler unhitched the stage and the men escaped on the horses. Wheeler was shot through the cheeks, the bullet passing through his mouth without doing serious damage. The Indians destroyed the stage and found $10,000 in currency among the cargo, but they threw the "worthless paper" into the sagebrush.

The trunk pattern on this gnarled western juniper in the Whychus Creek drainage denotes great age, probably dating from the 1860s clashes between Indians and white settlers.

To protect settlers and miners, the army eventually established small outposts at several sites in Oregon's interior regions. In the central area of the state, Camp Polk was situated along Whychus Creek, near the present location of Sisters. Still, continued skirmishes between soldiers and Paulina's raiders in the Crooked River–Ochoco area inflicted a number of casualties on both sides.

Not even aid from friendly Warm Springs Indians enabled the army to stop Chief Paulina. Ironically, it was an exasperated rancher, Howard Maupin, accompanied by three other settlers, who finally ended Paulina's renegade career on April 25, 1867. After Paulina's band had stolen cattle from the Andrew Clarno ranch, the four men joined forces to track the cattle and thieves through an entire night. They discovered the Indians the following morning in a rock-rimmed basin along Trout Creek, north of the present-day site of Prineville. Hiding in the rocks, the ranchers opened fire on the unsuspecting Paiutes, and Maupin reportedly shot and killed Chief Paulina. Although occasional Indian attacks followed Paulina's death, by the early 1870s, peace between whites and Indians generally prevailed.

Early Euro-American settlements

With relief from Indian hostilities, the influx of new settlers into Central Oregon began to accelerate. Spurred on by opportunities offered through the earlier Homestead Act of 1862, which allowed a U.S. citizen to acquire 160 acres of government land for a small fee and a few minimum occupancy requirements, more families arrived and organized communities. The first school in Central Oregon, a one-room, rough-hewn structure, was built in 1868 along Mill Creek in the foothills of the

Fourth-of-July parade in 1885 Prineville. Courtesy of the Bowman Museum, Crook County Historical Society

Ochoco Mountains. More schools followed throughout the area, supplemented by rustic churches. A few miles down Ochoco Creek from the Mill Creek school, Barney Prine and his family established a store on their ranch in the wild rye-grass meadows. These large, green flats invited tired travelers along the stage route and by 1877 other homes, a livery stable, hotel, and Baptist church had sprung up. Interior Oregon had its first true town, Prineville. Other small villages followed, including Ashwood, Antelope, and Mitchell, often little more than stage stops, possibly with post offices. Camp Polk, no longer a military base, picked up in 1888 and moved its post office to the new hamlet of Sisters, three miles to the south. Other communities formed toward the end of the century in the southern portions of the region: La Pine, Silver Lake, Lakeview, and Klamath Falls.

Bend, which eventually became the largest Oregon city east of the Cascades, was one of the later towns to develop, as were Redmond and Madras. In the meantime, Prineville became a thriving city and the hub of the region for many years. This bustling town, along with the ranches of the area, provided a background for many "Wild West" style occurrences. Most of these true stories seemingly could spring full-blown from the Hollywood scripts for classic western movies. In fact, local people called their section of Oregon "the West's last frontier," and with good reason.

For a period of about two years (1882–1884), before organized law enforcement protected this remote area, a group of vigilantes held sway with their own interpretation of law and order. With no court system to "slow the process" of dealing with supposed lawbreakers, the vigilantes handled situations quickly, usually with a six-shooter or a lynching rope slung over a convenient juniper limb. When, after a property dispute, two ranchers were found shot to death, these masked vigilantes efficiently dealt retribution to the two accused murderers. They forced their way into the town's hotel, where one suspect was being held for eventual trial in The Dalles, and killed him with pistol shots. The other alleged killer, not arrested because of lack of evidence, was captured by the vigilantes, dragged behind a horse down the dusty main street, and hanged from a bridge at the edge of town. Posing as a stockmen's organization, these masked law-enforcers anonymously ruled the area, punishing whatever they judged to be infractions with shootings, lynchings, and mysterious disappearances.

Tiring of this tyrannical rule, another (and larger) group of respected men, who wished to bring organized law to the Prineville district, banded together as a strong militia and publicly opposed the vigilantes. To demonstrate their serious intentions, the group of about seventy-five men rode down the main street of town fully armed. Apparently, this display had its desired effect: soon afterward the masked vigilantes disbanded and residents elected a town marshal and deputy.

Range wars erupt

Unfortunately, gunfire and bloodshed continued in Central Oregon. Trouble was brewing in the form of a range war. Since the late 1860s, enterprising men had been building cattle ranches in Central Oregon, some eventually becoming empires that encompassed millions of acres. Sheep were also grazing in the region; one operation, the famous Hays Creek Ranch near Madras, attained the same super size as the big cattle ranches.

Inevitably, grazing disputes erupted between sheep and cattle ranchers forced to share the open range. Some of the worst clashes flared into all-out range wars around the turn of the century. One group of cattlemen, wishing to rid the range of competing sheep, devised a solution: they organized themselves as the Crook County Sheep Shooting Association, named after their local county. The tactics were simple—upon finding a sheepherder using "their" range, the cattlemen donned masks, captured the herder at gunpoint, and he was blindfolded and tied to a tree. The sheep shooters then lived up to their name, killing every animal in the woolly flock. In 1903, one of the largest of these shootings occurred at Benjamin Lake on the high desert east of Bend, destroying more than 2,400 sheep. Government intervention finally settled the dispute by allotting and issuing permits for separate, designated grazing areas.

More communities emerge

While Prineville endured its turbulent growing pains, thirty-five miles to the southwest a small community quietly emerged. In 1879, John Y. Todd started a cattle ranch along the Deschutes where the river makes a large bend. This location at the edge of the Cascade Range was well known to countless generations of Native Americans who had camped there and, later, to dusty wagon trains coming off the high desert to the east. The attractive parklike setting of big ponderosa pines along the winding river, the grassy glades, views of the snowy peaks to the west, and plentiful fish and game made this a natural stopping place.

Early travelers named the site Farewell Bend because the stage road left the shady riparian zone of the river behind at this point and ran northward through many miles of dry, open country.

Other settlers soon built homes near Todd's Farewell Bend Ranch, and the little village in the pines began to grow. By 1886 a post office opened and postal authorities shortened the town's name to Bend. In June of 1900, Alexander M. Drake, a wealthy entrepreneur and fishing enthusiast from the Midwest, camped at Bend with his wife and a guide. Besides being on vacation, Drake was looking for business possibilities and a new place to live. He liked what he saw, decided to stay, and by autumn was building a large log home by this wide bend in the Deschutes River.

Undoubtedly, no other person exerted more influence upon the initial growth of Bend and the surrounding Deschutes Valley than this astute man. Drake realized the immense possibilities of the abundant waters of the Deschutes for irrigation and, with his planning and financial backing, three Bend pumping plants soon delivered water to the surrounding dry soil. Within the next several years, a network of irrigation canals began to spread outward into the open sagebrush and juniper country. As more and more land was cleared, plowed, and irrigated, word spread quickly throughout the nation of the opportunities available in the Bend area. A new influx of settlers swelled the population of Oregon's sunny heartland.

Sixteen miles to the north of Bend, the community of Redmond sprouted in 1905 as formerly dry rangelands gradually were nourished into green croplands and pastures. The Redmond area eventually became one of the largest sections of irrigated land in the Pacific Northwest and the agricultural hub of Central Oregon. Twenty-six miles to the north, Madras also took shape. Still farther north, a railroad track from The Dalles reached south to the little town of Shaniko in the heart of sheep country. Surrounded by grassy prairies and ridges, it quickly became one of the largest wool-shipping centers in the world. Central Oregon was thriving.

High desert homesteaders

Opportunity also brought tragedy. The federal government stimulated immigration with its 1909 Revised Homestead Act. This program granted settlers 320 acres of land for a ten-dollar fee and required only that they move onto the land within six months after filing and "improve" their claim within five years. Approximately 1.5 million acres of arid high desert land southeast of Bend was opened for homesteading. For a fee, unscrupulous real estate developers and "locaters" aided hopeful young families to find their bit of Uncle Sam's free land. It was all offered up as fulfilling the American egalitarian dream of rural independence. Many of these naive people, primarily fresh from eastern cities, had never seen such wild deserts and mountains. Rumors of future irrigation canals and a railroad line into the high desert never came true, and new settlers soon discovered that it was difficult to grow even a potato in the high elevation, arid climate.

A columnist for the *Fort Rock Times* newspaper in 1915 pointed out the humorous irony of this lack of self-sufficiency:

> Some of us Fort Rock Valley people get up at the alarm of a Connecticut clock, button our Chicago suspenders to our Phila-

A family of high desert homesteaders by their cabin in the sagebrush country east of Bend, 1916. *Courtesy of Deschutes County Historical Society*

delphia pants, wash our faces with Cincinnati soap in a Pennsylvania basin, sit down to a Grand Rapids table, eat Nebraska bacon, eat our biscuits made of Wisconsin flour and Kansas lard, walk out of a house plastered with Scotch mortgage, do business with money borrowed from the East, advertise with printed matter produced in Portland. At bedtime we read a verse from a Boston Bible, say a prayer composed in Jerusalem, crawl under a New Jersey blanket, and are kept awake by the yowling of a Fort Rock Valley cat, the only home product of the entire outfit.

Within a few dry years, most families left, disillusioned and exhausted, their savings gone. Today, lonely desert winds moan through cracks in the disintegrating walls of these homesteaders' cabins and shifting sands bury abandoned dreams.

Bend blossoms

While the high desert homesteaders were experiencing failure, the young city of Bend was prospering. In 1903, the *Bend Bulletin* newspaper began in a log cabin by the river. By 1904, the town was connected to the outside world by telephone and the first automobile chugged down its dirt main street. An "auto stage," the first inter-city bus in the United States, began shuttling passengers over a primitive road between Bend and the rail terminus at Shaniko. Gas streetlights, installed in 1907, had been converted by 1910 to electricity, thanks to a small power plant created by a dam built across the river.

The long-awaited railroad line finally reached Bend in 1911, and with this transportation connection the city evolved from an agricultural town into a mill town. Two of the most prominent commercial lumber companies in Minnesota, Shevlin-Hixon and Brooks-Scanlon, saw the enormous potential of the virgin forests surrounding the young town. With the railroad's arrival, they knew that a fortune in wood products could now be shipped to outside markets. In the spring of 1916, their mills, two of the largest in the world, started operation on opposite sides of the Deschutes River. The humming saws began serving an ever-spreading network of logging railroads that penetrated the seemingly endless stands of pine. A ready workforce was gleaned from the desperate ex-farmers coming to Bend from failed high desert homesteads, along with scores of other able-bodied men looking for work. With this boost to the local economy, records show that the community mushroomed from a 1910 population of just slightly over five hundred to more than five thousand residents within ten years.

Along with Bend's booming forest products industry, another major transformation came about during 1916. Huge Crook County, which had originally included most of the central portion of Oregon, was divided. Resultantly, Bend became the county seat of newly created Deschutes County. By this time, Bend was clearly the leader of growing Central Oregon communities and soon became the largest population center east of the Cascade Range.

Nineteen sixteen also saw the construction of the famed Pilot Butte Inn, built by Philip Brooks, a relative of Harry Brooks of the Brooks-Scanlon Lumber Company. Situated on the bustling corner of Wall Street

Early Bend boosterism, 1911. Courtesy of Deschutes County Historical Society

The famed Pilot Butte Inn, downtown Bend, circa 1920. Courtesy of Deschutes County Historical Society

and Newport avenues, the Swiss chalet-style lodge towered five stories above the rear gardens and Deschutes River. Its native pine and stone walls housed 150 rooms, a huge dining hall, massive lava-rock fireplace, and a wine cellar. The guest register contains the signatures of timber barons, railroad tycoons, baseball heroes, movie stars, President Herbert Hoover, and First Lady Eleanor Roosevelt. The Pilot Butte Inn eventually closed in 1965 and was later demolished in 1973, though a citizen group made a valiant but futile preservation attempt.

In later years, with improved transportation and modern highway systems, tourism and outdoor recreation added new resources to the area's rich assets. With the opening of a new ski development in 1958 on Mount Bachelor (or Bachelor Butte as it was originally called), Bend began to evolve into one of the nation's most popular ski and resort destinations.

The span of an eventful century had belied Henry Abbot's prediction that the remote wilderness he explored in 1855 would never be civilized.

Railroad wars

From 1909 to 1911, one of the most dramatic struggles in the West's saga of pioneer railroad expansion took place in Central Oregon. For two years, the construction crews of two of the nation's most powerful railroad magnates, James J. Hill of the Great Northern Railroad and Edward H. Harriman of the Union Pacific, fought their way up opposite

Sparks Lake nestles at the base of Mount Bachelor, historically known as Bachelor Butte prior to the late 1970s.

sides of the Deschutes River Canyon from the Columbia River to Bend.

One lucrative goal spurred this competition: the vast stands of ponderosa pine that bordered the young town of Bend. A long-awaited connection to this remote community promised transportation for this wealth of timber to the markets of the outside world. Large Minnesota lumber firms already had made long-range plans for the area. Both Hill and Harriman knew the railroad company that arrived at Bend first would win the shipping contracts.

The race was on. More than just a race, the long, grueling battle between these tycoons' rowdy work crews demanded stamina and masterful engineering skills. As early as 1855, the government's Pacific Railroad Survey had explored this frontier and reported that the deep, rugged gorges of this inhospitable land presented inaccessible barriers. It concluded that building a railroad up the Deschutes River was impossible. Undaunted by these negative pronouncements, both companies went into action.

Hill's Great Northern project was the Oregon Trunk Line, while Harriman's Union Pacific project was the Deschutes Railroad. Before construction began, both companies undertook legal maneuvers, buying stock to acquire important holdings and block each other. Hill scored an important coup when he

First Crossing over Crooked River Bridge. Central Oregon. 340 FT. up in the air.

A railroad crew works to finish the final bridge span over the Crooked River Gorge as they gradually extend the mainline south toward Bend, 1910. *Courtesy of Deschutes County Historical Society*

obtained a strategic site for a railroad crossing on a major Deschutes tributary, the Crooked River. Before legal surveys could be fully completed, both crews set up camps at locations along the canyon, the Deschutes Railroad taking the east bank of the river and the Oregon Trunk Line claiming the west side. Hill's men gained a head start by beginning work under the cover of darkness during the night of July 26, 1909. The following morning, the Harriman crew discovered that their wagon road for transporting supplies had been sabotaged and was impassable. The no-holds-barred battle had begun in earnest.

Through that first hot summer's work, each side used many tactics to discourage and slow the opponent's progress. Periodically, several men would swim across the river at night, find the other crew's store of blasting powder, and explode the entire supply. At other times shooting occurred, crews taking potshots at each other across the canyon. No one was actually hit, but the shootings did intimidate would-be workers.

Within a few months, as autumn's cooler weather arrived, the first heat of battle subsided. The companies now fully concentrated on the backbreaking work of blasting, digging, hauling, and clearing a railroad bed up both sides of the rocky gorge. Thousands of men labored with hand tools and wheelbarrows and laid track for two years, through summer heat and winter snow.

This warring, parallel contest raged on up the Deschutes until both lines converged near the small community of Metolius on the plateau above the east rim of the canyon. After an intense struggle in the courts, a truce was called. One line, jointly used, would be completed by Hill's construction crew.

After a total cost of twenty-five million dollars, James J. Hill drove in a final spike made of solid gold at the railroad's terminus in Bend on October 5, 1911. More than two thousand celebrants watched the ceremony that marked the end of this unusual railroad war. By 1928, the tracks had been extended south from Bend to connect with the Western Pacific Line in California.

To the east, Prineville needed its own connecting railroad, as this community also had large timber resources in the adjoining Ochoco Mountains. In 1918, this small town constructed its own line that extended west down the Crooked River to connect with the north-south mainline along the Deschutes. This unique railroad is still city-owned and in operation. ■

The Middle Ground: High Tech Meets Old West

There before me stretched the lovely panorama of the for-
ested Cascade Mountains skyline, centering on the snow-cov-
ered Three Sisters. I had seen snow mountains before, mostly
abroad. But on that first Oregon morning those mountains some-
how meant more to me than others ever had. There was a sense
of their being neighbors, a feeling of permanence about them. I
remember Stevenson's judgment that the three great moments
in a man's life are his first love, his first sunrise and his first is-
land. To that I would add seeing his first great mountain.

GEORGE PALMER PUTNAM
Wide Margins: The Autobiography of a Publisher, 1942

Modern Central Oregon occupies an equilibrium of the wild
and the civilized, the natural and the developed. Both its location within the state and the cultural characteristics of its people and their communities reflect this balance: to the east, extensive sections of remote sagebrush plains, deserts, canyons,
and mountains where people are comparatively scarce; to the
west, just beyond the Cascade Range, valleys brimming with
humanity. And the inhabitants of this middle ground proudly
declare their unique regional autonomy, as reflected in a promotional brochure that proclaims, "Central Oregon, at the
heart of it all!"

Within this long, north-south strip through the center of
the state, from the Columbia River to the California line, the

Mirror Pond in the
downtown district of Bend

Bend area in the midsection is the most developed and populated. Averaging approximately twelve inches of annual precipitation (the same as Tucson, Arizona), the cheerfully sunny climate, dramatic mountain views, abundant rivers, streams, lakes, and close-at-hand wilderness and recreation opportunities have attracted many new residents. Things are booming, and there's little indication of an immediate slacking off.

From 1995 to 2006, the tri-county population (Deschutes, Jefferson, and Crook) exploded by a whopping 65 percent. Much of this influx can be traced to dissatisfied urbanites from large cities, eager to trade smog and traffic jams for a smaller, progressive ski town. Additionally, the area's proximity to the Willamette Valley's ample populations allows easy access by vacationers, and the number of out-of-state visitors has skyrocketed in recent years. These swarms of recreationists contribute abundant tourist dollars to the region's economic stability. Indeed, it has sometimes been jokingly referred to as the Palm Springs of the Pacific Northwest by sun-starved vacationers from the famously rainy metropolises of Portland and Seattle.

Although mid–Central Oregon offers many of the amenities and cosmopolitan qualities of Western Oregon, the signs of human habitation diminish rapidly outward from Bend's environs. Many relatively wild areas still refresh the eye and spirit. Both the north and south portions of Central Oregon are predominately a mix of rural countryside, high desert, and forests. The scattered smaller communities located there, traditionally based on timber resources and agriculture, resemble those of the far-flung northeastern and southeastern regions of the state.

The Bend gateway

Introductions to Oregon's dry side usually begin in the Bend vicinity, for it's highly publicized. And with good reason—a mind-boggling array of outdoor-oriented enticements are nearby. Tourism boosters often tout the area's scenic and recreational wealth as if Bend is the gateway to Mother Nature's Disneyland.

This busy community, the largest east of the Cascades, has grown considerably since its incorporation in 1905. It's no longer a small, quiet mill town. Population numbers are climbing toward 100,000, and Bend is consistently listed among the fastest growing cities in the nation. The north-south/east-west positioning at the crossroads of two major highways makes it not only the service hub for more than 200,000 people from the surrounding area, but also a natural stop-off for travelers to and from Reno and Boise. Add to this the crowds attracted by four-season recreation, and the town tends to buzz with activity most of the time.

A stroll through Bend's downtown reveals why this idyllic site first drew Native American Indians for countless generations, and later, Euro-American pioneers. The cold waters of the Deschutes River flow directly through town, where towering old-growth ponderosa pines line the shore. Eye-catching views of the shining, snowcapped Cascade peaks form a background. Restaurants (including the famed Pine Tavern), brew pubs, a community art gallery, and boutiques overlook the broad, green lawns of Drake Park with its serene, river-dammed Mirror Pond. Particularly unique in a downtown area, this large park is a designated state wildlife refuge for flocks of ducks, Canada geese, and swans, along with the occasional gray squirrel, mink, river otter, osprey, or bald eagle.

A road that spirals to the top of Pilot Butte, about a mile east of downtown, provides an excellent vantage point to see the entirety of Bend within the surrounding landscape. It's something of a tradition among Bendites to cram visiting relatives and friends into the family car and whisk them to the summit of this city landmark. The usual "Wow!" response is easily triggered—the reddish volcanic cinder cone rises five hundred feet above the surrounding neighborhoods and affords a 360-degree view of nearly all of the upper Deschutes Valley. On a clear day, nine Cascade peaks are visible from its summit. Similar panoramic views of the Cascades are available at the western edge of Bend on Awbrey Butte, where a parklike setting is shared by both Central Oregon Community College and the Oregon State University Cascades campus.

Because of Bend's outdoorsy qualities and nearby multitude of recreational opportunities, the city attracts many athletic enthusiasts. Joggers, mountain-bikers, hikers, backpackers, downhill and cross-country skiers, snowboarders, dogsledders, rock-climbers, white water rafters, kayakers, and windsurfers abound. Any day of the week, scores of people, from children to ninety-year-olds, can be seen getting their daily aerobic workout by trekking to the top of Pilot Butte. Golfers enjoy their sport in a climate that can average 250 days of yearly sunshine, while choosing from any number of fine, uniquely scenic courses. *Golf Digest* recognized these attributes by listing Central Oregon among the fifty top golf destinations in the world. This collective fitness-minded segment of the population supports a noticeably large selection of exercise spas, ski shops, sporting goods

White-water rafting on the Deschutes River is a popular Bend area activity.

outlets, golf stores, and sports medicine clinics. A writer for *Sky West* magazine described Bend as "teeming with the fresh-faced and fit—poster children for an REI catalogue."

Annual athletic events have become community traditions and attract ever greater attendance. Notable is the world-class Pole-Pedal-Paddle Race of early May. Although composed of various divisions and degrees of involvement, it is the highly competitive elite category that sets a grueling pace through all phases of the multifaceted course. First comes alpine skiing down Mount Bachelor, followed by a cross-country ski component at the base of the mountain before twenty-two miles of bicycling on the Cascade Lakes Highway to Bend. Upon reaching town, contestants run a five-mile foot race along the Deschutes River Trail, and then paddle canoes and kayaks for 1.5 miles before sprinting a third of a mile to the finish line. Similarly, the Cascade Cycling Classic is held each July; throngs of devoted fans line the race's several

With the Three Sisters Wilderness and Pine Marten Lodge in the background, skier Ethan DeVoll enjoys the dry, powdery snow of Mount Bachelor. Photo: Kirk DeVoll

though, the name had switched to the currently preferred Mount Bachelor.

Encompassing nearly 3,700 acres leased from the Deschutes National Forest on a special permit, the Mount Bachelor ski area is now the largest facility of its kind in Oregon. With state-of-the-art electronic ticketing, seven high-speed quad-lift systems (considered the best in North America), and seventy-one runs, the slopes see a lot of smiling skiers and snowboarders. This high quality has not been overlooked by the U.S. Olympic Ski Team, which trains part of each winter on Mount Bachelor, as do Olympic snowboarders. There are also groomed trails for cross-country skiing and snowshoeing, plus a fun-filled area of inner-tube runs with its own lift. Calorie replacement after all this exercise is available at casual eateries in six day-lodges, along with ski equipment sales and rentals, child care, and ski schools. For fine dining with a jaw-dropping view of the adjacent Three Sisters Wilderness, visit the restaurant in the Pine Marten Lodge, which is perched at timberline on the mountainside.

routes, which may extend from Bend streets to highways that trace the shores of Cascade Range lakes. January brings sled dog championships, which attract more than a hundred of the world's top dog sled racers.

Mount Bachelor:
Bend's ski-slope backyard

Despite all of this sports diversity, every winter Bend becomes primarily a ski town, with snowboarding's popularity close on its heels. Depending upon the timing of November's first serious snowfall, the nearby Mount Bachelor ski area is open for business from around Thanksgiving to spring melt—and with Mount Bachelor topping-out at 9,065 feet, the revered white stuff usually doesn't disappear until Memorial Day. The Mountain, as locals call it, is located along the Cascade Lakes Highway, 22 miles southwest of Bend. Standing somewhat separated from the main Cascade Range, it has more the appearance of a huge, solitary butte. In fact, when a handful of Bend ski enthusiasts first constructed a humble rope tow there back in 1958, this volcanic promontory was historically called Bachelor Butte. By the late 1970s,

Eclectic Bend

With closure of the Brooks-Scanlon sawmill in 1994, Bend's sustaining economy has shifted to an eclectic blend of secondary-wood-products manufacturing (moldings and windows), high-tech research and development, retail and hospitality services, and the medical community, along with government jobs, such as the U.S. Forest Service. In recent years, a new component has been added at the Bend Municipal Airport, where aircraft and aerospace design-and-production companies have been established, and the well-known Deschutes Brewery's continued success requires a growing workforce. This varied job market in turn draws a broad mix of residents

Bend sunset from the summit of Pilot Butte

and creates something of a melting pot, rang- ing from lawyers and doctors through com- puter programmers, research technicians, architects, carpenters, roofers, landscapers, home-based telecommuters, chefs and art- ists, to the independently wealthy. The con- trasts are intriguing. A cowboy and his dog in a battered old pickup truck frequently wait at a stoplight beside a three-piece-suited busi- nessman in a Mercedes Benz. Additionally, because of a healthful climate, excellent med- ical facilities and other attractive qualities, Central Oregon consistently earns a rating as one of the most desirable retirement locations in the nation. As a result, a sizable segment of the population is comprised of older folks who have chosen Bend to enjoy their prover- bial golden years.

The area has a large pool of talented art- ists, who have contributed to a richly satisfy- ing array of galleries, community art show- ings, music concerts, and plays. Drawing upon these creative resources, Bend's flour- ishing art scene has generated an ongoing lineup of events each year: the Cascade Festi- val of Music, Bend Film Festival, Bend Gal- lery Association's Art Hop, Summer Sun- day Music Series, and Munch and Music are a few examples. Renovation of the historic Tower Theatre in the downtown district has provided a much-needed venue for plays, in- dependent film screenings, lectures, con- certs, fundraisers, and all manner of commu- nity events. Drivers can enjoy public art while navigating any of Bend's many roundabouts, where sculptures of various types (some con- troversial) are displayed.

Craving intellectual stimulation? Between nature-oriented slideshow presentations at the Central Oregon Environmental Cen-

The Cascade Festival of Music draws throngs of listeners to Bend's Drake Park.

Autumn at the Old Mill District of Bend

of any city in Oregon. Foodies and connoisseurs of regional wines and craft beers abound among the populace, savoring an astounding assortment of fine-dining restaurants (several of world-class ranking), small cafés, bistros, and diners, celebrated Northwest-style brew pubs, bakery-coffee shops, and ice cream parlors. Nearly every imaginable ethnic eatery is well-represented, along with a couple of family-owned 1950s Americana hamburger drive-ins (one boasting waiters who rollerskate to your car window in classic mode). And lest anyone grow faint between meals, almost any corner in Bend sports a drive-up espresso-coffee kiosk that offers locally made pastries with your favorite cup of joe. Central Oregon Community College contributes to this expanding gastronomic cornucopia by generating future talented chefs in their highly regarded Cascade Culinary Institute. Nevertheless, despite the sophistication of Bend's cultural offerings, a general casual style prevails. A plethora of just-plain-fun seasonal festivals, tented beer gardens, and farmer's markets in the streets and parks helps to ensure that folks do not take themselves too seriously.

Bend's roots in the timber industry are made clearly evident by three enormous smokestacks that soar high into the sky above the former sawmill site. Located just upriver from the downtown blocks, these historically familiar icons mark one of the city's latest additions, the Old Mill District. One of the original brick mill buildings at the base of the giant smokestack trio has been transformed into a home for REI (Recreational Equipment Incorporated). The remainder of the expansive site has many new structures filled with a variety of retail stores and galleries, a grocery, movie multiplex, medical buildings, office complexes, and riverfront restaurants with plenty of outdoor summer tables.

ter, the Nancy R. Chandler Visiting Scholar Program (which has brought Pulitzer Prize–winning speakers to Bend), and various lecture programs at the college campus and the High Desert Museum, there's plenty of food for thought. And the area's rich past can be explored at the Deschutes Historical Center, housed in the old Reid School building just a block away from the city's library.

As to the subject of food, Bend has the highest number of restaurants per person

Across a colorfully bannered footbridge, on the west bank of the Deschutes River, is the Les Schwab Amphitheater. This big, grass-carpeted bowl that fronts a stage is a warm-season outdoor venue for regional musicians and big-name acts—the Beach Boys, Bob Dylan, Crosby, Stills and Nash, Joan Baez, Willie Nelson, and Coldplay have all shared their music with appreciative Bend audiences; and Garrison Keillor has spun his humorous *Prairie Home Companion* tales. Next door to the amphitheater is the Art Station, an historic stone train depot converted into an art-education center. Throughout the Old Mill District, condos, town houses, and loft apartments provide living spaces mixed with marketplace storefronts. In the spirit of European cities and villages, this blending allows residents the convenience of walking and biking for shopping and other errands.

Bend growing pains

No doubt about it, the face of Bend has changed dramatically since the 1990s, from its riverside condos, trendy cafés, and shops to the multimillion-dollar mansions on Awbrey Butte. But not everyone favors these accelerated transformations of upscale urbanity. Many longtime residents remember quieter, simpler times and complain that big-city transplants have brought with them the same hectic pace and desire for helter-skelter development that they sought to escape. These cautionary Bendites have also expressed alarm at the demolition of several historical structures, and still lament the loss of the Pilot Butte Inn in 1973. Certainly, not all is perfect in this sunny Shangri-La. A typical "Anywhere America" conglomeration of national chain businesses crowds the fringes of town, complete with the ubiquitous big box stores, car lots, fast-food drive-ins, and motels. De-

spite the construction of a north-south parkway to shunt autos through town, rush-hour traffic still frequently congests the area's outgrown street systems. The large influx of new residents seeking their pieces of paradise has generated an explosion of new housing developments, and schools are bursting at the seams. Resultantly, grumblings and debates about property tax rates, water conservation issues, city planning, and school funding spawn heated discussions. Newcomers find that lucrative employment can be elusive, and "make-do" jobs test their initial survival. It has become a standard joke that Bend has the best-educated janitors in the state. Even with steady employment, things aren't always rosy: a recent *Bend Bulletin* headline declared, "Locked out: Many first-time buyers can't afford a house in Bend."

Despite such tarnishes, most Bendites will say that the enjoyments of skiing nearby Mount Bachelor, fly-fishing famed local streams, taking an evening stroll along the river trail, dining outdoors at an Old Mill café, or listening to classical music performed in Drake Park are livability positives that far outweigh any negatives.

Exploring south of Bend

Bend is an excellent jumping-off point to explore all directions in Central Oregon, and a good place to begin is 3.5 miles south of town at the High Desert Museum. Located just off Highway 97, this unique interpretive facility offers visitors a telescoped experience of the natural biodiversity and rich human history of the entire region east of the Cascades. Unquestionably, it's one of the finest resources available to equip visitors with a comprehensive understanding of Oregon's dry side.

High Desert Museum: Don's dream

"I'd like to take the side of the natural world," summarized the lean twenty-two-year-old man, tilting his head to gaze at the stars twinkling in the crystal-clear night sky. Everyone around the aromatic fire nodded agreement as more dead sagebrush branches were tossed into the fading flames. The flickering light illuminated the faces of the group of desert rat friends. Don Kerr, in his characteristic low voice, had been painting word pictures of a combination zoo and museum that would be an advocate for the natural ecosystems of the high desert country—not academic and stuffy, but a place that put visitors into the environment with the live plants and animals; a multi-sensorial experience that also clarified how humanity fit into these arid landscapes, from the past to the present and beyond. Such were Kerr's early glimmerings of the dream—imagined in discussions around remote desert campfires with a cadre of like-minded young naturalists in the late 1960s. These plans were further honed in his mind's eye during solo hikes, while experiencing moments of inspiration from the solitude of the sagebrush backcountry.

A native of Portland, during the 1970s Don worked at various jobs in that city, mostly for nature-related organizations, such as The Nature Conservancy and the zoo. All the while, he continued to formulate his ideas for a "living" museum. Eventually Kerr formed the Western Natural History Institute and seriously put into motion the initial solicitations for grants. A master of low-key, persistent fund-raising, the biologist successfully transmitted his zeal and idealistic vision to a num-

Don Kerr, age 25, 1971. *Courtesy of Kerr Family Collection*

ber of benefactors and eventually the needed money was acquired. The dream became reality when the doors of the High Desert Museum opened in 1982 with Donald M. Kerr at the helm as founder and first president.

Located 3.5 miles south of the Bend city limits, this is not a typical institutional collection of "look but do not touch" exhibits. The emphasis is on interactive experience. Live native animals, displayed in simulated natural habitats, are often adjacent to tables that provide touchable furry mammal hides, crinkly shed snakeskins, and sleek bird feathers. Augmenting these tactile encounter sessions are audio recordings such as owl hoots and the warning buzz of a rattlesnake. Other sections of the museum have dioramas of the area's human history, both Native American Indian and Euro-American. An excellent example is the Spirit of the West hall, which is a fascinating time-travel walkthrough that begins with a prehistoric scene of a Northern Paiute rock shelter above a Great Basin marsh. Piped-in early morning chill, sagebrush scent, and red-winged blackbird calls heighten the experiential authenticity. Farther along the walkthrough are period snapshots of early white explorers, trappers, ranchers, and miners, culminating in the re-creation of a typical 1885 settlement street, all with the proper sounds and climatic sensations.

Outside, various trails meander through pine groves and shrubby openings on the museum's 135 acres. One follows an aspen-lined, gurgling stream to a pond that harbors redband trout, Pacific treefrogs, and painted turtles. Other twists and turns of the paths reveal more wildlife—where a stream spills over rimrock, river otters cavort in their private pool (an underwater viewing window offers another entertaining perspective); chubby porcupines snooze in sun-warmed basalt alcoves; and on the limbs of snags, keen-eyed owls, hawks, falcons, and eagles observe passing visitors with equal interest. A bit farther on is a century-old sawmill, homesteader's cabin, mustang corral, and Native American tipi encampment. Throughout, knowledgeable volunteers answer questions and periodically give presentations with live creatures. Additionally, there are changing exhibits in the museum's Spirit of the West Gallery, high desert–related art showings in the halls, a variety of classes, field trips, a gift-and-book shop and café, plus an ongoing lecture series. The overall experience unfailingly imbues adults and kids alike with a greater understanding and appreciation of the region.

Although Don Kerr was physically incapacitated by illness in the mid 1990s, his dream continues to grow. The High Desert Museum has a long-range master plan that includes the creation of more outdoor natural habitat displays of live wolves, bobcats, cougars, bears, pronghorn, and bison. There will also be additional interactive cultural exhibits of a trapper's cabin, railroad logging camp, and pioneer ranch barn, with themes that relate to stewardship of the high desert region.

The remarkably naturalistic stream exhibit, with live cutthroat trout, in the High Desert Museum south of Bend

Don once commented, "I've raised a wolf and two great horned owls. I've been lucky to have these experiences that aren't possible for most people. I wanted to bring others closer to nature, to experience it, to learn to maintain it." A visit to the High Desert Museum will show that he succeeded grandly. ■

BEYOND the High Desert Museum, Highway 97 continues south into a tortured landscape of volcanic lava. This is Newberry National Volcanic Monument (see pages 36–38), 55,500 acres of extensive lava fields, cinder cones, icy-cold lava tunnels, and the imprinted molds of 7,000-year-old trees that were engulfed by molten lava. Dominating the monument is the nearly 8,000-foot presence of Newberry Volcano, with its expansive caldera containing two sky-blue lakes, obsidian flows, and hot springs. All of these geological marvels are accessible by good roads and viewing trails. The excellent Lava Lands visitor center with interpretive exhibits is located 10 miles south of Bend, off the west side of Highway 97 at Lava Butte. The monument

Interpretive trails lead from the Lava Lands Visitor Center into the adjacent lava beds.

is managed by the U.S. Forest Service, and as with many other public land locations, day-use fees, an annual Forest Pass, or other valid recreation passes are required.

Down the road from Lava Lands and about 15 miles south of Bend lies Sunriver. This large, planned community of around five thousand residents was built in 1968 on the former site of the old World War II military base Camp Abbot. The village was designed to complement its woodsy environment and manages to nicely blend disparate elements. Neighborhoods of homes are connected by winding streets and bike trails with another nearby component—one of the Northwest's most popular destination resorts, with its large, elegant lodge, award-winning golf courses, swimming pools, and tennis courts. And with Mount Bachelor only 18 miles away, skiers are much in evidence all winter. Serving the entire population, whether local inhabitants or vacationers, is a mall with stores and cafés, fire department, church, library, school, and an airstrip. Cultural happenings include the highly regarded Sunriver Music Festival, which features several concerts each year (from classical to pops), both in the Great Hall and outside at the community's Pavilion. Despite all these amenities

and peopled comings and goings, Sunriver remains surprisingly quiet and unhurried. This is probably due in large part to its natural qualities. Trees are thickly in evidence everywhere and provide a buffering effect between houses, businesses, civic centers, and recreational facilities. Adding further tranquillity is the defining heart of the community: a huge, aspen-bordered meadow and lake, along with the meandering Deschutes River, all accented by a backdrop of the green Cascade Range. The community even boasts its own excellent nature center, offering exhibits, classes, field trips, and an observatory for stargazing during Central Oregon's many crystal-clear nights.

SOUTH of Sunriver, Highway 97 cuts through more than a hundred miles of deep timber country. This is one of the world's most extensive ponderosa pine forests, interrupted only by the occasional grassy meadow. Human settlements, few and far between, consist of small towns with origins in the former logging glory days. La Pine now courts tourists as the "Gateway to Newberry National Volcanic Monument" and constantly seeks to magnify its longtime reputation as a prime fishing and hunting location. In recent years, as the Bend vicinity has become more upscale, retirees are increasingly choosing La Pine as a more affordable place to settle, swelling the population to over 10,000 residents. Gilchrist, however, has managed to hold on to its timber resources heritage. In 1938, Frank W. Gilchrist built a sawmill on the site, along with an entire company town of 135 houses, a grocery store, school, two churches, barbershop, restaurant, and bar. Crown Pacific purchased the mill from the Gilchrist family in 1991, subsequently updating the operation to process smaller diameter

Winter at Crater Lake National Park

logs in the wake of more stringent environmental regulations and dwindling old-growth trees. However, the beginning of the twenty-first century brought financial difficulties for Crown Pacific and the mill changed hands again in 2004, this time to a Canadian company, Interfor Pacific. Still, Gilchrist (along with Warm Springs in north Central Oregon) could claim the distinction of having one of the two surviving sawmills in operation along the vast eastern slope of the Cascades—formerly listed among the world's premiere logging regions.

After Crescent, more or less a southern extension of Gilchrist, Highway 97 traverses longer and longer stretches of pure pinewoods, passing through the small outpost of Chemult, and then reaching Diamond Lake Junction. The choice of a tantalizing side trip is offered at this point. There the Highway 138 turnoff heads due west, straight as an arrow, and accesses Oregon's only national park—Crater Lake at the top of Mount Mazama. Anyone who hasn't seen this member of our nation's collection of scenic crown jewels shouldn't hesitate to drive the extra 20 miles to the park's north entrance. As with the Grand Canyon, no matter the backlog in your mind of pictures conveyed through postcards, calendars, and television travelogues, the reality will far exceed your preconceived notions. Lingering anywhere along the rim of this gargantuan, flooded caldera of the high Cascade crest is time well spent.

Also well spent was the $15 million required to refurbish Crater Lake Lodge during the 1990s. The harsh, high-elevation years had badly deteriorated the historic structure since its opening in 1915, and it was scheduled for dismantling. Because of a public outcry, however, funds were eventually allocated for total reconstruction of the enormous four-storied building. Now, staying in one of the rooms is like going back in time to a former era of lodge grandeur. Situated on the brink of the crater, many rooms provide unforgettable views, as does dining in the lodge's restaurant. A scenic 1.5-mile-long trail leads from the lodge and follows the rim through alpine wildflowers to the 8,000-foot summit of Garfield Peak. This is an ideal vantage point to survey the entire caldera and contemplate how Mount Mazama literally blew its top 7,600 years ago. The eruption sent fifty cubic miles of pumice and ash into the sky, winds spreading an ash cloud as far east as Montana and northeast into Canada.

The Klamath Basin

The park's south entrance off Highway 62 is kept cleared of snow throughout the winter, allowing frigid, 7,000-foot-elevation sightseeing and cross-country skiing explorations. This highway will also provide a way to reconnect with our original southbound route. The road swoops downward into the enormous Klamath Basin (named for the Native American tribe of south Central Oregon), where it connects with Highway 97 near the community of Chiloquin. After the montane coniferous forests, interlacings of quaking aspen groves and broad meadows appear, and then sagebrush openings intermixed with an assemblage of pine groves, dry juniper woodlands, rimrock, lakes, marshes, and rivers. The historic importance of timber resources to the economy of the Klamath country is displayed at a museum in Collier Memorial State Park, just north of Chiloquin. It contains one of the largest collections of logging equipment in the nation and brings this period to life.

Continuing southward, Highway 97 traces the eastern shore of giant Upper Klamath Lake for nearly 20 miles. Its 133 square miles make it the largest body of fresh water in the Northwest region. The Upper Klamath National Wildlife Refuge and other local sanctuaries attract major flocks of migratory birds along the Pacific Flyway. Most ornithologists agree that the Klamath Basin has the largest concentrations of waterfowl in North America—more than six million ducks pass through each year, and one million may be present there during peak migration in autumn. Birders may enjoy the sublime evening spectacle of countless waterfowl against sunsets reflected in the lake and its marshes, with the alpine silhouette of Mount McLaughlin on the western skyline. Hundreds of bald eagles winter in the Klamath Basin, ranking it as the largest winter concentration of this regal national symbol in the lower 48 states. Each February the area hosts scores of nature enthusiasts who attend the Bald Eagle Conference.

The city of Klamath Falls, with a population of about twenty thousand, is situated at the southern end of the lake where it empties into smaller Lake Ewauna by the connecting, mile-long Link River. A small dam now blocks the large lake's outlet where the city's namesake falls was once located. If you take a walk through the historic downtown area, be sure to visit the Favell Museum. Its displays of work by more than three hundred western artists, along with a hundred thousand Indian artifacts, earn it a ranking as one of the three finest western art museums in the United States. Nearby is the 1906 Baldwin Hotel, where President Theodore Roosevelt signed the documents to create Crater Lake National Park. While strolling the sidewalks, don't be surprised if your feet feel toasty warm. The city straddles an underground pressure cooker of steaming water. Cleverly, this handy heat

Mount McLaughlin sunset at Upper Klamath Lake

is piped below city streets in winter to melt snow and ice. Thought to be one of the largest geothermal areas in the world, this natural source heats public service buildings and some private businesses and homes. The Oregon Institute of Technology, whose campus is located at the eastern edge of town, is internationally known for the innovative research done by its Geo-Heat Center. Indeed, the entire campus is heated by hot water pumped from the ground.

Klamath Falls exudes a strong Old West, outdoors atmosphere. Fishing and hunting stories are overheard on street corners and in barbershops and grocery stores. There is also a noticeable influence of Native American culture in the community, and an annual Pow Wow Days celebration features an Indian rodeo and traditional tribal dances. Exploring the town is made easy by a trolley bus that takes visitors on history tours in the old downtown district, and a fleet of public transit buses provides rides throughout the basin.

The Klamath watershed

Agricultural crops and cattle ranching lead the Klamath Basin's economy. Irrigation is a necessity in the semiarid climate, and killing frosts are possible even in midsummer at the basin's average 4,000-foot elevation. Therefore, most fields contain cold-tolerant potatoes, onions, barley, and alfalfa. Beginning in 1905, the Klamath Reclamation Project was put into motion by the U.S. Bureau of Reclamation. The resulting 1,400 miles of canals and drains diverted water from much of the area's vast wetlands, and the land was converted to agricultural uses. At present, less than 25 percent of the original marshes still exist and these remnants are extremely vital to the native waterfowl, fish, and other wildlife.

Dawn horse roundup at the ZX Ranch, Sycan Marsh

Predictably, the bone-dry years of 1992 to 1994 made it painfully apparent that there wasn't enough water to go around for both man and beast. Since those hard years, a passionate struggle has ensued between farmers and environmentalists. The issues are complex, involving not just the mega lakes and marshes of the basin, but management of the entire surrounding watershed of rivers, streams, tiny brooks, springs, and spongy seeps. After a century, family farms have sunk roots deep into the soils of former lakebeds. They now face issues that threaten the passing of hard-won livelihoods to the next generation. If environmental solutions involve diverting more water to wildlife habitat by shutting down farmland irrigation, the hackles rise on farmers' necks. Environmentalists counter this by contending that too much water has been promised to too many different interests in the Klamath Basin.

Beginning in the 1990s, partnerships between conservation groups and federal and state agencies have purchased thousands of acres of diked agricultural properties from farmers willing to sell. These lands at the northern end of Upper Klamath Lake have been restored to natural marshes. With more and more acquisitions returned to richly vegetated wetlands, this giant "sponge" increasingly conserves more water for both farmers and wildlife habitat. This may also help beleaguered Native American Indian tribes farther down the Klamath watershed in California. They claim that two local dams (both lacking fish ladders) on the Klamath River, along with lessened and degraded water from upstream in Oregon's irrigated Klamath Basin, have collectively caused major declines in salmon runs. Upper Klamath Lake was once one of the world's great fisheries; now Indians and some scientists are calling for removal of the Klamath's dams. It is hoped that this will allow the salmon to return, and a traditional Native American way of life will be restored.

Eastward from the Klamath Basin, the timbered heights of Fremont National Forest contain the headwaters of the Sprague River and the little-visited rocky pinnacles of the Gearhart Mountain Wilderness. Just to the north are the broad green flats of Sycan Marsh, and rising easterly is the summit of Winter Rim. This lofty prominence offered explorer John C. Fremont his first view of the northwestern portion of the immense Great Basin in 1843. There, where precipitation often slacks to just this side of nonexistent, tree growth largely ends. The panorama takes in the fault block humps of the basin and range country of Southeastern Oregon, with its alternating saltscrub desert lowlands and sagebrush-steppe uplands. Only a few tenacious junipers are sprinkled here and there on higher slopes, somehow managing to wring a sufficiency of moisture from the bone-dry terrain.

After peering over this brink into the eastern aridity, turn back north and retrace Highway 97 beyond Chiloquin, where there's a turnoff east on the Silver Lake Highway. This lovely drive takes you straight through the heart of the Klamath Marsh National Wildlife Refuge—watch for sandhill cranes and trumpeter swans—and then angles northeast up the Williamson River. Famed as one of the best fly-fishing rivers in the West, the Williamson's waters nourish the rich Klamath marshlands all the way to the big lake in the basin bottom. The road keeps gaining elevation along riverside meadows and through extensive stands of lodgepole pine, finally cresting out of the Williamson watershed to descend into the open Silver Lake Basin.

Fort Rock Valley

At this point, turn north on Highway 31, which follows along the pronounced contrast of an ecotone: the green borders of ponderosa pine forest abruptly end on the left, whereas to the right, grayish sagebrush steppelands sweep to the far horizon. After about 10 miles, begin glancing every now and then out the right-hand car windows. Soon, your vigilance will be rewarded by a sight that usually elicits an exclamation of wonder from first-time viewers—a startlingly huge stone monolith off to the east, jutting from the middle of the brushy plain. This is the starkly dramatic form of Fort Rock, which marks the beginning of an extensive volcanic landscape that contains several unusual geologic formations.

Access is easy. Just turn east on the paved Fort Rock–Christmas Valley Road, and use the rock itself as a guiding beacon in the distance. After 6 miles, the road enters the tiny community of Fort Rock, with its store–gas station combination, the Waterin' Hole Tavern, and the Homestead Village Museum, which tells the story of early settlers in the Fort Rock Valley. The route jogs north in the middle of "downtown," with the destination still clearly in sight. As the rock looms closer, a pronounced similarity to Australia's Ayers Rock readily comes to mind. The reddish-tan, sheer-faced walls tower three hundred feet high, and the entire crescent-shaped formation measures more than a half mile across.

A signature feature of Oregon's high desert country, Fort Rock was created in explosions of steam a bit less than 100,000 years ago. Picture a hundred-foot-deep Pleistocene lake so large that it submerged nearly six hundred square miles of the surrounding territory. Beneath are numerous faults. When this breaching of the earth's crust allowed magma to rise, it met abundant groundwater beneath the lakebed and a catastrophic detonation resulted. A lathery mixture of wet ash, rocks, lake mud, and vaporized water was spewed in great arcs and built a layered mud ring around an exploding crater. This hot glop cooled and hardened into a type of volcanic rock known as tuff. Judging by Fort Rock's height and layered composition, geologists say that several eruptions probably created this tuff ring. When things simmered down, the waves of Fort Rock Lake lapped the neonascent shores of an island volcano. Over the ensuing eons, the constant erosive action of the water gradually sculpted the huge, slope-sided hump into the vertical walls we see today. The south side was completely washed away, creating a wide entrance into the immense, bowl-like interior. From an airplane this ancient tuff ring looks like a stupendous horseshoe.

By around 13,000 years ago, Fort Rock was no longer an island. As the climate had become increasingly more arid, the lake finally dwindled away. Just to the west, there is a rocky promontory that contains Cow Cave, often called Fort Rock Cave. From this site and other nearby locations, archaeologists

Fort Rock

have unearthed sagebrush sandals and various other artifacts that date back as far as 13,000 years. Therefore, it's possible that early Native Americans paddled reed boats out to Fort Rock when it was still surrounded by water, but no clear proof of this yet exists. However, recent excavations 50 miles to the southeast in the Paisley Caves substantiate the probability of human occupation by a much larger Fort Rock Lake. Within these ancient rock shelters, Dennis Jenkins of the University of Oregon led an archaeological crew that found Native American artifacts mixed with the remains of now extinct Ice Age animals—bison, camels, and horses. These materials date from 14,300 years ago, pushing evidence of human presence in Oregon ever farther back into the Pleistocene period.

A visit to Fort Rock inspires a powerful sense of ancient earth transformations—volcanic upheavals, changing climates, evaporating Ice Age lakes, and the struggles of a vanished prehistoric people. Directly above the small Fort Rock State Park picnic area, you can climb out onto a large terrace that was cut by the long-gone lake's waves; and a hike through the amphitheater interior of the tuff ring might disclose an arrowhead half buried in Pleistocene beach sand.

Birdwatchers may want to visit Cabin Lake Campground, 10 miles to the north on the China Hat–Cabin Lake Road. Two wooden blinds, each with an adjacent concrete basin of water, have been provided. Located next to a U.S. Forest Service guard station, this spartan camp has no drinking water or toilets, so come prepared. The lake dried up long ago, but the site is pleasantly situated in the shade of ponderosa pines with views south into open shrublands. Therefore, bird species of both the desert and forest visit the water, which is piped from nearby aprons that collect dew and raindrops.

Exploring outward from Fort Rock will disclose some of the nearly forty other small, bowl-shaped volcanoes in the area. They, too,

◆ TRAILPOST
Springtime at Fort Rock

In late March through April, when your spring fever is running high, Fort Rock provides an excellent place to get outside for a much-needed, leg-stretching hike. This ancient volcanic formation is the perfect destination on one of those days when the sky is deep blue, but the early April sunrays are rather feeble, the breezes are a bit chilly, and the temperatures are barely making it to sixty degrees.

Dress in a warm coat and hat, pack a picnic lunch, including a thermos of steaming hot tea or coffee, and drive on Highway 31 to the Fort Rock–Christmas Valley Road turnoff. Take this route east across the sagebrush flats for 8 miles to the Fort Rock State Park picnic area. It's not advisable, though, to eat at the picnic tables this early in the season, as it will probably be uncomfortably windy and cold in this exposed site. Instead, stow your edibles in a daypack and walk the trail leading west from the parking area over a low rise into the enormous interior bowl of the Fort Rock formation. Although its south wall was eroded away eons ago by the Ice Age wave action of Fort Rock Lake, the remaining gigantic arc of 300-foot-high tuff walls forms a natural windbreak.

Here, with the body heat generated by this short jaunt, you'll be quite comfortable. The trail (much of it an old, closed dirt road) loops around the entire interior of Fort Rock, offering any number of pleasant spots to have a high desert picnic. Pick a sunbathed, comfy rock to sit on, and while munching a sandwich, soak up the surrounding grand scenery.

Fort Rock is a designated Oregon State Natural Area, and with good reason. It offers great opportunities for viewing wildlife and colorful spring wildflowers. After your fortifying lunch, continue the loop hike through the volcanic amphitheater, being alert for signs of life. Overhead, be watchful for the prairie falcons that nest on a high cleft in the vertical stone walls. You may hear this sleek raptor's "kyaah, kyaah, kyaah" before you see it, but use the repeating falcon's call as a directional aid in locating it with your binoculars. Red-tailed hawks and eagles are frequently seen as well. Fort Rock is well known among birders for its colony of white-throated swifts, and you can be assured of seeing and hearing these chattering little black-and-white birds shooting along the cliff faces. Sage

sparrows, green-tailed towhees, sage thrashers, and least chipmunks will no doubt be encountered among thickets of sagebrush and bitterbrush. If the midafternoon temperature happens to climb into the seventies, there's a good chance you'll see reptiles out basking—western fence lizards and side-blotched lizards on the rocks, with sagebrush lizards and pigmy short-horned lizards scampering on the warm pumice sand between shrubs. Don't worry about rattlesnakes; these venomous reptiles have never been reported in the immediate vicinity of Fort Rock. Also along the path will be frequent clumps of blazing-red Indian paintbrush blooms to cheer your outing.

Continuing the loop trail back toward your parked car, you may be tempted to clamber upward to the broad shelf of rock directly above the picnic area. This elevated perch, formed by the persistent wearing away of surging Pleistocene lake waters, gives expansive views of the Fort Rock Valley, south to the Connley Hills. There, in the crystal-clear, dry air, with sunshine on your face, winter will seem like a distant memory.

were caused by the explosive reaction of rising hot magma intersecting with underground water—usually called a maar. One impressive example is Hole-in-the-Ground, located about 6 miles, as the magpie flies, to the northwest of Fort Rock. Although it's possible to find your way there via a network of intervening pumice-sand roads, it's more dependable to simply return south and west on the paved road to Highway 31 and then turn north. At about 7 miles, watch for a sign pointing to "Hole-in-the-Ground," and take a right on gravel road number 3125 that leads 5 miles through pinewoods to the site. You'll know when you're there. Directly in front of you will be a mile-wide, 350- to 520-foot–deep depression that could understandably be mistaken for a giant meteorite crater. Fifty thousand years ago, a series of shattering steam eruptions brought up massive amounts of ash, cinders, and broken bedrock that created the high rim around the crater. This vantage point, situated at the forest edge, allows unobstructed views of Fort Rock far below in the open terrain to the southeast. Because Hole in the Ground's rimming perimeter rises over five hundred feet above the ancient bed of Fort Rock Lake, there was no wave erosion and this maar formation exhibits its nearly original gently sloping sides.

Fort Rock Valley Lava Beds

On the higher elevations to the north and east of Fort Rock, with few exceptions, no ground water caused steam-explosion maars. Instead, there is a collection of cinder cones with basalt flows that created miles of dark-toned, contorted lava beds. If your automobile and spirit of adventure are so inclined, there's a backcountry route that meanders for many miles through the heartland of this rugged volcanic landscape.

Drive east from Fort Rock to the small town of Christmas Valley and take a left (north) where a sign reads, "Crack in the Ground." After 7 miles on this gravel road, you'll arrive at the trailhead for this appropriately named natural feature—a seventy-foot-deep, two-mile-long narrow fissure in the basaltic landscape. Geologists explain that it's a tension fracture caused by an underlying fault zone. A footpath leads through the shady, cool aperture for almost a quarter mile, a pleasant hike during the heat of summer. A bit more driving brings into view the Pleistocene cinder cones of the Four Craters Flow, with close-at-hand lava beds that invite investigation. From there, the route becomes a dirt road that climbs through western juniper woodlands to the top of 5,200-foot Green Mountain, where there's a fire lookout tower. Just below the summit, a tiny, primitive campground (no water or toilets) has picnic tables in the shade of junipers. Lunch here affords grand views—and, coupled with a map, orientation for further explorations.

Down the other side of Green Mountain, take a left (west) on Sink Road and follow it out to the paved Derrick Cave Road and turn right (north). This luxurious paving soon ends, the subsequent gravel road continuing north along the lava beds of Devils Garden. This area has isolated sections of vegetation within the lava fields referred to as kipukas, a Hawaiian term. Because of their rough inaccessibility, these biotic islands have never been grazed by domestic livestock and contain undisturbed native bunchgrass-shrub communities with scattered junipers and pines. Along the route, left-hand pullouts lead to trailheads for unique points of interest, such as some large spatter cones called the Blowouts, and Derrick Cave, a lava tube that extends for a quarter mile (bring a flash-

Crack in the Ground

light and warm coat to probe its dark, chilly depths).

North to Millican and the Badlands

Still northbound, the route (Forest Service Rd. 23) passes through approximately 12 miles of cinder cones and rhyolite domes, such as Buzzard Rock, Burnt Butte, Fox Butte (Central Oregon's tallest cinder cone—900 feet high), and Quartz Mountain, eventually arriving at Sand Spring. This pool is trapped by a big, underlying bowl of lava buried under a layer of sand and popcorn-sized pumice granules. Naturally, being the lone bit of water amid many miles of dry sagebrush, juniper, and pine country, it attracts birds, bats, and deer along with Pacific treefrogs and western toads during the spring breeding season. In turn, wildlife watchers are attracted to the small campground located there (picnic tables and pit toilets, but no drinkable water), as well as other varieties of recreation. You are now just a few miles south of where Highway 20 passes through the Millican Valley, a popu-

lar outdoor playground for the nearby greater Bend area. On summer weekends, off-highway-vehicle (OHV) enthusiasts swarm to the area, where several hundred miles of trails on BLM (Bureau of Land Management) and Forest Service lands have been designated for this sport. Dirt-bikers out having exhilarating fun can be traced by their trailing dust plumes as they buzz across rabbitbrush flats and up cheatgrass slopes.

Meanwhile, other enthusiasts are enjoying their chosen sport 8 miles southeast of Millican on Highway 20. Launched from the 6,405-foot summit of Pine Mountain, multicolored paragliders soar on rising thermals. These minimalist pilots gain silent, eagle-eye perspectives far southeastward into the northern Great Basin. This open crest also provides a launching site for another kind of visual soaring—nighttime galaxy gazing that extends millions of light-years out into the universe. Taking advantage of the clear, dry air and the remote location's relatively uncontaminated darkness, the Pine Mountain Observatory houses three Cassegrain reflecting telescopes. The facility, operated by the University of Oregon Physics Department, conducts professional research and is open to the public on Friday and Saturday nights, late May through September. There's even an adjacent small Forest Service campground (no water) for visitors.

Back on smooth pavement again, set your course west over the north-south hump of juniper-covered Horse Ridge. Highway 20 crosses this rise along the upper edge of Dry River Canyon, where a pullout is provided on the north side of the road at a scenic overlook. Three-hundred-feet deep, this now dry gorge once contained a rushing Pleistocene river—the overflow from Ice Age Lake Millican, which was fed by meltwater descending from large glaciers on Newberry Volcano. A trail penetrates the canyon from the lower western end and gradually ascends through sagebrush and clumps of giant wild rye. There are Native American pictographs on some of the smooth, water-worn rocks, but these ancient paintings are faint and difficult to find. Now the highway descends into the Deschutes Valley, traversing the world's largest western juniper forests, and then enters Bend's suburbs of ranchettes with green, irrigated horse and llama pastures. Beyond is Central Oregon's distinctive skyline of the snowy Cascades backbone.

Before continuing back into town, though, make a stop at a place called the Badlands. There's a trailhead just off the north side of Highway 20, conveniently located only 12.5 miles east of the Bend city limits. Pathways wind through sandy hollows and alcoves in a labyrinth of picturesque lava outcrops and pressure ridges, intermixed with 1,000-year-old western junipers. The BLM has closed the Badlands to motorized vehicles, making

the 32,000 acres a zone of quiet that is managed for its unique natural values. Birdwatching, botanizing, interesting geology, Indian petroglyphs, and solitude have attracted appreciative hikers. It is already classified as a Wilderness Study Area, and many citizens and conservation groups are urging the BLM to combine it with Dry River Canyon and give the entire area permanent wilderness protection. These advocates point out that as Bend steadily expands in the direction of the Badlands, close-in natural areas are becoming scarce and need protection.

The Cascade Lakes Highway

Any explorations of the Bend area should include at least a day tour along the Cascade Lakes Highway, which is designated as a National Scenic Byway. It is also called Century Drive because of the approximately hundred-mile-long loop that can be made by following this road southwest from town into the forested Cascades. It threads its way south through the famed cluster of mountain lakes, finally jogging east to Highway 97 near La Pine, which provides a straight shot north for a return to Bend. Nevertheless, if time doesn't permit the entire grand loop tour, it's possible to do a shorter excursion to the nearest lakes for a quick picnic (about 25 to 35 miles from Bend) and then merely retrace your tire prints back to town. Indeed, some Bend restaurants and bakeries sell gourmet picnic lunches to go, complete with a bottle of Northwest wine or local craft beer—a delightful way to sample both the regional cuisine and the legendary Cascade Lakes ambiance. From mid November to late May, the Cascade Lakes Highway is snowbound beyond the Mount Bachelor ski area. But as soon as the spring thaw allows snowplows to open the remainder of the road,

Summer sailing on Elk Lake, below South Sister

it becomes a virtual recreational freeway and the high country summer season slams into gear. Even after the snow is gone, the ski area's Pine Marten Lift stays open for sightseeing rides, and "Sunset Dinners" are served in the Pine Marten Lodge restaurant.

Although some tourism brochures convey an impression that it's the "Highway to Heaven," a drive along this route will confirm that the hyperbole is nearly accurate. Beginning at Mount Bachelor, the Cascade Lakes Highway enters a subalpine world of eye-dazzling natural beauty. Be forewarned here: with mile after mile of pristine lakes, rushing streams, flower-filled meadows, and flabbergasting views of snow-encrusted 10,000-foot volcanic peaks, the choices of where to stop and recreate are almost overwhelming. It's a proverbial embarrassment of riches. Beginning with Todd Lake and its mirror reflec-

tion of jagged Broken Top, the road passes twelve more lakes: Sparks, Devils, Elk, Hosmer, Lava, Little Lava, Cultus, Little Cultus, Crane Prairie Reservoir, North Twin, South Twin, and Wickiup Reservoir. The drive also repeatedly crosses clear streams, and for a number of miles parallels the upper Deschutes River. Farther from the road, hundreds of other watercourses and lakes can be reached by side roads or via hiking trails.

Obviously, a three- or four-hour picnic outing up the Cascade Lakes Highway, though delightful, only hints at the possibilities. Loading an automobile with camping gear and venturing into this multifaceted backcountry for several days will provide an even richer experience. With a couple-hundred primitive campsites scattered about the area and twenty-five National Forest campgrounds along the route, there are plenty of

Fly-fishing at Sparks Lake provides the bonus of scenic views of South Sister and other Cascades peaks.

a fly-fisherman casting into the riffles of the Deschutes River, birders with binoculars at Crane Prairie Reservoir's osprey observation point, and a fit young couple unloading mountain bikes from an SUV's rack as they prepare to pedal Forest Service roads.

For those desiring the solitude afforded by more remote places, 260 miles of trail in the 242,400-acre Three Sisters Wilderness delights day hikers, backpackers, and horse packers alike. Signs here and there along the Cascade Lakes Highway point to the trailheads, but remember that most require a parking fee, annual Forest Pass, or other valid recreation pass. A wilderness permit is also required, but it's free and each trailhead is provided with a self-service box. For folks who like to explore the trails on horseback, there's a different fee system, along with established horse camps. Whether afoot or mounted on a horse, to sort out the complexities of all these varying and changing permits, contact the Deschutes National Forest offices for an update before heading into the outback.

And if roughing it isn't your style, let it be known that there are cushier accommodations along the Cascade Lakes Highway. Resort lodges, ranging from rustic to woodsy-plush, provide rental cabins and RV hookups at Elk Lake, Lava Lake, Cultus Lake, Crane Prairie Reservoir, and South Twin Lake. Most also have among their offerings a restaurant, small grocery store, showers, gas, fishing supplies, and boat, canoe, and kayak rentals. Elk Lake Resort is open in the winter, catering to cross-country skiers and snowmobilers, in addition to shuttling guests in and out with the resort's Sno-Cat. During midsummer, it's common to see suntanned backpackers enthusiastically chowing down in the Elk Lake Resort Restaurant. The famed Pacific Crest Trail, which

lodgepole pine groves to pitch a tent in, or lakesides ideal for parking a camper truck or travel trailer before hauling out the fishing equipment. When choosing a site, keep in mind that the more developed campgrounds charge a daily fee.

Pick any sunny summer's day to drive this mile-high section and you'll see people out enjoying the classic Cascade Lakes Highway charms—canoeing on sprawling Sparks Lake or photographing its scenic setting below the Three Sisters peaks, groups of day hikers setting off to trek into the popular Green Lakes Basin, sailboats and windsurfers on Elk Lake,

negotiates the entire spine of the Cascade and Sierra ranges—Canada to Mexico—conveniently passes nearby.

The Sisters–Camp Sherman area

A drive northwest of Bend on Highway 20 leads through the revitalized small community of Tumalo, across open stands of juniper mixed with sagebrush flats and ranchette lands. Looming ever closer, the snow-covered Cascade peaks attract photographers to a wayside along this road. Families dutifully line up in front of the scenic skyline, while an appointed member earnestly snaps a vacation memory. After 20 miles, the highway enters ponderosa pine forest and the town of Sisters. Seemingly at the very foot of the mountains, the picturesque village evokes thoughts of a western movie set. During the mid 1970s, the entire business district adopted a retro, non-neon, Old West architectural theme to attract tourism. Originally a lumber town, when the regional timber industry declined and local sawmills closed, the economy of Sisters sagged as well. This strategy of reinventing itself has been so spectacularly successful, that crowds of tourists and auto traffic frequently make it difficult to drive from one end of Sisters to the other at the height of the summer vacation season. Apparently, many of these people liked what they saw and decided to move to Sisters. Things are booming. There are increasing housing developments, new businesses, larger schools, plus a new city hall and library.

From about nine hundred people at the beginning of the new century, Sisters is moving toward tripling its population. Despite this accelerated growth and a touristy, resort town atmosphere, it has managed to retain an admirably strong sense of community. Taking

Sisters has adopted an Old West theme.

The annual Sisters Outdoor Quilt Show is the largest event of its kind in the world.

stock of Sisters' rich and varied music scene, volunteers came forward to coordinate annual events that tap this resource to raise thousands of dollars for the school district. Notable is the Sisters Starry Nights Concert Series, initiated in 1996. Along with local mu-

Music is a part of nearly every happening in Sisters.

stunning views of the tri-peaks of the Three Sisters. These snowy summits, known in pioneer times as Faith, Hope, and Charity, serve as the mega-landmarks of mid–Central Oregon. In the irrigated pastures below this landscape, llamas graze. These animals are now almost as common as cattle on local ranches, and the area is known as the llama-breeding capital of the United States. However, cowboys and cowgirls still hold sway each year during June, when the Sisters Rodeo takes place. The four days of events draw ever-larger crowds to the rodeo grounds 5 miles east of town. Other popular nearby attractions, in their proper seasons, include the drive west of Sisters on Highway 242 to enjoy autumn color along the scenic McKenzie Pass, winter skiing at the family-affordable Hoodoo Ski Bowl off Highway 20 on the Santiam Pass, an evening meal in the Lodge at Suttle Lake, or attending a theatrical performance by young students at the Caldera Arts Center along the shore of Blue Lake.

Although not readily apparent, more than twelve thousand people live just outside of Sisters in woodsy developments scattered through the surrounding forests. Among the most well known of these planned communities, Black Butte Ranch is just off Highway 20, 8 miles northwest of Sisters. A former cattle operation that was transformed into one of Oregon's finest resorts, it is situated in stands of ponderosa pine at the edge of a huge meadow and aspen-lined lake, with a panorama of the snowy Three Sisters and the matterhorn profile of Mount Washington. A main lodge houses a restaurant that offers fine dining with window views of the entire scene. Similar to Sunriver's design, there's a mix of both private and rental condos and homes among the pinewoods, along with resort facilities, such as several swimming pools, two

sical talent, big-name stars have contributed performances, such as Kim Carnes, The Nitty Gritty Dirt Band, Vince Gill, Amy Grant, Kathy Mattea, and Michael McDonald. Similarly, every year the popular Sisters Folk Festival and Sisters Jazz Festival generate financial contributions for music programs in the community's schools. All in all, the arts are flourishing in Sisters, and there's a plentiful selection of galleries that feature the works of painters, photographers, potters, jewelers, and a host of other artisans. Every July the largest outdoor quilt show in the world takes place in the downtown area, when well over a thousand of these colorful creations adorn the fronts of businesses along every street.

The source of the town's name is plainly evident at its western edge, where there are

Sand Mountain

If you're looking for a relatively short, family-friendly hike in the central portion of Oregon's Cascade Range, this trail fits the bill. It's a modest 1.25-mile loop that offers the reward of a spectacular 360-degree view of the volcanic peaks of the Cascade crest. Sand Mountain is a 5,460-foot cinder cone in the Santiam Pass area that erupted 3,000 years ago—the blink of an eye in geological time. Its views of timberlands in all directions didn't go unnoticed by the U.S. Forest Service. A fire lookout tower was first built on the summit in 1933 but was destroyed by an accidental fire in 1968. During 1990–91 it was reconstructed and has been staffed seasonally ever since, being one of Oregon's few fire lookout towers still in operation.

To reach the trailhead, drive 25 miles northwest of the town of Sisters on Highway 20 to the top of the Santiam Pass. Take a left (south) at the Hoodoo Ski Bowl turnoff on paved Forest Road 2690 (Big Lake Road). Continue south for 3 miles and turn right (west) on dirt Forest Road 810. Keep going west for about a mile from the pavement until you reach a primitive horse campground, where 810 briefly jogs south (left) and then immediately returns to its westward direction. At nearly the 3-mile mark, 810 turns sharply south (left) at a junction with Forest Road 866. Soon, 810 begins climbing Sand Mountain to the trailhead—

a total of 4.5 miles from where you originally left paved 2690.

NOTE Forest Road 810 is gated at the base of the mountain, 1.5 miles below the trailhead. The firetower staffer opens this gate every day at 9:00 a.m., and closes it at 6:00 p.m. Thus, if you miss the ungated period, plan on adding 3 miles to the total hiking distance. The road generally is free of snow and passable by early July, closing again with the return of the snowy season in autumn. Many sections of Forest Road 810 are rough, and a high-clearance vehicle and careful driving are advisable.

No parking permit is required at the trailhead, so merely strap on your daypack and filled water bottle (no drinking water is available on the mountain) and stride up the path. Beginning in larger conifers at the parking area, the route climbs steeply for .4 miles to the crest, quickly entering the more open terrain of a stunted, high-elevation forest of subalpine fir,

noble fir, Engelmann spruce, and whitebark pine. At the top, don't be surprised if a friendly fire lookout invites you to climb the stairs of the tower to its observation deck. From this vantage point, you can marvel at the panoramic vista that encompasses extensive lava flows, Big Lake, Clear Lake, Black Butte, the Three Sisters tri-peak array, Mount Jefferson, and Mount Washington. On especially clear days, Mount Hood might be visible far to the north.

From the tower, follow the trail south down the barren pumice sand slope, watching for the three-inch pigmy short-horned lizards that manage to live in this lofty, harsh environment. Shortly, you'll arrive at Sand Mountain's crater, where the trail continues on around the perimeter of the rim, connecting with an unused jeep road directly below the tower. From here, the loop follows this old road north, descending back to the trailhead.

The Sand Mountain fire lookout tower offers unsurpassed views of the high Cascade crest in Central Oregon.

Catching a morning updraft, a hot air balloon drifts toward Black Butte.

The ponderosa forests of the Metolius Basin, below Mount Jefferson

The Metolius bursts forth from the earth as a full-sized river, only a stone's throw upstream from this vantage point.

golf courses, canoeing, kayaking, bicycling, and a scenic system of horse trails.

As Highway 20 continues northwest, it passes through magnificent stands of ponderosa pine with their jigsaw patterns of golden, cinnamon hued bark. Not far from Black Butte Ranch, take a right-hand turn-off on a paved side road at the western base of cone-shaped Black Butte. This leads 5 miles through the pines to the tiny village of Camp Sherman (population 250), situated in a spectacular setting of green meadows and pine forests, below the snowy mountains. Nearby, the crystal-clear Metolius magically bubbles forth from the ground as a full-blown river. Camp Sherman's name hails from a time around the turn of the last century when Sherman County farmers, from the open wheat country to the northeast, traveled here to camp and refresh themselves after hot summer harvests. The Camp Sherman Store and Fly Shop is located just a stone's throw from the river, and has been the hamlet's heartbeat since 1918. This little business, adjoining the post office and mini lending-library, somehow manages to supply everything from groceries, deli takeout, clothing, hats, and gas to fishing equipment and the latest news on how the local trout are biting. Surrounding it are a collection of private cabins and homes, several small rustic resorts, the Kokanee Cafe (topnotch Northwest-style cuisine), two-room school, miniature chapel, fire hall, and a community center.

Downstream (north) from Camp Sherman, is some of the most beautiful riparian environment in Oregon. The Metolius has a federal designation as Wild and Scenic and is a world-famous fly-fishing river. Unless it's the dead of winter, rare is the day that you won't see someone casting for trout in the icy, 45-degree waters (catch and release only for this stretch). A number of Forest Service campgrounds are situated here and there in pleasant pine groves along the river, and some particularly beautiful trails lead both up and down the Metolius from the Wizard Falls Hatchery. This hatchery, located 5 miles downstream from Camp Sherman, is open to the public and has large ponds and holding tanks full of trout and salmon. Because of the unique geographic location of the Metolius Basin, nestled between Black Butte, Green Ridge, and the eastern slope of the Cascades, localized weather patterns often bring more precipitation here than anywhere else in Central Oregon—some thirty-three annual inches, which is comparable to famously rainy Portland. Consequently, in places, there's the moist, mossy look of Western Oregon, with ferns and cedars. A short trail that leads into the head of Jack Creek, a Metolius tributary, provides a good example of this. Nearby Jack Lake Road accesses trailheads for the Mount Jefferson Wilderness, where the easy 4.3-mile loop path into Canyon Creek Meadow is popular with families. It offers magnificent views of Mount Jefferson and Three Fingered Jack, along with plenty of summer wildflowers in an alpine setting.

Redmond

North of Bend, the Deschutes Valley widens and gradually decreases in elevation. There, it is a more open landscape of semiarid sagebrush flats, extensive juniper woodlands, rimrock-edged buttes and ridges often juxtaposed with the contrasting green of irrigated farmlands and pastures. The diverted Deschutes waters make the area the agricultural hub of the valley, where there are plentiful crops of alfalfa, rye, oats, wheat, barley, peppermint, potatoes, grass, and hay. Dairy cows, beef cattle, and horses as well as the ubiquitous Central Oregon llamas graze in wide pastures.

The city of Redmond, 16 miles north of burgeoning Bend, is also booming, currently nearing a population of thirty thousand. Future growth predictions indicate that nearly twice that number could be living in Redmond by mid century. With its hometown, all-American personality, Redmond has attracted families who are increasingly finding nearby upscale Bend to be unaffordable. Something of a renaissance is occurring in the historic downtown area, with new retail shops appearing in the stately old-brick buildings, while restaurants, brew pubs, and coffee shops now occupy refurbished Craftsman houses. Inevitably, there has also been a creeping growth of commercial malls and box stores along Highway 97 at both the north and south ends of town. Locals frequently speculate as to how many years will pass be-

The Redmond Hotel in the historic
downtown section

fore the sagebrush, juniper, and agricultural
lands between Redmond and Bend vanish,
the two cities being connected by an umbil-
ical cord of typical urban sprawl. In this regard, controversies keep erupting over proposed changes in land-use regulations for the
rural areas surrounding Bend and Redmond.
Proponents are in favor of an increase in the
number of large destination resorts that could
be developed on lands presently zoned for
ranch, farm, or forest use. Many Deschutes
County residents, however, think there are
already plenty of existing resorts, such as
Eagle Crest, Pronghorn, and Ranch at the
Canyons. They argue that many of these resorts are nothing more than upscale residential subdivisions that will lead to a spreading
elitist suburbia. Rather than help the local
economy, they contend the change would
make Central Oregon ever more unaffordable
for the average wage earner.

Regardless, people keep coming, either as
new residents, to vacation, or to attend local
events, and they are increasingly arriving via
commercial air flights. Redmond Municipal
Airport, at the southern edge of the town, is
conveniently situated at the center of the Deschutes Valley. It offers daily direct connections with Portland, Seattle, San Francisco,
and Salt Lake City, and is billed as "The Aviation Gateway to Central Oregon." The exit
doors of the airport terminal are commonly
the point of introduction to the region for
many first-time visitors. Besides passenger
service, the airport is home to air cargo companies and Lancair, a manufacturer of high-
performance general aviation aircraft. Additionally, the U.S. Forest Service uses this airfield as a base from which to fight forest fires.
Further reflecting Redmond's handy central-
ized location, the Deschutes County Fairgrounds neighbor the airport. The large covered arena there hosts many events, including
livestock shows and rodeos, indicative of the
region's ranching roots.

Prineville

Central Oregon's ranching heritage is especially evident 20 miles to the east in the small
city of Prineville—"The Cowboy Capital of
Oregon" is their promotional slogan. It's a
town nestled among green, irrigated pastures
and fields in a rimrock-bordered valley, with
the Crooked River flowing through its central neighborhoods. Historically, because of
the nearby pine-clad Ochoco Mountains,
there was a dual economy of timber resources
and beef production. As with so many Northwest communities, though, the local sawmill closed in 2001. Loggers in tin hard-hats
and brightly colored suspenders have become
few and far between, and now the streets are

dominated by cowboy hats, western boots, and Wrangler jeans. Every year at the end of June, buckaroos abound in Prineville when the well-known Crooked River Roundup rodeo and races are held at the Crook County Fairgrounds, the events being kicked-off by a cattle drive through the middle of town. Another notable presence is the huge Les Schwab Tire Distribution Center, Prineville being the birthplace and regional headquarters for this Northwest business empire.

Prineville is the oldest city in the mid–Central Oregon area. Its rich history is displayed in the Bowman Museum, housed in a vintage stone bank building on Main Street in the downtown area. East along the street you'll see a classic stone-and-brick 1909 courthouse surrounded by trees and lawns—Prineville is the Crook County seat. Additionally, it's interesting to note that Prineville is the county's only incorporated city; and with a population growing toward ten thousand, it's the largest. Located at the far western edge of its nearly 3,000-square-mile rural kingdom, it has a big backyard. This positioning also makes Prineville the gateway to the recreational delights of these vast eastern hinterlands. The Crooked River and the Prineville and Ochoco reservoirs provide ample fishing opportunities; and among deer and elk hunters, the forested Ochoco Mountains are famous for their bounty of game. These same timbered heights of the Ochoco National Forest offer an abundance of pleasant campgrounds, such as ponderosa-fringed Walton Lake, linked by an extensive system of Forest Service roads that entice mountain bikers. Refreshingly untrammeled trails await backpackers and horse packers in the little-known Mill Creek Wilderness, or the equally obscure Bridge Creek Wilderness. Likewise, winter brings snowmobilers, cross-country skiers, and snowshoe

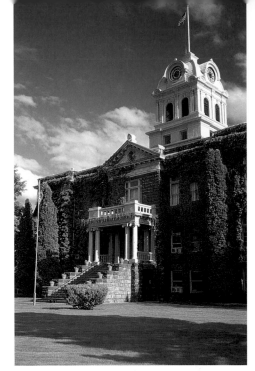

Prineville's historic Crook County Courthouse dates from 1909.

enthusiasts to explore remote trails in the Ochoco backcountry.

The entire Prineville area is also a rock hound's mecca, with a number of locations that yield thundereggs, green jasper, agates, petrified wood, limb casts, obsidian, and other geological enticements. Many of these sites are on federal lands where digging and collecting are allowed—check with the local U.S. Forest Service and Bureau of Land Management headquarters for details.

From the Painted Hills and Clarno Fossil Beds to Shaniko

For an outdoors lesson about the area's geology and paleontology, take a 45-mile drive northeast of Prineville to the Painted Hills Unit of John Day Fossil Beds National Monument, near the little community of Mitchell. Interpretive signs and brochures describe

The Painted Hills, John Day Fossil
Beds National Monument

what the constant erosion of these brick red, pale yellow, and greenish banded ashbeds have progressively revealed. The numerous leaf prints and fossilized wood fragments reflect millions of years of volcanic upheavals and shifting climates, with resulting changes in flora and fauna. Several footpaths lead along the eroded borders of the barren, fossil-bearing mounds. A picnic area with tables, restrooms, and drinking water is located near the entrance of the monument.

About 60 miles to the north, via Highway 19 through the towns of Service Creek and Fossil, is the Clarno Unit of the John Day Fossil Beds National Monument. Located along Highway 218, this is the smallest of the monument's three units (the main Sheep Rock Unit and headquarters is to the east, near Dayville, along the John Day River; see "The John Day River drainage" in Part IV). The Clarno picnic area is situated among junipers with shaded tables, drinking water, and restrooms. The self-guided Trail of the Fossils leads a quarter mile along the base of the nearby towering cliffs, known as the Palisades. Interpretive signs enlighten hikers as to the identity of these eroded reddish-tan spires. They represent a solidified, 45-million-year-old conglomeration of volcanic glop that

was originally composed of ash, rocks, and other debris. This mudflow from a Clarno volcano engulfed a subtropical forest of palms, avocado trees, ferns, and other exotic plants as proven by petrified logs and limb casts along the path. Other fossils found in the area show that animals were also trapped in the mud, such as miniature primitive horses and early rhinolike creatures called titanotheres.

Just around the corner of the Palisades is Hancock Field Station, operated by Portland's Oregon Museum of Science and Industry (OMSI). The field station is a rustic science camp for youngsters, founded in 1953 under the expert guidance of Lon Hancock, a Portland amateur paleontologist who made many important discoveries in the Clarno formation. Specializing in the teaching of paleontology and other natural science subjects, Camp Hancock has launched many beginning students upon successful careers as paleontologists, biologists, and naturalists.

Continuing west on Highway 218 through this dry landscape of sagebrush, juniper, and rimrock, you complete a big loop that will eventually bring you back to the Deschutes Valley. Along the way, we'll briefly stop off in two interesting backcountry villages.

The first is Antelope (population 35, give or take a person or two), once a bustling frontier stagecoach stop with over two hundred residents. It's now a very quiet place. However, from 1981 to 1985 things got pretty lively again because of a bizarre series of incidents that catapulted Antelope into the international news. It all began when the wealthy Indian guru Bhagwan Shree Rajneesh purchased the nearby hundred-square-mile Big Muddy Ranch and converted it into a religious commune, called Rajneeshpuram. Soon, the population of orange-clad followers grew to more than seven thousand people, drawn to the remote location by the leader's freeform blend of esoteric Eastern philosophies that included permissive sex. By sheer overpowering numbers, the cult began taking over Antelope's politics and businesses. They even renamed the town Rajneesh. Almost everything in the town was eventually theirs, except for the two churches. When a remnant of original townsfolk resisted "annexation," an armed, thuggish Rajneesh police force intimidated them back into line. Rajneeshpuram finally self-destructed when the leaders were arrested for plotting to take over Wasco County's government and conspiring to murder the U.S. Attorney heading a federal grand jury investigation of the commune. Now the Big Muddy Ranch is a Young Life Christian Retreat Center and Antelope is again peaceful, just the way the locals seem to prefer it. Visit the friendly little café and try one of their delicious hamburgers made from the local brand—Painted Hills Natural Beef.

An 8-mile drive northwest brings you to Highway 97 and the high-plains outpost of Shaniko. Formerly one of the world's major wool-shipping centers, it's now largely just a shadow of former boom times. At the turn of the last century, scores of sheepherder camps with their wooly flocks grazed the surrounding hundreds of square miles of rolling grasslands. From 1900 to 1910, trainloads of wool (sometimes as much as 4 million pounds yearly) were shipped along a track that ran sixty miles north to a mainline railroad along the Columbia River, and then on to the East Coast. Shaniko prospered, and the population grew to six hundred people. In 1911, however, Shaniko was bypassed by a new railroad line to the west that followed the Deschutes River to Bend, and the town faded. Today, the old brick hotel has been beauti-

The restored Shaniko Hotel and Cafe, on the quiet main street of "Oregon's Best Known Ghost Town"

fully restored and the other surviving buildings spruced up. Travelers along Highway 97 are stopping more frequently to see "Oregon's Best Known Ghost Town," browsing the antique shops, touring the museum, and eating in the hotel's café.

Madras

Now it's a straight shot southwest on 97 back to the Deschutes Valley, where you enter the city of Madras. This community of around seven thousand people is located at the northern end of the valley's agricultural lands, which grow the most extensive crops in Central Oregon. A summer drive on the surrounding roads will take you past field after field of mint, alfalfa, sugar beets, carrots, radishes, potatoes, onions, and garlic. Seed production is a major purpose of these crops, along with seed from lawn bluegrass and flowers. In fact,

Irrigated croplands near Madras, the agricultural hub of the Deschutes Valley

the Madras area produces 80 percent of the nation's carrot seed. The area's ranching influence is evident at the south end of town. On the east side of Highway 97, an old-fashioned livestock auction arena facilitates the sale of cattle, horses, and other animals. Anyone unfamiliar with this fascinating ritual of the American West should experience it at least once. The auctioneer orchestrates the bidding in traditional hyperstaccato style, which is incomprehensible to the uninitiated. Nevertheless, the attending ranchers understand and often indicate their bids to the auctioneer by nothing more than a nearly imperceptible tip of the hat. Yet in some mysterious fashion communication takes place and sales are made.

The Madras area is unquestionably the most culturally and ethnically diverse place in Central Oregon. Along with farming and ranching families, many descended from original pioneer stock, the Warm Springs Indian Reservation is only fourteen miles to the northwest; and in recent years more and more Hispanics have been settling in the area.

Many first came to work in crop harvests and then decided to stay, some establishing farms of their own. These members of the community have added a noticeably rich variety of authentic Mexican restaurants, bakeries, and grocery stores. Because Native American youths from Warm Springs attend high school in Madras, all of the area's ethnicities share the same classrooms. Every May, this diversity is celebrated with the Collage of Culture Festival, held in Friendship Park, where a broad mix of music, dance, art, and foods from the world's ethnic traditions is presented along with the yearly colorful hot-air balloon liftoff.

Madras has been an agricultural hub from the start. The city was incorporated in 1911 when the railroad arrived, followed by access to irrigation water from the Deschutes River. This combination allowed the area to realize its potential as a prolific grower of crops that could be shipped to outside markets, and Madras began to grow. There was another boost during World War II when the U.S. Army established an air base there. Most recently manufacturing enterprises of various types have introduced a new element to the economy. This is apparent near the Madras Municipal Airport where a progressively expanding industrial park is home for several businesses. Notable is the Bright Wood Corporation, the largest molding plant in the world and Central Oregon's second largest provider of jobs. Madras and the surrounding Jefferson County area are usually considered to be primarily laid-back farming country. However, the region is now counted among the fastest growing areas in Oregon, both in employment and population.

Additionally, merely being in Central Oregon ensures that a good portion of the Madras area's economy will be derived from recreation and tourism. Nearby, of course, is the outdoor sports bounty of the Cascade Range, with its Mount Jefferson Wilderness. Even closer, though, is the Deschutes River Canyon and its two large reservoirs, just a stone's throw west of town. And the Deschutes River leads to the next explorations of Central Oregon—a trip down the Deschutes drainage, culminating at the Columbia River.

Composed of volcanic tuff and rhyolite, the dramatic cliffs of Smith Rock State Park rise above the Crooked River.

Down the Lower Deschutes

The trip begins about 20 miles south of Madras, near the small community of Terrebonne, where the Crooked River flows past the startling spires of Smith Rock State Park. These immense, reddish-tan cliffs of volcanic tuff and rhyolite tower above a sharp bend of the river and offer dramatic views for picnickers, hikers, and photographers. Smith Rock has become famous among rock climbers, and scores of people commonly clamber and dangle by ropes on the sheer precipices. Stop and listen; you will frequently hear voices speaking French, German, Japanese, and other languages, indicating how this park draws climbers from all over the planet. It has also attracted Hollywood, and several movies have been shot at Smith Rock State Park over the years.

Tracing the water's current ever downward into the Crooked River Gorge, passing beneath the soaring bridge spans of Highway 97 and the north-south railroad line, you at last break out into the enormous main canyon of the Deschutes River. Here the Crooked River from the east and the Metolius River from the west both connect with the Deschutes in a deep mega-chasm confluence. Far above

The Monkey Face formation and other challenging routes at Smith Rock attract climbers from around the world.

and out of sight are the level, irrigated agricultural lands and juniper woods of the mid–Deschutes Valley, with the snowy presence of 10,495-foot Mount Jefferson to the west. But in the canyon bottom, the views are confined to a world of towering, strikingly layered basalt walls and impounded water. In 1963, 440-foot-high Round Butte Dam was constructed just downstream from the three river forks, creating ten-mile-long Lake Billy Chinook (named for the nineteenth-century Indian scout who guided John Fremont through the area). Water was backed into the three connecting river gorges, where it now laps at the base of the 300-foot-high sheer cliffs of the Cove Palisades—a knife-thin, flat-topped dividing ridge between the Crooked River and Deschutes arms of the lake.

A road leading from the small community of Culver switchbacks down into the gorge to Cove Palisades State Park. Picnic and camping areas, with marinas, accommodate a Cen-

tral Oregon aqua-playground of swimming, boating, water skiing, jet-skiing, and fishing. Anglers on houseboats and motorized fishing boats delve westward for miles into the Cascade foothills along the Metolius arm of the lake, trying their luck for bull trout and kokanee salmon. Scattered along these remote shorelines are cabins belonging to outdoor folks who savor peaceful solitude. Next in line down river from Round Butte Dam is Lake Simtustus, backed up behind Pelton Dam, near Madras. Roads follow the eastern rim tops above these lengthy reservoirs, occasional pullouts giving eagle-eye views of the canyon and the Cascade peaks. Utilizing these lofty vantage points, every February an entire weekend is devoted to welcoming bald eagles as they migrate in from the north country to spend the winter in Central Oregon. Jointly organized and hosted by the Oregon Department of Parks and Recreation, the Confederated Tribes of the Warm Springs, and Portland General Electric, there are two days of guided birdwatching, nature talks, and traditional Native American dance performances. Also, the High Desert Museum brings their live birds of prey.

Below Lake Simtustus and where Highway 26 crosses the river at the town of Warm Springs, the Deschutes Canyon takes on a progressively more remote quality. For the remainder of its nearly hundred-mile journey northward to join the Columbia River, the lower Deschutes, unencumbered by dams, is designated as a Wild and Scenic Waterway.

Nearly half of this stretch borders the Warm Springs Indian Reservation on the west side. After initially losing most of their traditional tribal lands in an 1855 treaty with the U.S. government, the Warm Springs Confederated Tribes transformed loss into success. Because of the rich natural resources of the 640,000 acres they now possess, theirs is one of the most self-sufficient reservations in the United States. More than 150 years later, the Warm Springs Reservation now boasts a lumber mill, plywood plant, large, modern administration center, a plaza with retail shops and a restaurant, a 25,000-square-foot cultural museum, and a tribal radio station. Perhaps most impressive is a multimillion-dollar resort lodge, Kah-Nee-Ta, with its dramatic hillside architecture. It offers a hot-springs-warmed swimming pool, convention facility, golf course, and tennis courts. As many other Native American tribes have done, in 1996 Warm Springs added a gambling casino to their resort lineup. Other income is derived from the tribe's share of hydroelectric revenue generated by the Round Butte and Pelton Dams that border their side of the river, along with a third Deschutes dam owned by the tribe. Despite these modern touches, Indians still fish for salmon with nets from traditional wood platforms on the river, gather native plants for food and medicinal purposes, and capture wild horses locally for use each year at an all-Indian rodeo in nearby Tygh Valley.

The lower Deschutes, besides being a legendary steelhead, trout, and salmon fishery, is also famed for its premier white-water rafting. There's mile after mile of free-flowing river with periodic rapids, ranging from relatively easy to white-knuckle rough-and-tumble. Several commercial guide enterprises in the Central Oregon area offer float trips with guaranteed white-water thrills. In all this lonesome stretch of water roiling between basalt cliffs, from Warm Springs to the Columbia, there's only one town. It's the pint-sized village of Maupin, perched on a steep hillside directly above the Deschutes. When it's the height of the season for both fishing and rafting, this little river town is abustle with the comings and goings of river-runners and anglers stocking up on supplies. Just down river is the dangerously impassable falls at Sherar's Bridge, a good place to watch Native American Indians balance precariously on wooden platforms, salmon nets in hand, above the roaring white water.

Lake Billy Chinook in the Deschutes River Canyon, at Cove Palisades, with Mount Jefferson on the skyline

North Central Oregon's appearance changes noticeably as the elevation diminishes from 3,623 feet at Bend to around a hundred feet where the Deschutes empties into the Columbia River. Groves of Oregon white oak begin to appear in some of the side can-

Mount Hood sunset

Using the ages-old traditional method, a Native American pulls in a netted steelhead at Sherar's Bridge.

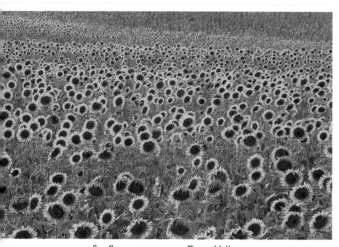

Sunflower crop near Grass Valley

Columbia Gorge Discovery Center's display of historic fruit boxes reflects the area's world-class reputation for growing apples, pears, peaches, cherries, and other crops.

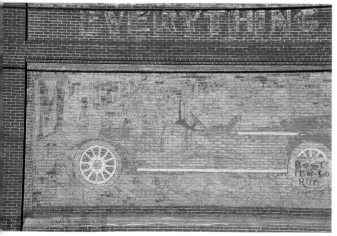

A brick wall of Wasco's old mercantile has a faded 1920s auto advertisement.

yons and along the lower flanks of 11,235-foot Mount Hood, with some places having a resemblance to the open oak savannas of the Rogue Valley in Southwestern Oregon.

Above the Deschutes Canyon's eastern rim are the margins of the rolling Columbia Basin wheat country—seas of grain, flowing like green waves in the spring breezes or standing silently golden in the still, hot days of summer. The few-and-far-between human outposts are diminutive farming communities that sport large grain elevators, wonderfully quiet places like Moro and Grass Valley. Well worth a short side trip is little Wasco, bypassed by time and the modern pace of Highway 97. On the main street, watch for a long-vacated mercantile building dating from the late 1800s, next door to the lovingly restored Oskaloosa Hotel. There, painted on the old store's brick wall, is a large advertisement for a 1920s vintage auto. The image is so faded that it's like seeing a haunting shadow from another era. Slow down or you'll miss it.

The Dalles–Eastern Columbia River Gorge area

At the northern border of Central Oregon, The Dalles has the distinction of being the state's oldest city east of the Cascades, and it is saturated with history. The name dates back to early French-Canadian fur company employees who described the location's narrow basalt channel through which the Columbia flowed as *Les dalles*—literally, "the stone trough." The Lewis and Clark expedition camped at this location in 1805; and during the 1840s, The Dalles marked the end of the long overland portions of the Oregon Trail. Before Mount Hood's Barlow Pass offered pioneers an alternate route, their dismantled wagons and belongings were loaded on rafts and floated down the hair-raising rapids of the Columbia River Gorge to reach the Willamette Valley. The Fort Dalles Museum, housed in the surviving 1856 surgeons' quarters, has exhibits related to this military post, and in the downtown area is Klindt's Booksellers, the oldest bookstore in Oregon (1870). Take a walk just about anywhere in the old-town district of The Dalles and you'll see homes and churches from the nineteeth century.

Just to the west of The Dalles is the Columbia River Gorge National Scenic Area. However, before exploring there it's a good idea to first visit the Columbia Gorge Discovery Center, which does an excellent job of living up to its name. Located at the western edge of town, its varied, high-quality interpretive exhibits provide an impressively thorough understanding of the area's natural and cultural history. The Wasco County Historical Museum is housed in the same facility, and the center's Basalt Rock Café serves quality lunch and snack foods.

Although Interstate 84 follows the river through this gigantic breach in the Cascade Range, the more enjoyable way to tour it is along the remaining sections of the original road. Built between 1913 and 1922, the Old Columbia River Highway picturesquely meanders along cliff faces and past wind-bent oaks on high overlooks between the small communities of Rowena and Mosier. On the summit of Rowena Crest, it passes The Nature Conservancy's Tom McCall Preserve. If you're there during April or May, be sure to stop and hike out across the high, level-topped bluff. Masses of spring wildflowers cover the sanctuary, several being protected endemics that are found nowhere else in the world. When the trail reaches the promontory's edge, you'll be rewarded with jaw-drop-

Along the Old Columbia River Gorge Highway, the Rowena Crest
overlook gives tremendous views east toward the The Dalles.

The Nature Conservancy's Tom McCall Preserve in the spring season.

ping views down the gorge. Far below, you might see brightly colored sails skimming across the river's surface—the Columbia River Gorge is a stupendous geological wind-tunnel, making it one of the finest windsurfing sites in the world.

The entire eastern gorge district, including the Washington side, has a famously ideal climate for growing apples, cherries, pears, and peaches. Additionally, in recent years, local grape crops have been transformed into prize-winning wines. Country drives in April provide stunning views of fruit trees in blossom below snowy Mount Hood; and during the summer and autumn harvest seasons, roadside fruit stands abound. An especially enjoyable way to see some of the area's orchards and vineyards is to catch a ride on one of the Mount Hood Railroad's historic trains. Beginning in the town of Hood River, the four-hour excursion travels 15 miles up the Hood River Valley to the little town of Parkdale, where an hour layover allows time to visit shops, a museum, cafés, or the acclaimed Elliot Glacier Public House brew pub. Back in Hood River, you might want to visit a fascinating landmark at the western city limits— the Columbia Gorge Hotel, now restored to its former historical grandeur. It was built in 1921 by wealthy lumber baron Simon Benson, who hired Italian stonemasons to craft a European-style inn. "The Waldorf of the West," as it was called, sits on a lushly landscaped, panoramic cliff edge where a 208-foot waterfall plunges to the river below. Fine cuisine with a Northwest flare is served in the dining hall, and overnight guests enjoy being pampered in luxurious rooms, followed by a complimentary four-course breakfast in the morning.

The Columbia River Gorge is definitely a different place than it was in the early 1800s.

The Columbia River Gorge is one of the premier windsurfing sites in the world.

Roger Woosley, a lifelong Gorge resident, proudly sells his crop of apples from a vintage Chevy pickup in Hood River.

The Dalles Dam on the Columbia River, along with many other dams within this enormous drainage, produces abundant electricity for the Northwest region. Photo: Brian Robb

The fearsome rapids that challenged the pioneers now have been tamed by a series of dams and navigation locks, transforming the river into a string of long, placid reservoirs. Just outside the eastern end of the gorge, The Dalles Dam spans the Columbia, and twenty-four miles farther upstream, near the mouth of the John Day River, is the namesake John Day Dam. All totaled, there are about two hundred dams of various sizes in the Columbia drainage, from the Pacific Ocean to its source in the Canadian Rocky Mountains, along with the numerous tributaries.

Harnessing the awesome power of the mighty Columbia has created obvious benefits. Northwesterners enjoy abundant electricity at half the average U.S. price—the John Day Dam alone is capable of supplying the equivalent of twice the power needs of Seat-

tle! The list of positives also includes the fact that irrigation from these reservoirs has converted the dry Columbia Basin into a major agricultural region, along with allowing the barging of goods up and down the river and mitigating the threat of floods.

But this extensive network of dams has collectively generated problems as well. The eons-old salmon and steelhead runs have faltered, with many biologists tracing a hefty portion of the blame to these impediments. There have been cultural and economic ramifications as well. Water impounded by The Dalles Dam in 1957 inundated Celilo Falls, where generations of Native Americans fished for thousands of years, and commercial and sports fisheries have declined with the dwindling wild salmon runs. Despite complex, costly fish ladders and bypass systems being

After passing through navigation locks, a barge works its way up the Columbia River.

installed at these dams, the problems persist and worsen. Coalitions of conservation groups, fishing associations, river groups, and Native American tribes are increasingly calling for a breaching of some of the less-important dams in the upper reaches of the Columbia drainage. They cite studies indicating that a reduced number of these concrete obstacles would allow more salmon to successfully complete their migratory anadromous cycles.

The issues are complex, and certainly the dams cannot be blamed for everything; cities, industry, and agricultural runoff leach toxic pollutants into the river, riparian damage on upper tributaries from improper grazing and logging take a toll, and there has been a history of commercial overfishing before strict regulations came into effect. Ultimately, it's a question of how nearly a century of engineering in the Columbia watershed can be workably fine-tuned and reconciled with elegantly successful natural systems that evolved over millions of years.

PART III

Southeastern Oregon

Southeastern Oregon

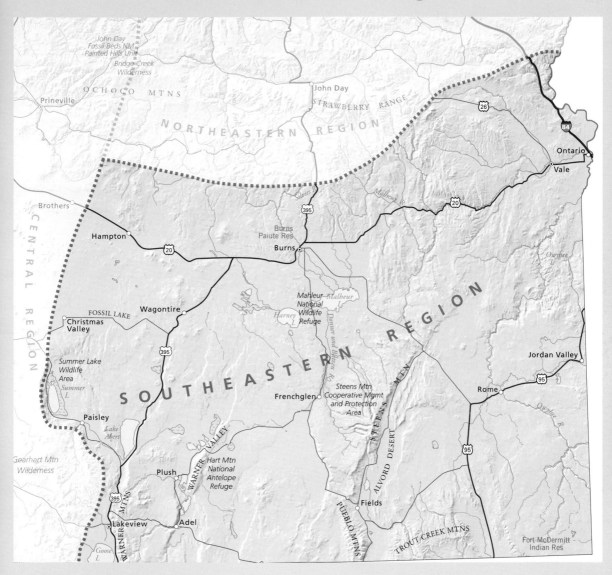

From Covered Wagons to Horseless Carriages

*The reason I've been able to produce some fast
horses, is that where I graze them, they have to
feed at thirty miles an hour to get enough to eat.*

Reub Long, *The Oregon Desert*, 1966

As this humorous anecdote attests, the high desert country of
Oregon can be a difficult region for raising horses and cattle,
as well as for other agricultural enterprises. Reub Long, the
well-known philosopher "sage" of the desert, spent his entire
life ranching these sparse drylands and observed many poorly
prepared, would-be homesteaders come and go.

Others, however, have managed to survive in this arid region, with some family-run ranches being in operation over
several generations. The longtime resident of Southeastern
Oregon learns that nature must be met here on its own terms.
A climate with less than ten inches of annual rainfall can have
a profoundly humbling influence. Anyone not recognizing the
wisdom of a sound stewardship ethic will eventually have unproductive land, ruined by bad grazing practices. Although
seemingly stoic and practical on the surface, when asked about
the country he or she resides in, a rancher often waxes poetic
with deep convictions about this expansive, sagebrush-covered
land.

Human presence is not the dominant element in Southeastern Oregon. The open, sweeping terrain and measureless sky
take center stage, while the profound silence is a blank sheet

Pages 178–179: Low-water year
in Warner Valley. Inset: Alvord
Desert playa detail, Southeastern Oregon. Page 180: An
old, weather-ravaged settlers'
cabin in the Catlow Valley

Opposite: The Alvord Desert
playa, below the eastern escarpment of Steens Mountain

upon which the desert winds write their subtle background music.

Desert hunter-gatherers

The first prehistoric aboriginal groups arrived in this far corner of Oregon at the close of the last Ice Age and became masters of desert survival. Over the course of many centuries, their evolving lifestyles and cultures gradually became uniquely identifiable as the bands now collectively known as the Northern Paiutes.

During pre-Columbian times, large bands of Paiutes were uncommon in Southeastern Oregon. Their social structure emphasized small, widely separated family groups because the meager offerings of the arid Great Basin generally could not provide sufficient food, firewood, and other supplies to support large tribes. Some archaeological investigations indicate that there may have been only one Paiute family group for every one hundred square miles before the coming of Euro-American settlers. Their lifestyle was simple, nomadic, and unencumbered. Food consisted of nearly anything edible: roots, shoots, berries, seeds, birds and their eggs, lizards, snakes, fish, insects, rabbits, marmots, ground squirrels, mule deer, pronghorn, and bighorn sheep. The Paiute groups of the Harney Basin apparently hunted American bison (buffalo) as well—the journals of early white explorers reported the finding of skulls and other bones of these huge animals around Malheur and Harney lakes. Why bison disappeared there remains unknown. The Paiutes netted and snared small animals, or used deadfall traps, augmented with bows and stone-tipped arrows for larger game.

Ancient Paiute petroglyphs adorn rocks throughout Southeastern Oregon. This boulder's artwork in the Pueblo Mountains is accompanied by a Great Basin collared lizard.

Historically, Paiutes used bows and stone-tipped arrows to hunt larger game, such as mule deer.

Winter, a time of scarcity, demanded supplies of dried foods accumulated through the warm months. Starvation probably was all too frequent in severe, extended winters. Paiute camps were rather austere and unadorned compared with the artfully elegant tipi assemblages of the larger tribes of plains Indians to the east. Temporary, lean-to shelters of local plant materials were constructed on the spot, and caves were sometimes inhabited as well. Mats, usually woven from cattail leaves,

Chief Jimmy Louie of the Wadiatika band of Northern Paiutes, Harney Basin. Courtesy of Harney County Historical Society

formed bed pads or chairs to recline against when propped up by short pole frames. Various sizes of woven baskets served for gathering, storing and cooking foods, or even as women's hats. The indispensable, all-purpose rabbit-skin blanket doubled as bed covering and warm clothing. Twisted sagebrush bark fiber made tough sandals.

Such was the elegantly simple, admirably proficient lifestyle of these early Oregonians. In this harsh environment, a modern-day person with adequate clothing, boots, and a knife, might die within a few days of dehydration and exposure to heat or cold. Conversely, these skilled desert dwellers survived generation after generation for thousands of years—and they did so mostly naked, wearing sandals, and using only primitive tools

and shelters through blazingly hot summers and snowy, subzero winters.

However, this millennia-old aboriginal society surrendered within less than a century to the arriving white men and women whose coming heralded the eclipse of an ancient way of life that could be traced back across a vanished land bridge to Asian roots.

First white explorers and migrating settlers

Three Frenchmen—La Valle, Charbonneau, and Nadeau—may have been the first whites to see Southeastern Oregon. Embarking upon an incredible adventure across an unmapped, wild continent without supplies or guns in 1750, they left a ship on the southern California coast, at the present site of San Diego, and attempted to walk to Quebec in eastern Canada. Whatever prompted this hopeless trek, history does not say. Two of them survived long enough to arrive in what is now Idaho, where they abandoned their fiasco and lived with the local Indians.

In 1818, Donald McKenzie, while investigating the Snake River drainage for the Northwest Fur Company, reached the head of a river in what is now southwestern Idaho. He sent three Hawaiian members of his crew down this unknown watercourse that flowed toward the west and the present-day Oregon boundary. These South Sea islanders never came back from the wild canyon and it was named in their honor, using the native pronunciation for their islands, "Owyhee."

The first documented nonnative exploration of Southeastern Oregon was in 1825–26, when Peter Skene Ogden led about a hundred members of a Hudson's Bay Company brigade into the Snake River area to trap beaver. Six of his men followed a tributary river into

Alvord Desert twilight. John Work, a Hudson's Bay employee, was the first white explorer to see the eastern side of Steens Mountain and the arid Alvord Basin.

the Harney Basin. When Indians wounded and killed several members of the party and stole their furs, these French trappers named the river Malheur, meaning "bad times." Later, the large, shallow lake that dominates the basin was given the same name. In the fall of 1826, Ogden himself explored the Harney district, the first of several such trips that continued through 1829. The next white explorer to enter this arid region, in 1831, was another Hudson's Bay employee, John Work. He investigated as far south as the eastern side of Steens Mountain, which he referred to as Snow Mountain.

In the winter of 1843, that far-ranging path-finder Lt. John C. Fremont, with his scout, Kit Carson, led a government survey party through Central Oregon and southeastward, exploring and naming Summer and Abert lakes. The group then progressed south into California and crossed the Sierra.

Indians attack wagon trains and military troops

That same year of 1843 saw the beginning of huge migrations of settlers coming west on the Oregon Trail. This famous route crossed the Snake River into Oregon near the present sites of Nyssa and Ontario, progressed northwesterly over the Blue Mountains and down the Columbia River to The Dalles.

In 1845, the Blue Bucket Train was the first to attempt a southerly shortcut through the middle of the high desert. It was not the last to suffer hardship on this alternate pathway. Near the Snake River in Idaho during 1851, Indians attacked one small group of emigrants, composed mainly of the family of Thomas Clark. His nineteen-year-old sister was wounded by a gunshot and partly scalped; Clark's mother and younger brother were killed. The survivors endured a miserable trip across the Oregon desert, eventually camping by the Deschutes River at the present site of Bend, where they rested for several days while the injured girl regained her strength.

In 1859, the year Oregon became a state, the military began surveying a route to Salt Lake City, Utah, that passed through Southeastern Oregon. Like the preceding wagon trains, they, too, encountered hostile Native Americans. In 1860, Captain A. Smith and his men were attacked by Indians. Major Enoch Steen, who was also surveying in the area, brought his cavalry troops to the rescue in the proverbial "nick of time." The Major and his soldiers pursued the Paiutes across the slopes of a lofty fault block escarpment in the area and, now, Steens Mountain bears his name.

Commerce: Ranching and gold!

In 1861, the traffic of white travelers through Southeastern Oregon accelerated when gold was discovered in the Blue Mountains to the north. More strikes soon followed at other sites in the same general area and to the east in Idaho. The following year brought an additional gold discovery near the Snake River in the Mormon Basin, north of the present-day site of Ontario, Oregon. Excited gold seekers streamed through the region on military roads and small settlements coalesced in the Mormon Basin. The first permanent residence in the Harney Basin was built by trappers in 1862—a simple sod house, near the current location of the Malheur National Wildlife Refuge headquarters. A way station began business in 1863 at the Ruby Ranch on a road along Jordan Creek. By the following year, a short distance to the east, John Baxter built a hotel-store combination. At first this settlement was called Baxterville, but the name later changed to Jordan Valley.

The Paiutes observed this increasing ac-

Wildhorse Creek Canyon, Steens Mountain

tivity with concern. When most U.S. Army troops left Oregon during the Civil War, Indians used the situation to their advantage by making frequent attacks on unprotected settlers and travelers. After the war, troops returned and established a number of military camps in the region to quell unrest. By 1868, Indian resistance to white settlement ceased and, with more peaceful conditions, new communities began.

Cattle empires emerge

In 1867, another gold strike in the Mormon Basin caused an influx of miners and two villages sprang up: Eldorado and Amelia City, followed by a third, Malheur City. Just across the Idaho line, Silver City was overflowing with nearly five thousand inhabitants. This abundance of hardworking folks with big appetites created a demand for beef. Although a few settlers on this wild, young frontier were raising cattle, their endeavors utilized only a small fraction of the immense rangelands. Wealthy entrepreneurs from California and elsewhere noted the potential of Southeastern Oregon's unclaimed millions of acres of bunchgrass plains and shrewdly acquired vast holdings. Powerful empires of beef production were born.

This period saw the beginning of a century of overzealous rangeland practices. Completely unregulated, season-long livestock grazing that far exceeded the carrying capacity of the land took place year after year. The resulting ecological damage to native grass species, riparian zones, and the interre-lated native wildlife has had long-term consequences that extend to present times.

As cattle ranches appeared in the region, more supply and trade centers were needed. In 1872, a stone house built on the lower Malheur River catered to wagon trains on the Oregon Trail, and fostered the growing community of Vale. At the western edge of the region, the town of Lakeview was born in 1874. Paisley and Summer Lake emerged during this period as well.

The desert cattle barons

In the early 1860s, the vast rangelands of Southeastern Oregon had largely escaped white settlement. Only a few bands of Paiute Indians wandered the sagebrush plains. Then, in 1869, John S. Devine came to the Alvord Basin in the arid reaches east of Steens Mountain. He was the first permanent settler to inhabit this remote section of desert wilderness and would build Oregon's initial cat-

Peter French (far right) and his buckaroos, circa 1890. Courtesy of Harney County Historical Society

tle empire. This marked the beginning of a period of unbridled exuberance in the youthful years of the region's Euro-American settlement. Because the land and its bounty seemed so limitless, a general frontier bravado prevailed that led to a century of reckless overgrazing.

Devine, a thirty-year-old Californian, came equipped to immediately start a working ranch. He had the financial backing of a wealthy Sacramento meat-company owner, W. B. Todhunter, and arrived in Oregon with three thousand head of cattle, a herd of horses, six vaquero cowhands, a cook, and a wagon full of supplies. Devine fancied himself as an aristocrat in the mold of the old Spanish dons and dressed and acted the part.

After claiming the lands of an abandoned military camp, where he established his famed Whitehorse Ranch, Devine greatly expanded his holdings. His stock grazed most of the country below the east face of Steens Mountain. Before long, he had added a second operation, the Alvord Ranch, in the northerly section of his territory. Despite the isolation of his spread, two hundred miles from the nearest settlers, Devine was able, with the use of his wealth, to create an outpost of refinement. He rode a beautiful white stallion fitted with a silver-adorned saddle and impressed guests with his stable of top-rate racehorses and a well-stocked game farm, while lavishing on them sumptuous meals of fine foods and wines.

By 1872, however, Devine was no longer alone in his far-removed, private kingdom. Peter French, a young man of twenty, started the P Ranch about eighty-five miles to the northwest in the Blitzen Valley. Like Devine, French also came to the region completely outfitted for ranching. He was backed by the rich assets of Dr. Hugh Glenn, an influential landowner in the Sacramento Valley and the largest wheat grower in the nation.

Eventually, the P Ranch engulfed most of the grazing lands along the western side of Steens Mountain and generated several satellite ranches, the largest at Roaring Springs in the Catlow Valley. Although Pete French became a wealthy, powerful man and a legend of the Old West, his private life was less than peaceful and pleasant. He married partner Glenn's daughter, but she refused to live on his remote ranch and their marriage ended in divorce. In the tumultuous years that followed, Glenn was murdered by an employee, leaving French with legal problems and debts that resulted in the loss of land and other assets. Adding to these woes, Indians attacked some of the P Ranch cowhands and houses. When more settlers came to the area, French's terse, uncompromising manner caused bitter disputes over boundary claims and water rights. Serious animosities developed with most of the nearby ranchers. Peter French lost his life in 1897 when a neighboring ranchowner shot him during a heated argument. Although there were witnesses at the slaying, French had been so widely disliked that a jury set the murderer free.

Meanwhile, following forfeiture of illegal landholdings and enormous losses of cattle during the severe winters of 1887 to 1890, John Devine filed for bankruptcy. Henry Miller, a shrewd and powerful German cattleman from California, bought out Devine. Nevertheless, Miller retained Devine as manager of the Oregon properties and gave him back the deed to the Alvord Ranch and all its livestock. Miller must have admired the proud pseudo-nobleman, allowing John Devine to retain part of his former honor and desert domain, where he lived the remainder of his life.

An old stone cabin in the Pueblo Mountains is a reminder of an earlier era.

After Peter French's violent death, Henry Miller added some of French's former lands to his ever-growing holdings throughout the West, and founded the famous Pacific Land and Livestock Company. When Miller died in 1916, he owned the world's largest cattle empire. A colorful epoch came to an end.

The Whitehorse, Alvord, and Roaring Springs ranches are still in operation, and Pete French's famous round barn, which he used for breaking horses, can be seen near the Malheur National Wildlife Refuge. ▪

SHEEP ranching also played a large role in the settling of Southeastern Oregon. Besides beefsteak, hungry miners liked a meal of mutton, and there was a demand for wool as well. To supply this market, enterprising sheepherders brought their woolly flocks into the region. These early herders were predominantly of Scot and Irish origins, and later many Basque sheepmen arrived.

The vicinity of the Jordan Valley was particularly noted as sheep country. Outright range wars between cattle ranchers and sheepmen, like those in Central Oregon, occasionally arose. Most of these conflicts, however, involved wandering "tramp sheepmen" (and tramp cattlemen as well) who moved onto ranges used by established ranches. In fact, some large cattle operations also ran their own flocks of sheep.

The Paiute-Bannock uprising

In 1878 one final Indian uprising occurred. The Paiutes in Southeastern Oregon and the Bannocks of southern Idaho had been established on reservations, which the U.S. government believed solved the earlier hostilities. However, during the Civil War years, government funds for these reservations had been largely rerouted to the military effort. The Indians, inexperienced as farmers and denied access to most of their tribal hunting and gathering grounds, were left to starve. When a "clerical error" opened a traditional Bannock camas bulb gathering area in Idaho for white settlement, these Indians reacted with violence at the loss of this important food source.

Under the leadership of Chief Buffalo Horn, the Bannocks influenced the Paiutes of Oregon to join them in a war against the whites throughout the entire region. The combined forces of Buffalo Horn's Bannock warriors and the Paiutes, led by Chief Egan, swept through southern Idaho and the eastern portions of Oregon. Homes and way stations were burned, and many settlers, travelers, miners, sheepherders, and cattle ranchers were killed. The consolidated efforts of the army, a citizen's volunteer militia, and friendly Indians finally ended the uprising. The Paiutes of the Harney Basin were banished to a reservation in Washington, where many died of illnesses, and the government claimed their Oregon reservation lands. When a small remnant group of Paiutes even-

The new community of Burns, 1884. Courtesy of Harney County Historical Society

tually returned, only a fraction of their original reservation lands remained.

By the late 1800s, the region was well known for producing horses, one man's enterprise in particular adding to this reputation. Bill Brown, beginning in 1882, operated a large horse ranch on the rangelands between the present locations of Bend and Burns. Brown, known as the "Horse King," sold millions of dollars worth of livestock over the years, but could not maintain his wealth due to excessive generosity and haphazard, poor business practices. Reportedly, he wrote checks on whatever happened to be handy, whether it was a piece of newspaper or the back of a food can label.

The first railroads and horseless carriages

For many years, cattle and other stock that were to be marketed had to be trailed overland long distances to railheads in northern Nevada or as far as Wyoming and, beyond the Rocky Mountains, to Kansas. By 1884, however, the railroad reached the Snake River area of Oregon and spawned the community of Ontario. With this rail connection, Southeastern Oregon opened itself to the markets of the outside world, and its era as a remote frontier drew to a close.

Things changed quickly in the region. A new community near the military base of Fort Harney, called Burns (after Scottish poet Robert Burns), opened a post office in 1884. In June of 1903, the first "horseless carriage" drove through the town. This was a 20-horsepower Winton, piloted by its owner, Dr. Horatio Jackson, on his historic quest to complete America's first successful transcontinental road trip by automobile. Accompanied by his co-driver–mechanic Sewall Crocker and a bulldog mascot named Bud (who, like the men, wore driving goggles), the trio traveled eastward at the blistering pace of twenty miles per hour. Roadside spectators were so impressed that they christened the contraption "the Go-Like-Hell-Machine."

The Bend to Burns auto-stage, circa 1914. *Courtesy of Deschutes County Historical Society*

By 1913, there was an "auto stage" making jouncing trips with passengers and freight along more than a hundred miles of primitive road between Burns and Bend. Dallas Lore Sharp, visiting from Boston, gives a 1914 account of one of these harrowing, dawn-to-dark journeys:

> The desert was entirely new to me; so was the desert automobile. . . . I thought I knew an automobile, but I found that I had never been on one of the Western desert breed. The best bucker at the Pendleton Roundup is but a rocking-horse in comparison. I doubt if you could experience death in any part of the world more times for twenty dollars than by auto stage from Bend to Burns.

Later, in 1924, transportation to and from the outside world became somewhat easier and more comfortable when a railroad connection came to Burns. This boon, matched with abundant pine resources in the nearby Blue Mountains, spurred creation of a small neighboring mill town four miles to the west —Hines, the Edward Hines Lumber Company's namesake.

Desert farming, for better or worse

Beginning in 1909, the offer of government land to U.S. citizens under the Revised Homestead Act brought a wave of new settlers to the high desert. Small communities sprouted almost overnight, even in the most remote sections of this sprawling land. By 1921, most had become ghost towns when starry-eyed farmers discovered that rainfall was miserably scant and the sandy soils produced more dust than crops. Mining boomtowns had long since passed their zeniths when the mines played out in the late 1800s. Amelia City, Eldorado, Malheur City, and other such villages died or deteriorated toward ghost-town status.

Although still primarily a "cow town," Ontario was beginning to diversify its economy by the turn of the century. Water from the adjacent Snake River, combined with good soils and a sunny climate, was helping produce ever more vegetable and fruit crops. In 1928, the government funded the construction of irrigation canals in the surrounding Treasure Valley on both the Oregon and Idaho sides of the Snake. This attracted an even greater influx of farmers. With the benefits of irrigation, they achieved considerably more success than the previous would-be agriculturalists who came to Oregon's parched high desert country. Dams built on the Owyhee and Malheur rivers, along with other tributaries, impounded reservoirs that fed the ever-spreading canals and transformed the area into a green oasis of croplands.

When a connecting paved highway between Burns and Bend opened in 1929, the modern age truly had arrived in remote Southeastern Oregon. Where weary nineteenth-century wagon trains struggled westward across the baking high desert day after

Highway 20, near Brothers, with the Three Sisters peaks of the Cascades in the distance

day, an air-conditioned automobile can now make the 130-mile trip in less than three hours.

Sagebrush and Elbow Room

Fortunately, the American desert remains open to all, most of it still our public domain. No passports needed, no examinations to undergo, no special equipment required, no experience necessary. A journey into the wilderness is the freest, cheapest, most nonprivileged of pleasures. . . . Open space was the fundamental heritage of America; the freedom of the wilderness may well be the central purpose of our national adventure.

EDWARD ABBEY, *Beyond the Wall*, 1984

Along with the persistent odor of sagebrush lingering on their hiking boots, desert enthusiasts also share the soul-deep love of solitude and nature's wide-open spaces. And the southeastern region of Oregon is tailor-made for them, as its little-known deserts are relatively lightly visited.

This far corner of the state comprises the northernmost reach of the Great Basin and offers a wealth of elbow room. In this regard, Edward Abbey's words here touch on something that this renowned desert rat highlighted frequently in his writings: the importance of public lands—places where it is possible to wander freely and experience primordial pleasures that our crowded cities preclude. This unbounded outback is, according to Abbey, a primary contributor to the shaping of the American character and has made us who we are as a people. "Vast and democratic vistas" was how Abbey put it.

As the pace and clamor of contemporary American life increases, a general sensory overload can result. Consequently, the quiet solitude of wilderness is becoming one of our most

Iron Point, along the Owyhee Canyon, north of Rome

A new morning begins at the Alvord Desert

UNQUESTIONABLY, Southeastern Oregon is totally opposite from the state's popular image of rainy weather and lush forests. It's a dry, scratchy, prickly, rough place. You don't go there to recline in soft meadow grass. Instead, it presents an invitation for a sagebrush stroll and easing into refreshing spaciousness. An awareness of the region's sometimes subtle attributes deserves its own focus.

Gaining greater familiarity with the high desert country will reveal an intriguing dual character. The widespread basalt formations, which are geologically more recent, convey an impression of rimrock-lean, raw-boned youth—this terrain has known rough times and passed through trials of volcanic fire and gut-wrenching, inner turbulence. On the other hand, the exposed underlying strata are unmistakably ancient and present an eroded, cracked dessication that lends a wizened appearance to its countenance. You'll understand its age if you walk the ancient, wave-cut sedimentary terraces rimming the Alvord playa and watch for rocks bearing the leaf imprints of early Miocene maples and walnuts. This sun-baked basin is a monumental trace of the eons—a long-vanished Pleistocene lake whose waves lapped the fossilized desert shorelines you see today. In quiet moments of contemplation, you can sense an inscrutable quality of the land; a timeless backwash where there's almost the whisper of wind across Ice Age waters.

Overhead, a wide sky achieves the deepest shade of clear, dry-air blue. Few clouds obscure the scintillating light, which blinds with its midday ferocity on a white alkali flat. The desert is married to the sun, its shadows mirroring the bright orb's arc across the sky. The slanting rays of morning and evening reveal the contrasting textures of the landscape,

valued natural resources. Deserts especially provide these sorts of opportunities, and the largest portion of Southeastern Oregon's unfettered vistas are public lands, available to be explored and enjoyed. These arid environments are often referred to as wastelands, probably meaning they lack the propensity to produce food crops. But deserts harbor great value for our species as reservoirs for spiritual renewal. It's no accident that many great prophets through the ages have returned from lonely wilderness vigils with messages of inspiration. Nothing is wasted in nature.

Still, not everyone is attracted to these sparse drylands. So the question arises, why visit the desert? Can its parched, starkly open spaces compare with the pleasant qualities of forests, meadows, and ocean beaches? True, the sweeping enormity and lack of trees can be unsettling, sometimes making a visitor feel small and insignificant. However, the trick is to get past the nagging expectation of green piney woods and embrace what the desert actually contains, rather than what it lacks. Because the primary plant growth is low shrubs, the eye quite naturally scans above and beyond to the distant horizon. Unaccustomed to the desert, we may literally overlook what is directly in front of us. A true irony: not being able to see the desert for lack of trees.

while at the solar zenith it appears bleached and homogeneous.

Further explorations soon make it clearly evident that the spectacular fault-tilted geology is a prime contributor to Southeastern Oregon's rugged scenic beauty. The often rapidly shifting weather adds atmospheric drama, with evening's rimrock shadows creeping across sage flats and dissolving into blood-red sunset clouds. Surprises abound: topping a sagebrush ridge discloses a huge, salty lake in the basin beyond; the lingering desire for trees finds relief by a trickling spring in the shade of a grove of quaking aspens; a wet April and May paints the uplands velvety grass-green, intermixed with persistent patches of snow; and blooming amid fleeting sun showers and rainbows, the high desert transforms into a a flower garden for a season. There's much to discover, but where does one begin in a sprawling region that's roughly the size of all the New England states combined?

Steens Mountain

One of the best places to gain a broad perspective on the lay of Oregon's southeastern land is from atop Steens Mountain. Born of tremendous convulsions deep within the earth, this ancient massif shoulders its glaciated bulk 9,733 feet into the desert sky. As the highest point in the entire region, Steens Mountain provides panoramic views of Southeastern Oregon and sections of Idaho and Nevada. The summit is largely open with only scattered groves of quaking aspen. There are almost no conifers; two canyons contain small stands of white fir, and one of these groupings appears to have nearly died away, as of this writing.

Ascending to this high-altitude world does not require days of strenuous backpacking.

High desert skies are deep, dry-air blue.
Eastern flanks of Steens Mountain

Prince's plume in bloom at the Pillars of Rome formations, Owyhee River Canyon

Evening thunderstorm over the summit of Steens Mountain

The historic Frenchglen Hotel, built in 1916

A 66-mile-long gravel and dirt road, known as the Steens Mountain Loop, winds its way upward to the summit, rewarding motorists with one of the most awe-inspiring scenic drives in all the Northwest—and also the experience of driving the highest road in Oregon. The outstanding natural qualities of this range were recognized by Congress in 2000 with the approval of the Steens Mountain Cooperative Management and Protection Area. This 500,000-acre chunk of ecologically diverse high desert landscape is divided into various designations. Included are 100,000 acres of cow-free, roadless wilderness and a redband trout reserve in the Blitzen River watershed.

The usual departure point for a Steens Loop drive is the small community of Frenchglen, located 60 miles south of the city of Burns, along Highway 205 in the Blitzen Valley. Although gas can be purchased at a café-grocery about 28 miles south of Burns (by the Malheur National Wildlife Refuge turnoff), none is currently available in Frenchglen. Always remember the cardinal rule of travel in Southeastern Oregon—top-off your gas tank whenever possible. Towns with service stations are often 50 miles or more apart, and low-gear backcountry driving rapidly burns gas.

Frenchglen (population about 15) makes a good base from which to explore not only Steens Mountain but the entire surrounding area. Named for the famed local cattle baron of the 1800s, Peter French, and his California partner, Hugh Glenn, this hamlet keeps the picturesque frontier era alive. The Frenchglen Hotel, built in 1916 and a state historical wayside, offers eight rental rooms and is open from mid-March to mid-November. Homestyle meals, served at two large communal tables in the lobby, are also available to non–hotel guests. Reservations for hotel rooms and dinners are usually required well in advance (the quality of the food is well known!). Breakfasts and lunches are served on a walk-in, order-from-the-menu basis. Additional rooms with private baths are available at the newer adjunct Drovers Inn. For more rustic accommodations, drive 3 miles southeast of town, where the Steens Mountain Resort offers cabins, tent spaces, and RV hookups, and a bit farther down the road is the Page Springs BLM Campground.

The Steens Loop Road is usually free of snow from mid-July through October, although rapid and unpredictable weather

Sagebrush and paintbrush on the western slope of Steens Mountain

changes at the higher elevations can quickly alter things. Generally, the road is in good condition, but the southern half is somewhat rougher and narrower, unsuitable for trailers and large motor homes. If you're planning on completing the entire loop, a vehicle with adequate clearance and good traction is recommended. Otherwise, ordinary passenger cars can usually negotiate the northern leg and then return the same way.

Launching our high country explorations, the road leads southeast from Frenchglen and soon crosses the cold, snow-fed waters of the Blitzen River by the Page Springs Campground. The upper portions of this free-flowing watercourse are designated as a Wild and Scenic River. As an interesting historical tidbit, the actual full name is the Donner und Blitzen River—German for "thunder and lightning." As the story goes, in 1864 Captain George B Currey, leading a regiment of U.S. cavalry troops in pursuit of warring Indians, forded the river during a thunderstorm. Apparently Currey was so impressed with the intensity of the meteorological booming and electrical flashes that he named the watercourse accordingly.

Immediately after the bridge, the climb up Steens Mountain begins. Not a classic cone-shaped peak, it is instead an enormous, fifty-mile-long rugged ridge. This fault block range formed some 10 million years ago during the late Miocene when a gigantic fracture developed, uplifting it with a westward tilt. Thus, while the western side of the mountain gradually inclines upward, the eastern face drops away in a dizzying precipice to the Alvord Basin, which is more than a near-vertical mile below.

The Loop Road first traverses numerous sagebrush openings and a belt of fragrant juniper woodlands. For miles, magnificent views are afforded across the steppelands to the west. After climbing still higher, the route passes through patches of mountain mahogany and more sagebrush openings, which in July are profusely decorated with the red and yellow of paintbrush growing among the shrubs.

At about 7,000-feet elevation, we enter a subalpine zone where the mountain manages to pluck about twenty-five inches of annual precipitation from the atmosphere—rather moist, compared with the six to ten inches of the surrounding lowlands. This change is reflected in the occurrence of grove after grove of quaking aspen, along with meadows and small lakes. Two BLM campgrounds—Fish Lake and Jackman Park—are along this pleasant stretch, both nestled among these white-barked trees. The camps have drinking water, picnic tables, and toilets, with the additional appeal of Fish Lake being well stocked with trout. Birders should be alert for hummingbirds of several species around these aspen-bordered lakes, including the occasional broad-tailed hummer, this being one of the few spots where it is seen in Oregon.

In autumn, these groves transform themselves into a brilliant gold and reddish-orange blanket spread across the Steens's lofty slopes. For many high desert enthusiasts, it's an an-

Fish Lake sunset

September aspens on Steens Mountain

The first streaks of autumn. Quaking aspen groves near Jackman Park

nual tradition to make a pilgrimage to Steens Mountain and revel in this colorful extravaganza. There are few experiences so sublime as reclining on your back among the white-barked trunks and peering up through the whispering yellow foliage set against an intensely blue, high-altitude sky. As the wind-blown golden leaves float down toward your face, the hurry-scurry twenty-first-century world seems far away. Photographers delight in these groves, with tripod-mounted cameras much in evidence at scenic turnouts. Visits in mid-September usually coincide with the initial transformations to fall color, creating photogenic patterns of yellow and orange intermixed with aspens that are still green.

Shortly, the road breaks out above tree line and ascends along the enormous crest of Steens Mountain. This alpine bunchgrass tundra supports several endemic plant species, such as the large, showy Steens Mountain thistle and the more subdued Steens Mountain paintbrush, among other kinds (see "High elevation endemics of the desert ranges" in Part I). When walking through these areas, try to stay on established paths to avoid needlessly trampling these plants in their fragile, high-elevation ecosystem. Keep your eyes peeled and your binoculars ready for wildlife. Orangish brown Belding's ground squirrels seem to be everywhere, scurrying across the road or alertly watching from the tops of rocks. Small herds of pronghorn spend the summer grazing the mountain's summit, often allowing close approach of visitors in cars. Red-tailed hawks, prairie falcons, golden eagles, and other birds of prey can frequently be observed soaring on thermal updrafts, sometimes flying below you where the road negotiates high overlooks.

Continuing southeasterly, at about 6 miles from Fish Lake a side road turns off to the left. Whatever you do, don't miss this diversion from the main loop route. After you turn left it's a half mile to the Kiger Gorge Viewpoint, at 8,800 feet elevation. At this north-facing vista the land literally drops away at your feet into one of the world's colossal, textbook-perfect U-shaped glacial valleys. In fact, it's not uncommon to encounter a college geology class at this site, contemplating the abyss, and a teacher, arms waving in expansive gestures, describing the river of Pleistocene ice that sculpted this wonder of nature. Although the word *awesome* is frequently overused in our culture, this is a place that warrants the description. Scan your eyes to the right, along the eastern rim of the gorge, and you'll see a huge notch there. This geological oddity was created when a smaller Ice Age glacier eroded through the dividing ridgetop from neighboring Mann Creek Canyon.

Back on the Loop Road again, the drive takes you past two more deep, glaciated canyons, not quite as stupendous as Kiger Gorge but nonetheless quite breathtaking. Both open out to the west—Little Blitzen Gorge and Big Indian Gorge. Here the road negotiates the narrow "hogback" summit between the heads of these chasms and the eastern side of the mountain. In places, it's possible to simultaneously have views both east and west off the mountaintop. Patches of snow begin to appear, which is a good place to watch for an uncommon bird, the black rosy-finch. These little summer residents of the alpine zones breed on Steens Mountain and can often be seen foraging for insects and seeds along the borders of snowmelt or flying in flocks along the highest barren sections of the summit.

Where the main Loop Road takes a bend to the west and begins to meander down the open mountainside, there's a three-way junction that offers two short scenic side spurs.

Contemplating the deep morning shadows of Kiger Gorge

The left turn leads .3 mile up to the East Rim Overlook, with more vertigo-inducing grandeur. Far below the sheer escarpment, Mann Lake is visible with the Sheepshead Mountains on the northeastern horizon. Some people find this panorama so captivating to investigate through binoculars or a spotting scope that they set up a comfortable folding chair and are content to gaze for hours. If you're more inclined to stretch your legs with a stimulating hike, follow the middle spur road south. It will take you 2 miles, ending at the Wildhorse Lake Viewpoint and Trailhead, directly below the highest point of Steens Mountain. Leading from the south edge of the parking area, a gated, very steep, rough road ascends to a radio repeater station. Following this track, it's a distance of only .4 mile to the topmost Steens summit. If you begin to huff and puff, realize that you're climbing to nearly 10,000 feet elevation, where oxygen gets a bit scarce.

The Steens Mountain East Rim Overlook

Wildhorse Lake

The eastern view from the Steens summit, with the Alvord Desert far below

Steens summit panorama

From this lofty vantage point, the seemingly endless views in all directions encompass a magnificent high-altitude realm of bighorn sheep, and these surefooted reintroduced animals sometimes appear along the rocky chasms that drop away below the summit. Down the southern side of the mountain, a large glacially excavated hanging valley (the geological term is cirque) cradles Wildhorse Lake. Still farther to the south, the broken ridges and humps of the Pueblo Mountains give way to northwestern Nevada's remote Pine Forest Range and the vast Black Rock Desert.

Westward, as far as the eye can see, are alternating basins and tablelike ranges—Oregon's allotment of the immense Great Basin, which has no drainage to the sea. The few watercourses that flow from the region's higher elevations are more often than not inexorably pulled by gravity to extinction in dry alkali playas. The massive humps and depressions of this geologically faulted basin and range country seem to march on endlessly. Place-names such as Catlow Valley, Lone Mountain, Antelope Butte, Sagehen Butte, Blizzard Gap, Dry Valley, Lonegrave Butte, Coyote Gap, Rattlesnake Butte, and Wildcat Mountain paint word-pictures of a classically wild outback of the American West. The land's enormity dwarfs the scant human population and the handful of settlements: Wagontire, Alkali Lake Station, Plush, and Adel.

The view to the north of Steens Mountain takes in the Blitzen Valley and Frenchglen, where we began our explorations. In that green, oasislike basin, the Blitzen River can be seen flowing into the lushly vegetated marshes of the Malheur National Wildlife Refuge. More northerly is the Harney Basin, which holds Malheur and Harney lakes along with the town of Burns.

To the east, directly below, you can survey the entirety of the Alvord Basin, north to south. This huge trough once held an Ice Age lake, but a 10,000-year-long climatic shift toward greater aridity has dramatically changed the scenery. Through binoculars and heat waves, you can see brushy sand dunes along the edges of white alkali flats in the barren Alvord Desert. Still farther east are more dunes and alkali in the Coyote Lake Basin; and beyond that, drylands stretch to the wild Owyhee Canyonlands and eventually Idaho. From the mountain's perspective, the Alvord Desert resembles a gigantic paved parking lot shimmering in the sun. Situated in the Steens rainshadow, this bone-dry Alvord country is the truest desert area within Oregon.

AT THIS point in the drive, it's time to decide if your vehicle is suited to completing the remaining rougher section of the Loop Road, which connects with Highway 205 about 10 miles south of Frenchglen. If retreat seems more sensible, retrace your earlier route back to Frenchglen. An advantage of continuing onward along the loop is that it passes South Steens Campground (drinking water and vault toilets). Not only does this offer

◆ TRAILPOST
Wildhorse Lake

If an invigorating hike in the Steens Mountain alpine zone is tantalizing, there's a scenically dramatic trail that leads from the southwestern corner of the Wildhorse Lake Viewpoint parking area. Although relatively short (about 2.8 miles roundtrip) this is a fairly strenuous, difficult hike. For a preview of what's involved, amble down a moderate grade for a mere .2 mile along the trail's beginning to a saddle ridge that borders Big Indian Gorge on the north. This provides an overlook of the path's goal and a chance to decide if you want to continue, or return to your car. Facing south, you'll be looking down into a glacially carved cirque containing Wildhorse Lake, a thousand feet below.

Listed among the highest elevation lakes in Oregon, and also one of the most beautiful, it's well worth the effort. Be forewarned, however, that the rocky trail is unimproved, very steep, and in places more like a rough goat path—a walking staff or trekking poles for added stability are almost requisite. The most challenging section begins shortly after the trail descends the steep incline, but at about the halfway mark the pitch lessens. Upon reaching the lake, your reward is lolling in green grass and wildflowers, perhaps refreshing your bare feet in the icy water and soaking up the gloriously wild solitude. When ready to leave, just remember that the lake's elevation is 8,400 feet and you'll be

climbing back up to the parking area at 9,500 feet. Unless you're acclimated to hiking high elevations, expect needed stops for breath-catching.

Wildhorse Lake, at the outlet of Wildhorse Creek

a good place to pitch a tent, it's also the trailhead for Big Indian Gorge, a 17-mile, round-trip hike. Hailed as a topnotch backpacking or llama trek, the trail traverses the bottom of the spectacular glacial canyon, through aspen groves and past waterfalls, finally returning via the same path to the parking area.

The Alvord Basin

To reach the next destination, follow Highway 205 south of Frenchglen along the western foothills of Steens Mountain. The route passes the historic Roaring Springs Ranch; at the southern end of the Catlow Valley it veers east over Long Hollow Summit, a pass between Steens Mountain and the Pueblo Mountains. When you break over the top, there will be an outstanding view of the Alvord Basin. If you have a hankering to experience a true Great Basin desert environment at its arid best, this is the place to go in Oregon. The Alvord Basin lies within double rainshadows; located not only east of the Cascade Range, it's also situated on the dry side of the nearly 10,000-foot, moisture-trapping barrier of Steens Mountain. The average annual rainfall can drop below six inches, so if you're unaccustomed to this type of climate, bring along plenty of sunscreen lotion and lip moisturizer, plus a good hat. Also, in summer, carry extra water and drink often.

The paved highway descends into the basin and swings south through the tiny outpost of Fields, and then onward for another 23 miles, where it crosses into Nevada at the small community of Denio. A wide, well-maintained gravel road runs north through the basin, but otherwise only a few secondary dirt-gravel roads, sand tracks, and rough jeep trails extend into the more remote sections. Note that any of the side roads may provide good driving in dry weather but will become completely impassable during spring rainstorms or after a severe summer thundershower. However, a majority of the primary points of interest can be reached on the better roads by the average auto.

The area's two major scenic wonders are the huge alkali flats of the Alvord Desert and the looming presence of Steens Mountain towering a vertical mile directly above. First things first, though. Obeying the high desert explorer's rule of always filling your gas tank whenever possible, start with a stop at the venerable Fields Station, established in 1881. This business is the little hamlet's version of a shopping mall—grocery store, café, ice, gas pumps, tire repair shop, motel, and small campground.

While your auto is being refueled, don't miss the chance to eat in the café. Owner Sandy Downs can make you one of her famously delicious thick milkshakes (many experienced desert rats especially recommend the chocolate malt) or an old-fashioned Americana cheeseburger. While eating your meal, you will readily notice that this is the social hub of the surrounding area. Ranching families stop in for lunch, exchanging local news and engaging in friendly banter. Next, a van disgorges Oregon State University biology students, hungry and thirsty after their field trip in the desert. Two alkali-dusted government geologists make the doorbell jingle as they walk in and sit at the counter, enthusiastically ordering a milkshake each. By now, the small café is totally packed with good cheer. A young couple from Portland, out doing some Great Basin birding, sit down at one of the outside tables. After asking for grilled-cheese sandwiches, they use binoculars to scan the large willow grove surrounding a spring across the road—well known among the Oregon birdwatching community as the Fields Oasis. A pair of great horned owls regularly nest in these trees, and unusual vagrant birds are often sighted, such as rose-breasted grosbeaks, blue jays, common grackles, yellow-billed cuckoos, and eastern warblers of several species.

Now pleasantly fortified for exploring, how about observing desert fish? Although that may seem incongruous, it's possible at The Nature Conservancy's Borax Lake Preserve. It's a bit out of the way and unmarked, but well worth the visit. Drive about 1.5 miles north of Fields, and where the paved highway curves west, keep going straight north on the broad gravel road that traverses the length of the basin—sort of a localized "Alvord Freeway." Just beyond that junction, turn right (east) on the dirt power-line road, and at 2 miles take a left (north) on a sandy road. Within another 2 miles, you'll reach a gate at the edge of the preserve. After parking, a short hike of slightly under a mile will bring you to Borax Lake.

Just before reaching the main Borax Lake, you'll pass Lower Borax Lake with evidence of some interesting human history. Both of these small lakes are fed by hot springs that contain large amounts of sodium borate, a substance used in soaps and other cleaning agents. The crusty, white crystals that form here once supplied the borax industry during the late 1800s. Chinese laborers, working for the Rose Valley Borax Company, collected and processed the deposits into purified borax crystals. The sacked product was then transported 130 miles by 16-mule-team wagon to the railhead at Winnemucca, Nevada. Some of their relic equipment, long rusting vats used to boil down the borate, is still to be seen just off the trail. It can only be imagined how miserable this work must have been in the heat of the desert summer, gathering greasewood and sagebrush to feed fires under the

Borax Lake

The high desert explorer's rule: always top-off your gas tank whenever the opportunity presents itself.

Chinese laborers in the Alvord Basin look on as a load of borax departs by 16-mule-team for a 130-mile trip to the railhead at Winnemucca, Nevada. Courtesy of Harney County Historical Society

vats. One of the small sod houses where Chinese workers lived still exists nearby.

Just beyond these vats, you'll reach Borax Lake. However, refrain from walking right up to the shoreline. Instead, get down on your hands and knees and carefully peer over the edge into the water. In that way you won't scare away the small fish that swim the lake shallows. Although rather unimpressive, this is the federally protected two-inch golden-tan Borax Lake chub. Found nowhere else in the world, this endemic species has evolved the ability to live in the slightly alkaline, hot-spring-heated 93-degree water. Their environment constitutes the largest thermal lake in Oregon. During the frozen winter, these two warm lakes are the only open water in the basin. Consequently, water birds are attracted, making this is a good spot for birding at that time of year. On the surrounding salt-encrusted flats, look for the low-growing iodine bush, which reaches the northern limits of its range in the Alvord Basin. Like the Borax Lake chub, this unusual plant is adapted to survive in alkaline habitats. Its fleshy, water-conserving segments resemble

strings of miniature green pickles, earning it another common name: pickleweed. By September, the plant's color shifts to red, adding a bit of autumn color to the desert flats.

RETURNING to the main gravel road and continuing north through the Alvord Basin will take you through the little community of Andrews, located 13 miles north of Fields. Originally known as Wildhorse, this was a lively place from 1898 to 1924 when the population swelled to 135. The store, hotel, saloon, and stone dance hall drew buckaroos and Basque sheepherders from miles around, but now it is nearly a ghost town. The abandoned dance hall still survives, along with two homes; and the stone one-room schoolhouse is no longer in operation. If you're driving through the Andrews area during June to August, watch along the roadsides for the lovely white blooms of the thistlelike prickly poppy, growing here at the northernmost limit of its range.

After Andrews, the road jogs northeast for about 4.5 miles and then tops a ridge. Suddenly the entirety of the Alvord Desert will come into view. The first time you experience this huge expanse of totally barren Pleistocene lake bed, it's somewhat startling. While lingering to feast your eyes on this arid scene, also be alert for black-throated sparrows in sections of taller "old-growth" sagebrush off the road. This is a well-known spot among birders to see this typically Great Basin species. The white-tailed antelope squirrel is also frequently seen on this ridgetop as it zips across the road. This desert-dwelling mammal resembles a large, pale chipmunk. While moving about through the shrubs and rocks, this species characteristically holds its tail arched over its back like a sunshade.

Approximately 1.5 miles down the hill,

watch for a short dirt road on the right that accesses the desert's edge. It's a bit rough, so negotiate the uneven sections very carefully if you're driving a passenger car with low clearance. Like most playas, the Alvord Desert is usually covered with shallow water during the winter and spring seasons, but by late June most of it is dry and can be safely driven on. This is an experience not to be missed, providing awesome views back across the cracked alkali-mud surface to the precipitous Steens escarpment on the western skyline.

There are some precautions, however. The federally protected snowy plover, a small, grayish tan shorebird, nests on these alkali flats. The eggs (laid on bare ground) are difficult to see because they blend with the environment. Therefore, try to avoid driving in areas frequented by the plovers. The northwestern side of the Alvord playa tends to be more wet because of bordering hot springs, and these birds bring their chicks there to forage for insects. Common sense dictates that venturing into these muddy places will result in a mired auto, and it needlessly endangers the plovers.

There are also other recreationists to consider. Ultralight planes are often taking off or landing on the generously wide "airstrip"; and the Alvord Desert has become increasingly popular with land sailors—wind jockeys on wheeled sailboards. Unless it's a dead-calm day, their bright-colored sails will be seen shooting across the alkali as they catch a strong gust. And for several years, a group of kindred-spirit hot-air balloonists have come every June to launch off the playa and silently float past the face of Steens Mountain.

However, if you're a seeker of solitude, drive across the playa to the less-visited eastern sections of the desert (again, mindful of the snowy plovers). Stepping out into the silent nothingness—not one blade of grass

Silent soaring over the Alvord Desert

Dawn's first rays on the cracked surface of the Alvord Desert playa

There's a great hike available on the far eastern side of the Alvord Desert that is about a 3-mile round trip. It will take you to one of the most starkly picturesque, arid environments in Oregon. September and October are good times to go because the playa is dry, and the daytime temperatures are moderate. Binoculars and a daypack containing snacks and a couple of full water bottles are required. You're going to explore desert-style, where the lack of trees allows trailless hiking by sighting-in on a goal and beelining your way to it. Scan the eastern horizon beyond the dry lake bed for a natural feature called Big Sand Gap. You can't miss it. Just as the name describes, it's a large gap in the rimrocks where sand dunes have drifted in. Use binoculars to pick out details and familiarize yourself with the site. Then drive straight toward it until you reach low, brushy dunes at the eastern edge of the playa. Park your car and simply hike for about a mile across the strip of dunes to Big Sand Gap. Watch for several interesting species of Great Basin reptiles that inhabit this sandy, saltscrub habitat: long-nosed leopard lizards, desert horned lizards, and western whiptails. Once you're there, continuing on to the upper end of the gap provides panoramic views across the Alvord Desert to Steens Mountain, with the Sheepshead Mountains to the north and the Pueblo Mountains in the south. Be alert for rattlesnakes while traversing the rocky slopes, although these unique reptiles are not as dangerous as is popularly believed (see "Rattlesnake! Is it dangerous?" in Part I) The lithe, nonvenomous striped whipsnake also inhabits these rocky slopes, along with side-blotched lizards, Great Basin collared lizards, rock wrens, reintroduced bighorn sheep, and possibly the rarely seen kit fox. When you've enjoyed enough rejuvenating elbow room, merely retrace your footprints in the sand back to the waiting car.

Dune and greasewood at Big Sand Gap

anywhere—is consciousness altering. Claustrophobia is definitely an alien concept here.

BACK on the main gravel road on the west side of the playa, you'll now travel to the north end of the Alvord Basin, and then angle northeast into the Mickey Basin (more or less a smaller sub-basin extension of the Alvord). At about 3 miles north of the Alvord Ranch, start watching for a gravel road that turns due east. Take that road, and after approximately 2.5 miles stay left (northeast) at a fork. Progressing nearly 4 miles more brings you to the parking area for Mickey Hot Spring, with its thirty-foot-deep blue, green, yellow, and orange algae-colored "glory hole." Surrounding this gaudy centerpiece are an array of smaller steaming, bubbling, spurting vents and gurgling mud pots. These springs are dangerously hot (over 200 degrees F), so small children should be under constant adult supervision and all dogs restrained by leashes. The area is captivatingly surreal, being something of a miniature Yellowstone. The sandy, shrubby habitat around Mickey Hot Spring is also well known for its abundant lizard populations, with the same mix of species encountered at Big Sand Gap.

Returning south through the Alvord Basin, you will pass conspicuous stream drainages lined with cottonwoods and willows that spill out of canyons on the eastern face of Steens Mountain. One of these, Pike Creek (3.7 miles south of the Alvord Ranch), has a nice trail that ascends about 2 miles up the canyon into the Steens Mountain Wilderness. The path leads to a high, rocky point that gives spectacular views back to the Alvord Desert below and the snowy alpine heights of the Steens summit above. During May and June, many sections of the trail are lined with the purple-blue blooms of lupine and the sunny yellow of arrowleaf balsamroot. Additionally, some of the same unusual vagrant bird species seen at the Fields Oasis also turn up in the riparian growth along Pike Creek. There are several primitive camping spots along the lower creek near the trailhead that offer some shade under the cottonwoods.

After your hike, finish off the day with a relaxing soak in the Alvord Hot Spring, 2 miles south of the Pike Creek turnoff. Located below the east side of the road near the edge of the playa, it boasts both an outdoor pool and a second enclosed pool in a rustic, tin bathhouse. There's even a small annex that offers privacy for changing clothing. Cares will melt away as you bathe in funky splendor, while enjoying grand views of towering Steens Mountain and the vast Alvord Desert. Although

When chukars are heard clucking high on the Steens slope above, both dogs and hunters go on the alert.

Alvord Hot Spring

Dawn over the Alvord playa and hot spring

Autumn in Cottonwood Creek Canyon, Pueblo Mountains

Green ephedra ("Mormon tea"). Eastern foothills of the Pueblo Mountains

Hairy yellow paintbrush and purple sage along the Domingo Pass Road

Alvord Hot Spring, the desert rat's rustic day spa

Cowgirls are working ranch hands, too. DaeNell Douglas, out rounding up stray cattle south of Fields

the spring is open to the public, it's on private land, so do not abuse the privilege. Those preferring a morning bath often soak while the sun rises over the playa, and then drive to the Fields Café for a hearty breakfast.

If you're exploring the Alvord area during May and early June, be sure to take a drive that showcases the native wildflowers. About 3.5 miles south of Fields is a right-hand turn (west) that leads to the top of Domingo Pass in the Pueblo Mountains. During the height of spring, Indian paintbrush, purple sage, lupines, orange globemallow, buckwheats, penstemons and many other species will be in bloom along this entire stretch of road. The panoramic view from the top of the pass is icing on the cake.

The Pueblo Mountains contain some unique natural history, including 200-million-year-old greenstone, some of the oldest rock in the state. Geologists say that this represents exotic terrane—sections of Jurassic islands that were offshore in the Pacific Ocean when Southeastern Oregon was a coastline. The Pueblo Mountains are also botanically interesting in that both green and Nevada ephedra occur here at the northern extreme of their ranges.

The Owyhee Canyonlands

To the east, beyond the wild Trout Creek Mountains, human settlements become even more scarce. In an arid, open basin, the small community of McDermitt straddles the Oregon-Nevada border along Highway 95. Originally called Dugout, it was established by the military during the 1860s Indian hostilities as protection for the stagecoach route from Virginia City, Nevada, to Boise, Idaho. For many years, until it closed in 1984, the Whitehorse Inn served thirsty buckaroos, tired and dry from their work on the range. This colorful

establishment—hotel, saloon, and brothel—was famous for being half in Nevada and half in Oregon, with a line painted across the middle of the floor to separate the two states. Customers wishing to play the slot machines and gamble merely had to step over the demarcation into the Nevada side of the building. East of McDermitt in Oregon, there are no more settlements, just far-flung expanses of high desert.

This little-traveled far corner of the state is often called the ION country, because Idaho, Oregon, and Nevada all meet there. For hardcore desert travelers seeking immersion in the true outback, the country east of Steens Mountain and the Alvord Basin fits the bill. Here we enter the remote Owyhee River drainage. As it winds through rocky corridors and thousand-foot sheer-walled gorges, age-old Indian petroglyphs silently witness its northward journey to rendezvous with the Snake River.

These exquisitely lonely canyonlands comprise some of America's wildest remaining backcountry south of the Canadian border. It's certainly much less visited than many heavily used, officially designated wilderness areas. The feeling of isolation from the outside world is quite pronounced. Frequented mainly by seasonal river runners, an occasional rockhound, or a rancher tending his cattle, the Owyhee possesses a mysterious, haunting beauty all its own, with extensive sections designated as Wild and Scenic. In many respects, where the river has eroded sculpted badlands of multicolored spires, arches, and balanced rocks, the landscape is reminiscent of the sandstone canyon country of Utah. The dramatic reddish and yellowish cliffs are composed of volcanic tuff, many resembling the ruins of castles or coliseums. There is a beguiling beauty to these chasms that entices

The Pillars of Rome formations

one farther and farther into their depths to see what may be hidden around the next bend of the river.

Near the small riverside community of Rome along Highway 95, some especially picturesque formations can easily be accessed by the average passenger car—a rare situation along the Owyhee. The Pillars of Rome resemble ancient Roman architecture and give the settlement its name. Composed of pale tuffaceous deposits with a thin layer of basalt at the top, these eroded battlements tower several hundred feet high. The cliffs are located about 3.5 miles northwest of "downtown" Rome, via a good gravel road. While at this tiny outpost of around fifteen people, remember to top off your gas tank. There's also a friendly café that serves good food—breakfast, lunch, and dinner.

Except where Highway 95 crosses the river at Rome, just a few, mostly unmarked dirt roads and jeep trails penetrate the upper Owyhee drainage. Only those outfitted with good maps, extra gas and water, and a four-wheel-drive vehicle should venture into much of this rugged backcountry. A passing thunderstorm can quickly turn these dirt tracks to sticky gumbo mud, and resulting flash floods can obliterate a road where it crosses a formerly dry wash. A hopelessly mired auto could mean a 30- to 50-mile walkout from some locations—a dangerous proposition in hot weather, as these meandering jeep trails rarely follow the often sheer-walled river. Therefore, self-reliance is the key to safe exploration and camping there.

Access by boat is possible along Lake Owyhee, where the lower river has been impounded behind the Owyhee Dam; and river-running with rafts and kayaks is common along the free-flowing upper sections during springtime high-water. Guided wilderness float trips are available, which put in at Rome or farther upstream in Idaho and end at the reservoir. A shady, grassy state park is located near the dam and offers an oasis for camping, including hot shower facilities. It can be reached by a paved road from the Vale-

Nyssa area. Fishing enthusiasts tout the little-known Owyhee for its generous catches of bass, crappie, catfish, and trout.

However, it's the wilder, inaccessible portions of the canyon that offer the truest flavor of the Owyhee Canyonlands. To get a taste of this, first drive 33 miles east of Rome to Jordan Valley at the Idaho state line, where there are stores, cafés, motels, and gas. This town of about three hundred folks is known for its generations of Basque sheepherders. In fact, there's an excellent and authentic Basque Restaurant at the eastern end of the little city, near the rodeo grounds. Every spring, during late May, Jordan Valley fills with as many as ten thousand people when the Big Loop Rodeo takes place. Parked all around the arena are double-cab pickups ("rigs") with attached horse trailers. From many miles around, buckaroos and ranch families converge in the usually quiet community and there's a festive feeling in the air.

After stocking up on supplies and refueling, retrace Highway 95 west for 16 miles and turn left (south) on the gravel Three Forks Road. However, if it's raining do not attempt this drive, as the roads become very slippery. If the weather is dry, follow this route (which progressively becomes more dirt than gravel) for about 28 miles to a junction and turn right (southwest). Within 3 miles you'll arrive at the rim of the Owyhee Canyon, where the road plunges over the edge and switchbacks down to the river. At this point, the Three Forks Road becomes more rough and narrow. If you're not driving a vehicle with high ground clearance, it's best to not proceed farther and turn back, or else park and hike the remaining 1.5 miles to the bottom. Actually, the drive in and out from Highway 95 alone is very scenic, with a viewpoint that affords a spectacular overlook of the Owyhee Canyon.

Jordan Valley's annual Big Loop Rodeo gathers together the ranch community from many miles around for a festive celebration.

During the spring season the route passes through the green bunchgrass prairies of the Owyhee uplands, with wildflowers sprinkled throughout. Burrowing owls, golden eagles, coyotes, and pronghorn are commonly seen in these open grasslands. Nevertheless, continuing down to Three Forks will take you to one of the most remote places in Oregon that's accessible by road. The sense of isolation is quite profound. Other than on a holiday weekend, such as Memorial Day or Independence Day, few people are to be seen there.

As the place name indicates, this broadened, bowl-like section of the canyon is at the confluence of three watercourses—the main, middle, and north forks of the Owyhee. A pleasant grassy area near a corral and boat ramp offers good camping spots, with views up the yawning gorge of the main Owyhee River. Hiking beyond this point is difficult; there is nothing that could be called a well-maintained trail. A rough jeep road crosses a small bridge over the north fork and then shortly fords the middle fork. It then climbs to a high ridgetop that gives access to hikes along the eastern rim of the main river canyon. Meandering southeast toward nearby

A remote section of the Owyhee River Canyon, upstream from Three Forks

Idaho gives views of the most remote upper slot canyon sections, accessible only by river rafts and kayaks. There's also a trail that penetrates directly into the main river gorge from the camping area at Three Forks. Following an old wagon road along the eastern side of the river, it traces the base of the soaring thousand-foot cliffs. This is a summer hike when the river is low, as there's a bit of wading at times when the trail fades out along the riverbank. Two miles upstream, beyond the chasm, is a nice hot spring that makes the canyon scramble well worth the effort. The tantalizing details await your discovery.

BEFORE leaving the Jordan Valley area, there are two more places you should visit.

The first point of interest is a little-known National Historic Site, located 18 miles west of Jordan Valley near the tiny community of Danner. This is the grave of Jean Baptiste Charbonneau, the son of famed Sacajawea. He was born while his mother was a member of the Lewis and Clark expedition, and was a baby in her arms when she first saw the Pacific Ocean in 1805. Charbonneau became severely ill with pneumonia during a journey from California to Montana in 1866, and died

while staying at the old Inskip way station. Now only crumbling stone walls remain, but some of the rifle ports (slots) used for shooting in defense against Indians are still visible.

Secondly comes some local geology. Like most of Oregon's dry side, the Owyhee country exhibits many volcanic features, such as hot springs and extensive lava beds. The Jordan Craters contains some of North America's most recent lava flows—eruptions estimated to date from 4,000 years ago, though some geologists speculate that one section of lava may be much younger than that, perhaps dating back only one hundred years. To reach the area, drive north from town on Highway 95 for 8 miles, and watch for the Jordan Craters Road turning left (west). Continue west on this gravel road for approximately 25 miles until you arrive at Coffee Pot Crater. Interpretive information is available at the parking area for the mile-long path that loops around the entire crater. You'll enjoy the views down into this fascinating vent, along with vistas across miles of surrounding black lava beds. About 8 miles cross-country to the southeast are Upper and Lower Cow lakes, formed by a natural lava dam. A BLM campground has picnic tables and a vault restroom; it is best reached by driving west of Jordan Valley about 5 miles on Highway 95, and then turning northeast (right) on Lower Cow Creek Road.

Next, head northward and visit another one of those rarities—a good road that accesses the interior reaches of the Owyhee Canyonlands. Taking Highway 95 north for 18 miles brings you to a left turn (northwest) onto the gravel Succor Creek Road. This more or less traces the original route of the old pioneer stage road through the upper Succor Creek drainage, passing through the diminutive community of Rockville, and beyond to a left turn (west) on the Leslie Gulch

Road. Like the earlier Three Forks Road, this fairly steep grade can become quite slippery when wet. During dry weather, though, the 14.5 miles down to a boat ramp at the Owyhee River provides great driving. Be forewarned that you'll want to keep your camera ready on the trip through Leslie Gulch. On all sides there are huge golden and reddish formations of eroded tuff and rhyolite. Astoundingly diverse in their shapes, there are tall domes, razor-thin crags, gargoyle-like shapes, columns, castles, and pinnacles. These bizarre badlands are composed of 15-million-year-old ash flows from an eruption on Mahogany Mountain, just to the south.

While taking in the scenery, also keep your binoculars handy to observe bighorn sheep. These agile animals were successfully reintroduced into Leslie Gulch a number of years ago and can often be seen feeding high on the canyon sides. At about 10 miles down the canyon is a pullout for the popular trail up Juniper Creek. Wander as far as your sense of wonder will carry you, up the sandy bottom of this crinkled and pitted side canyon. In places, the cliffs appear to be composed of Swiss cheese—weathered tuffaceous rocks, often referred to as honeycombs. Leslie Gulch is named after cattle rancher Hiram E. Leslie who, during the spring of 1882, was struck by lightning and died while in the canyon.

Resuming explorations northward along Succor Creek, the route follows the stream through the colorful, narrow aperture of Succor Creek Canyon. The towering stone walls often overhang the road and are similar in appearance to Leslie Gulch, with warm tones of golden-pink, pumpkin-orange, and even purplish-gray. The unusual name for this watercourse has had two different spellings over the years, depending upon the supposed source of the name. One version main-

The Owyhee uplands, north of Jordan Valley

A November skiff of snow in the upper Succor Creek drainage

Late evening in Leslie Gulch

Leslie Gulch with a frosting of snow

tains that pioneers found aid there—"succor"—from either thirst or attacking Indians. Another tells of early miners who were played for "suckers" in some sort of swindle. Still another says that the name is merely derived from the fish of that species that swims the stream. An 1895 stage-stop post office in the canyon spelled it "Sucker," perhaps indicating the correct version. A state campground, nestled within the canyon along the creek, provides shade, vault toilets, and tables, but no drinking water. Rockhounds frequent this camp and use it as a base to look for the area's famed thundereggs, along with jasper, sunstone, agate, and petrified wood.

The Treasure Valley

A few miles more and we leave the canyonlands, break out into rolling sagebrush slopes, and then continue down into the green, irrigated fields of the western Treasure Valley along the Snake River. This watered oasis, where the Owyhee and Malheur rivers flow into the Snake, forms the agricultural hub of Southeastern Oregon. The local centers of commerce include Ontario, Nyssa, Adrian, and Vale. Crops of russet potatoes, onions, sugar beets, corn, peppermint, fruits, and other produce thrive here. South of Ontario along Highway 201, colorful summer crops of zinnias can be seen in roadside fields, where much of the world's supply of zinnia seed is produced.

The area's population consists of several different ethnic groups that include Native American, Basque, Japanese, and Hispanic. Historically, the area attracted Euro-American immigrants by virtue of its location along the Oregon Trail. Wagon wheel ruts from this famous route can still be seen south of Vale at a designated interpretive site. Basque sheep ranchers and Dutch immigrants came to the region around the turn of the last century, and during World War II, the government established a Japanese internment camp in Cow Hollow. The Japanese were allowed to work in the fields of local farms and, after the

Onion fields in Oregon's Treasure Valley

Onion harvest near Vale

war, many stayed in the area and purchased land. Now Japanese families operate some of the largest, most successful farms in the area. In more recent years, many farmworkers of Mexican origin have settled in the valley and integrated into the local communities, as reflected in authentic Mexican restaurants and grocery stores. This cultural diversity is celebrated annually with the Japanese Obon Festival and Mexican Cinco de Mayo festival.

Ontario is Southeastern Oregon's largest city, with steady growth bringing its population to nearly 15,000 people. In the downtown area, the Four Rivers Cultural Center has museum displays about the area's ethnic influences, along with providing office space and classrooms for Eastern Oregon University satellite programs. The Treasure Valley Community College campus is also located near the heart of the city.

Twin Springs and the Owyhee Wilds beyond

Before we leave the Treasure Valley area, a final possibility for Owyhee backcountry adventure should be mentioned. This only applies to those with high-clearance, four-wheel-drive vehicles, good topographic maps, and the time required to explore rough dirt roads. The launching point is about 5

Political commentary, Eastern Oregon–style, in the small agricultural community of Adrian

miles southwest of the town of Vale, where the Twin Springs Road turns south (left) off Highway 20. As with earlier precautions, don't try this if it's wet weather because of the slippery mud-quagmires that develop. Follow this dirt road (BLM 7320) for approximately 30 miles across the big sky vistas of the rolling, bunchgrass-sagebrush prairies of the Owyhee uplands. This will bring you to Twin Springs Campground, undoubtedly one of BLM's most far-flung camps. The accommodations are minimalist, but it has some of the basics that are hard to come by in the desert: water and shade trees. The hand-pump spring is only for washing, unless it's rendered safe by purification through filtering or boiling. Picnic tables under poplar and aspen trees round things out to make this a great spot from which to explore the surrounding wild landscapes. Just keep in mind that this is big country with virtually no road signs. It's even more remote than Three Forks, and you're on your own here. Study your maps well to get an idea of the lay of the land before setting out, but expect to get lost a time or two anyway. Or you may have to spend an hour tossing rocks into a washed-out section of road before continuing on. It's all part of the fun of poking about in truly primitive places. Staying on the established roads to avoid tearing up natural habitat is proper, commonsense outback etiquette.

The road leading south from Twin Springs accesses a vast territory of interesting locations west of the reservoir created by the Owyhee Dam—Grassy Mountain, Dry Creek Canyon, Sand Hollow, Deadman Gulch, Pelican Point, Red Butte Canyon, and the Owyhee Breaks— enough possibilities to keep a desert rat happy for years. When it's time to return to civilization, a northeasterly road through the Oxbow Basin loops back to the Treasure Valley via a connection with the paved road below the dam. Plus, there's the added enticement of a hot shower at Lake Owyhee State Park.

The Burns-Malheur area

On Highway 20 again, drive southwest up the Malheur River, 100 miles to Burns. A population of just over three thousand makes this the second largest town in the Southeastern Oregon region. Named after the famed eighteenth-century Scottish poet Robert Burns, the community describes itself as the "most away from it all town in the nation." This dubious distinction refers to the fact that surrounding Harney County is one of the largest, and least populated, counties in America, larger than many eastern states. Also a self-proclaimed "cowboy town," it's the business center for the area's ranches. However, the times are rapidly changing, even in remote Southeastern Oregon. Traditional cowboy hats, boots, and horse tack share the range now with high-tech accoutrements. A modern rancher may now spend as much time managing business in front of an Internet-linked computer as out on the range in a saddle. Instead of three or four powerful nineteenth-century cattle barons dominating the ranching scene, three or four huge agribusiness corporations hold the power. Located far from the Southeastern Oregon region, these enormous meatpacking companies efficiently monopolize the market. Little of the profits trickle down to the small ranches that sell cattle to these distant megacorporations. Similarly, hometown meat-packing companies can't compete with these giants of the beef industry. Nevertheless, some collective family ranches have successfully formed their own cooperatives and sell directly to the more profitable grass-fed, "natural beef" niche-market, utilizing the services of the small, regional feedlots and meatpackers.

Burns, though, is still strongly anchored in its historical roots. In the downtown area, the Harney County Historical Museum features displays of the area's Old West beginnings. Boasting considerably older roots in the region, the Wadatika band of Paiute Indians has inhabited the Harney Basin for many centuries. Today, there are nearly three hundred members of the Burns Paiute Reservation, located north of town, and the tribe operates the Old Camp Casino in Burns. Four miles to the west, the small town of Hines (population about 1,600) is rooted in a different history—the timber industry. In the late 1920s, spurred by a new rail connection to outside markets and the vast ponderosa pine forests in the nearby Blue Mountains, Edward Hines constructed a sawmill and a complete adjoining community for the workers. Thus, the new city of Hines came into existence full-blown—designed by his wife, it includes gracefully meandering streets and a large, green central park. The Hines Lumber Company operated until 1981, when it finally went out of business due to a declining market and more restrictive environmental regulations in the national forests. Under new ownership, the mill reopened in 1983 as the Snow Mountain Pine Company and continued operation until 1994. Now the site is an industrial park, containing a laminate-veneers mill and a motor home manufacturing company.

Farther to the west of Burns spread more than a hundred miles of open sagebrush rangelands, sparse juniper woodlands, and scattered rimrock promontories, culminating at the slopes of the Cascade Range in Central Oregon. This is the former territory of the famous "Horse King," Bill Brown; and wild horses still roam the high desert expanses to this day. At Glass Buttes, between the Highway 20 way-stations of Riley and Hampton, countless generations of Paiute Indians gathered volcanic obsidian glass for arrowheads and other implements. The dirt road that winds to the summit is sprinkled with chips of this volcanic glass, which sparkle in the sun. This is a much-recommended drive during May and June when sagebrush steppe wildflower species bloom in colorful abundance.

Next, come full circle and journey south of Burns on Highway 205 toward Frenchglen. Along the way are some not-to-be-missed places. The drive takes you across a connecting strip of land between Malheur and Harney lakes, a mosaic of mud flats, dryland, marshes, and alkali playa, collectively called the Narrows. Many water birds are to be seen off both sides of the highway, and the tops of old wooden fence posts along the roadside often have red-winged blackbirds, yellow-headed blackbirds, and Wilson's snipes perched on them.

Just to the south of this isthmus is a left-hand (east) turnoff that leads 6 miles to the Malheur National Wildlife Refuge Headquarters. Famed bird authority Roger Tory Peterson considered this to be among the top dozen birding hot spots in the nation. With many hundreds of square miles of surrounding drylands, this huge collection of marshes attracts great numbers of waterfowl on their seasonal migrations along the Pacific Flyway. Information and displays at the headquarters along the south edge of Malheur Lake provide materials for understanding the area's complex ecology. Another excellent resource for the study and protection of Southeastern Oregon's ecosystems is the nearby Malheur Field Station, operated by a consortium of Northwest regional colleges and universities. It offers field courses in various natural science subjects and provides dormitory and cafeteria services. Located in ideal outdoor-classroom surroundings, it takes full advantage of the wildlife refuge, Diamond Craters, Malheur Cave, Steens Mountain, and the Alvord Basin to teach about the fascinating local natural history.

Malheur National Wildlife Refuge: a natural heritage

In the early glimmerings that portend a high desert spring, when the ice begins to melt on Malheur and Harney lakes in February, the ages-old cycle recurs. The first northern pintail ducks come winging in on their annual migration north. And, as if a floodgate had opened, a virtual deluge of many thousands of winged, feathered bodies soon arrive in their wake. Canada geese, snow geese, Ross's geese, white-fronted geese, sandhill cranes, tundra swans, and many other species descend in large flocks and the marshes come

White-faced ibis

alive with the movements and sounds of both migrating and nesting birds.

By early summer, the variety of birds at the Malheur National Wildlife Refuge is astounding. Broods of young explore the vegetation of the marshes. Observant birders and photographers focus their binoculars, spotting scopes, and camera lenses on such species as great blue herons, white-faced ibis, double-crested cormorants, American white pelicans, many kinds of ducks, black-crowned night herons, American avocets, willets, long-billed curlews, Wilson's phalaropes, Franklin's gulls, Wilson's snipes, snowy egrets, western grebes, American bitterns, northern harriers (marsh hawks), marsh wrens, yellow-headed blackbirds, and red-winged blackbirds. Nesting birds of prey, such as golden eagles, red-tailed hawks, and great horned owls, frequent surrounding trees and rimrocks.

The honking of Canada geese heralds the southward migration in the golden autumn, and the quacking and whistling of mallard ducks, tundra swans, sandhill cranes, and other migrating species join the cacophony. Anyone visiting this refuge during these seasonal migrations will be amazed and uplifted by this spectacle of birdlife. Yet these birds represent only a small portion of the immense migrations along the West Coast of North America on the great Pacific Flyway, from the Arctic Circle to south of the Mexican border. Equally impressive, as well as sad, is the fact that this congregation of birds does not compare to the numbers the first white explorers saw when they entered the Harney Basin in the early 1800s.

At the end of the 1800s, hunters shot birds in unrestricted numbers while plume hunters killed egrets, swans, herons, and grebes nationwide to provide decorative feathers for women's stylish hats. Egrets were totally ex-

Malheur wetlands, with Steens Mountain on the horizon

terminated at Malheur, while populations of other species sank to dangerous lows. Early naturalists and the fledgling Oregon Audubon Society in Portland, decrying this unlimited slaughter, publicized the situation in newspapers and magazines. When pioneer wildlife photographers William L. Finley (who later became a prime mover and initial director of the Oregon Fish and Game Commission) and Herman Bohlman sent their Oregon bird photos to President Theodore Roosevelt, he was outraged. The pictures of vast flocks of nesting birds and the shocking evidence of decimations by plume hunters moved Roosevelt to include Oregon's first preserves as part of a new federal wildlife refuge system. Three Arch Rocks on the Oregon Coast became a refuge in 1907, and Lower Klamath and Malheur refuges were created in 1908.

In 1935, President Franklin Roosevelt purchased an additional 65,000 acres in the Blitzen Valley, extending the Malheur refuge southward and making it one of the nation's largest bird sanctuaries. In 1940, the Double-O Ranch was obtained, adding to the west 14,751 acres of wildlife habitat around Harney Lake.

Today, Malheur National Wildlife Refuge consists of nearly 187,000 acres. More than 320 species of birds have been observed on the refuge to date, along with 58 species of mammals. At one point, though, wildlife populations were on the decline late in the twentieth century. Livestock grazing has always been allowed in the refuge, and this practice came under fire during the 1970s when visitors began strongly protesting that the environments there were being damaged and bird counts were resultantly down. This public outcry elicited a response and refuge management reduced the number of cattle. However, environmental groups continue to call for a complete elimination of cows on the refuge, such has occurred at Hart Mountain National Antelope Refuge.

During peak times of the spring and fall migrations, some experienced birders report seeing as many as a hundred bird species in

Birding Malheur

a single day. Especially recommended for beginning birders is the annual John Scharff Migratory Bird Festival, held during the first week of April in the nearby town of Burns. Considered a top birding event in the Northwest region, it provides a concentrated experience of all the ornithological wonders of the area. The program includes birding tours, workshops, educational presentations, an art show, and a banquet. The festival honors the legacy of John Scharff, who was the refuge's highly respected manager for thirty years, until he retired in 1970. Additionally, this birding celebration attracts increasingly larger numbers of participants and has proven to be a much-needed economic boost for the Burns vicinity.

Malheur National Wildlife Refuge is located at the northwestern base of Steens Mountain, thirty miles south of Burns, where the lovely stone headquarters buildings overlook the southern shore of Malheur Lake. During the 1930s, Civilian Conservation Corps stonemasons and a work crew quarried the rock on the refuge and did all the construction. Besides housing offices, a visitor center offers informational brochures, checklists, and guide maps, along with a bookshop, restrooms, and drinking water. An adjacent small museum manages to contain within its

stone walls an impressive collection of two hundred mounted specimens of native birds. The surrounding grounds of watered lawns and many large deciduous trees attracts both unusual bird species and attendant avid bird-watchers. Examples of past rarities sighted there include magnolia warbler, Cape May warbler, rose-breasted grosbeak, indigo bunting, yellow-billed cuckoo, red-eyed vireo, northern parula, scarlet tanager, and painted bunting. After checking the posted bird-sighting reports and getting suggestions from the helpful staff, take the self-guided Malheur birding tour south on the famed Central Patrol Road—the CPR, as it's affectionately known among birders. Have your binoculars ready, because this drive takes you straight through the heart of the refuge's wetlands, which are teeming with life. The Buena Vista Overlook off Highway 205 is also a must-visit location, where you might see the reintroduced trumpeter swan. Go to Malheur National Wildlife Refuge in late May and you're guaranteed to have a watchable wildlife experience you'll never forget. ■

CONTINUING east of the refuge headquarters and taking a right (south) on Lava Bed Road will take you to the Peter French Round Barn Historical Site. This unique structure, built by the infamous cattle baron sometime during the late 1870s to early 1880s (the available historical records aren't precise), has a diameter of one hundred feet. The juniper post-and-stone barn has a domed shingled roof and was used during the long, cold winters to break and train horses. Standing quietly inside you can almost imagine the clopping sound of circling horse hoofs and snowy gales whistling outside. The Jenkins family (fourth generation Harney County ranchers) donated this section of land to the state in 1970 and now operates an adjoining visitor center, complete with historical tours. Just southwest down the same road is the Diamond Craters Natural Area—26 square miles containing a multitude of fascinating cinder cones, volcanic bombs, pressure ridges, lava gutters, tubes, spatter cones, maar craters, and strange, ropey-shaped lava formations with glassy surfaces. Many geologists consider this site to be one of the most diverse, textbook-perfect examples of basaltic volcanism in the nation. Considered to be less than 25,000 years old, this lava flow can be explored along roads and trails that wind through the area, using a kiosk-dispensed tour brochure. Don't miss the maar crater that contains a small lake.

If you have time for a side jaunt up the northwestern slope of Steens Mountain, check out the Kiger Mustang Overlook. Some experts speculate that the wild herd roaming this remote section of the Kiger Creek drainage (below Kiger Gorge) may be descendants of escaped horses brought to North America by the Spanish conquistadors more than four hundred years ago. Showing the "primitive markings" distinctive of ancestral European stock, the Steens horses are called Kiger mustangs. They represent one of only four herds in the United States designated as Spanish-type mustangs. To reach the site, drive southeast of Diamond Craters to the little community of Diamond, where about 12 miles of dirt road lead eastward to the wild mustang country. Keep your binoculars ready; you may be lucky enough to spot these beautiful horses with their unusual dun (tan) coloring, zebra-marked legs, and flowing dark manes and tails. However, the road is rough and suited only to vehicles with high-ground clearance, and only in dry weather. On returning to Diamond, you may want to have a meal or cold

Interior ceiling view of the Peter French Round Barn. Photo: Buck Jenkins

drink at Frazier's Pub, attached to the historic 1898 Hotel Diamond. Although the pub serves on a walk-in-and-order basis, rooms and meals in the hotel are by reservation only, mid March to mid November.

Arriving back in Frenchglen, you've completed a very big loop, but there's still more to be seen of Southeastern Oregon—it's a big place! To the west is the vast basin and range country you saw from the summit of Steens Mountain. Therefore, since these alternating humps and depressions run north–south, setting a course westward will cause you to cut across the grain, so to speak. These will be up-and-down explorations over high fault block upthrusts, followed by plunging switchbacks down into ancient lake beds, only to be repeated at the next fault block range. Just make sure your gas tank is full. It's going to be about 150 miles to the next gas pump (side excursions included), and most of it on gravel and dirt roads.

The varied Hart Mountain landscape—a high plateau of sagebrush, bunchgrass, scattered quaking aspen groves, riparian willows, and moist meadows

Hart Mountain

After driving 7 miles south of Frenchglen on Highway 205, you will make a right-hand turn on Rock Creek Road and head west on this graveled route for 42 miles. The elevation gain on this particular stretch of undulating, open steppelands is deceptively gradual. When the miles are covered and the dust settles, you arrive at the mile-high headquarters of the Hart Mountain National Antelope Refuge. This is the place to start a tour of these ecologically rich plateaulands, consisting of 278,000 acres within the refuge's boundaries. Near the stone cottage staff residence is a smaller building (open 24 hours) that houses interpretive displays and a public restroom. Informative brochures provide a refuge map and descriptions of the various points of interest, along with details about the local wildlife, where to camp, regulations, and other pertinent facts. Also be sure to read the wildlife sightings register, filled out by

other visitors. It will give good tips on where animals have been seen recently. Besides getting you oriented, this is the only location in the refuge offering safe drinking water, so fill up here if you're running low.

Usually, visitors immediately want to see the notoriously fleet pronghorn. But where to go? Spreading from the plateau's 5,000-foot-elevation plains to the 8,000-foot summit of Warner Peak is an array of habitats: bunchgrass prairie, sagebrush-rabbitbrush-bitterbrush shrublands, riparian willows along streams, small lakes, hot springs, moist meadows around springs, mountain mahogany thickets, quaking aspen groves, a stand of ponderosa pine, and a bit of white fir at the highest zones. More than three hundred different species of animals are native to the area, each with its own unique behavior patterns and needs.

One factor, though, greatly improves your chances for success. To see wildlife in this dry environment, find water. It's a magnet for thirsty animals, with exceptions, such as lizards and kangaroo rats, which derive sufficient moisture from their foods. One good spot is Petroglyph Lake, about 3 miles northwest of the headquarters, at the end of a dirt road. Although the first stretch is usually in good condition (unless it has been raining), the final half mile is rocky and rough. Unless you're driving a vehicle with high ground clearance, it's best to park and walk the final distance. Petroglyph Lake is nestled in a depression directly below the southeastern slope of Poker Jim Ridge. Therefore, it attracts animals from both the open country on one side and the rocky highlands on the other. The best times to arrive are at dawn or in the evening, but be sensitive to the needs of the wildlife. It is critical for them to become rehydrated, particularly in the heat of summer. Quietly remain at a considerable distance, just beyond the end of the road where the initial view of the lake is gained. Bring a comfortable folding chair, along with water bottle and snacks, settle in, and savor your wild surroundings. Before long, you'll probably be rewarded by the appearance of pronghorn trailing in from the grasslands or bighorn sheep warily descending from the rocky ridge beyond the lake. Mule deer are commonly seen coming in for a drink, and sage grouse often visit as well. The peaceful quality of witnessing this eons-old natural rhythm of life at a watering place is profound.

You may want to return to the lake during the mid-portions of the day and hike around its perimeter. Search the bordering rocks and if you're observant you'll find the ancient Native American petroglyphs for which it's named. For a great day hike, continue northwest past the lake and ascend to the crest of Poker Jim Ridge. The view off the other side is breathtaking. You'll be looking down

Pronghorn in typical surroundings at Hart Mountain National Antelope Refuge

Evening wildlife-watching at Petroglyph Lake

A pronghorn has an evening drink at Petroglyph Lake

a nearly vertical 3,600-foot escarpment to the scattered lakes and marshes of the Warner Valley far below—startling visual proof that Hart Mountain is a massive fault block range. This is prime bighorn sheep habitat, so be alert for a chance to observe them nimbly moving along rocky ledges. These magnificent animals were extirpated from Southeastern Oregon by 1915, victims of overhunting and the twin pressures of competition for forage and diseases brought in by domestic sheep. Twenty bighorns were successfully reintroduced at Hart Mountain in 1954, and now the population is one of the largest in the state. Prairie falcons and golden eagles nest along this enormous rim and may soar into view.

Other areas of the refuge are equally fascinating to explore. Follow Blue Sky Road south

Autumn quaking aspen grove on Hart Mountain

from the headquarters through the exhilaratingly expansive steppelands, which offer good opportunities for seeing more pronghorn. If the air temperature is above 70 degrees, watch for gopher snakes crossing the road or even a western rattlesnake. During spring into midsummer, varieties of high desert wildflower species will be in bloom along these meandering roads. Stopping anywhere in these open environments and walking out through the shrublands may turn up pigmy short-horned lizards or sagebrush lizards in sun-warmed sandy places, or possibly a burrowing owl. The road eventually leads to Blue Sky, a delightful place with an isolated, relic stand of ponderosa pine and an adjacent quaking aspen grove. The South Boundary Road will take you to a more far-removed section of the refuge where a cluster of lakes often attracts sizable herds of pronghorn, along with other wildlife. However, the roads are rough, so driving there in a passenger car is not recommended. Touring by mountainbike is another inviting option at Hart Mountain, although it's a refuge stipulation to cycle only on the roads. For the adventurous, backpacking is a way to see some of the more remote sections. But be advised that bona fide trails are virtually nonexistent and filling out a free backpacking permit form at the headquarters is required.

If you stay overnight on Hart Mountain, there's a treat in store. Hot Springs Campground, 4.5 miles south of the headquarters, has thirty sites scattered along Rock Creek in shady groves of quaking aspen. Although it's primitive, with only pit toilets and no drinking water, as the camp's name indicates, there's a delightful hot spring. Surrounded only by a low wall, it's pure pleasure to soak under the clear-air sky and rinse off the road dust.

Prior to Euro-American settlement, vast herds of pronghorn roamed the open landscapes of North America. Hart Mountain National Antelope Refuge was established in 1936 in response to an alarming decline of pronghorn. Populations have rebounded from a low of approximately 15,000 in America by the beginning of the twentieth century to a present population of around 500,000 nationwide. At Hart Mountain National Antelope Refuge there are currently from 1,500 to 2,000 pronghorn in residence across the grassy steppelands.

Nevertheless, other species have not fared as well. Reflecting the fact that healthy, diverse habitat means an abundance of wildlife, by the 1980s it was noted that sage grouse and mule deer populations were declining from historic levels. Subsequent in-depth studies showed that riparian growth along streams had greatly lessened. This caused deteriorating water quality and bank erosion, which negatively impacted native redband trout, as well as a host of other creatures. Bunchgrass prairies had declined, too, being extensively replaced by sagebrush and western juniper. In the final analysis, it was the majority opinion of the involved wildlife biologists that this collective decline in habitat integrity had resulted in a serious reduction in the wildlife-carrying capacity of the refuge. They concurred that this was primarily the result of two factors: more than a century of heavy domestic livestock grazing and the routine practice of extinguishing natural fires.

As a result, a new resource management plan was put into effect in 1993. First, it excluded livestock grazing from the refuge. Secondly, a program of periodic prescribed burns was established to mimic naturally occurring fires that reduce shrub cover and stimulate the growth of native grasses. This initially caused an uproar within the local ranching community, but the controversy seems to have settled down in recent years. Because this plan is limited to a fifteen-year trial period, both the beef industry and environmental groups are watching this ongoing biological experiment with great interest. So far, riparian willow and aspen growth have noticeably increased along Rock and Guano creeks; and as controlled burns are continued, there is greater diversity of mixed bunchgrass, herbaceous forbs, and sagebrush. Additionally, nearly all the fences formerly used to control cattle on the refuge have been removed by volunteer groups, freeing pronghorn dispersal. Concurrent with these changes have been significant increases in the populations of sage grouse, songbirds, and pronghorn. It should be added, though, that another variable is involved. Shortly after the new management plan was put into motion, a long drought period ended. The accumulating facts gleaned by the ongoing monitoring at Hart Mountain will establish whether these management decisions were sound.

Warner Valley to Lakeview

You now leave Hart Mountain along one of the most panoramic drives in the state— down the precipitous basalt ramparts of Poker Jim Ridge. The gravel road west of the refuge headquarters suddenly dives off of this classic fault rim, down a series of sharp switchbacks, to the Warner Valley at about 4,400 feet elevation. On the way down, pullouts beckon with their splendid views westward across the long north-south basin. Again, like so many other Southeastern Oregon valleys, this trough, sunk low by an underlying fault, was brimming with water during Pleistocene times. In the present regional aridity, this has dwindled to a thirty-mile-long series of lakes—Pelican, Crump, Hart, Ander-

The Warner Valley below Poker Jim Ridge

Rocks with Native American petroglyphs are fairly common throughout the Warner Valley area.

Large-leaved lupine along the shore of Goose Lake

son, Swamp, Mugwump, Flagstaff, Campbell, Stone Corral, and Bluejoint. Crump and Hart lakes are the largest and, therefore, most permanent. In between are shallow vegetated marshes, dry alkali playas, saltscrub flats, sand dunes, and sagebrush plains. During wet years, many of these bodies of water rise and connect, but then shrink back with the next drought. Like the marshes of Malheur to the east and Klamath to the west, this extensive wetland complex ranks as one of the most important stopover places for migrating birds along the Pacific Flyway, as well as for nesting species in spring. Indeed, it's a grand spectacle as flocks of ducks and geese, along with white pelicans, egrets, terns, tundra swans, gulls, and sandhill cranes wing their way over the lake chain, all with the gargantuan stone wall of Poker Jim Ridge forming a backdrop.

Only two outposts exist in this out-of-the-way basin. Plush, more or less in the center of the Warner Valley, has one of those "full service" establishments—the Hart Mountain Store. They'll fill up your nearly empty gas tank, offer water and geographical directions, plus sell you groceries, cold beer, a sandwich, and ice cream. And if you're wondering about the little community's name, as legend has it, in the 1880s a local Paiute Indian was playing poker with some buckaroos and got a royal flush. He announced this development, with slight mispronunciation, by exclaiming, "Plush!" The humorous incident was told and retold until it became high desert lore and the town name. Whether the Native American in this incident has any connection to the nearby Poker Jim Ridge, history does not say. At the southern end of the valley, you come to Highway 140 and the even smaller community of Adel. This is the last chance for gas, groceries, sandwiches, cold beer, and directions before venturing west over the Warner Mountains.

After days of desert travel, crossing the Warners comes as something of a visual shock. The forests of pine and fir, broken occasionally by large, grassy meadows, glow with intense green in comparison to the many former miles of subdued sagebrush gray-green. Over the summit, by way of wide Camas Prairie, purple-blue in springtime with the blooms of camas, we descend past the Warner Canyon Ski Area. This small facility offers fourteen downhill runs, and trails are provided for enthusiasts of cross-country skiing and snowmobiling. Highway 140 soon breaks out into a lovely, open valley of sagebrush flats and ranchlands, bordered by forested mountains to the west and east. Just after noting the change in surroundings, you reach the main north-south interstate route of Highway 395.

Turning south on 395 brings you to Lakeview within 5 miles. The largest city in this westerly section of Oregon's basin and range corner, it musters a population of about 2,500. Billing itself as the "tallest town in Oregon," at 4,800 feet this is the state's highest elevation incorporated city that has year-round residents. The community is also proud of its ranching heritage, made apparent by a huge cutout billboard of a smiling cowboy greeting visitors as they enter town. Old West ambience aside, the primary employment comes from federal, state, and county jobs: the city is the local headquarters for the Bureau of Land Management, Forest Service, Oregon Department of Fish and Wildlife, and the Lake County seat.

This is a timber town, too, surrounded by extensive coniferous forests. Lakeview's innovative Freemont Sawmill has retooled to process smaller diameter logs, a good portion of the supply coming from a nearby sustained yield unit of the Fremont-Winema National Forest. This half-million-acre section of timberlands is managed and monitored in a low-impact, sustainable manner by the Lakeview Stewardship Group, a diverse consortium that includes, among others, local forestry workers, the Collins Companies, scientists, environmental organizations, the U.S. Forest Service, Lake County Chamber of Commerce, Oregon Department of Economic and Community Development, and Lakeview High School.

Like Klamath Falls to the west, Lakeview sits over an active geothermal area and boasts Oregon's only continuously spouting geyser. "Old Perpetual" is located at the north edge of town in front of the Hunter Hot Springs Resort. It's actually not a natural geyser, having been accidentally created many years ago during a well-drilling endeavor. Now there's a steamy spouting every two or three minutes, rising over fifty feet into the air. However, during the lazy days of summer, it slows down to every five to ten minutes. Lakeview's name refers to huge, neighboring Goose Lake, which extends south into California. Along the shore, 15 miles south of town, there's a nice state campground with all of the usual amenities, including hot showers. Adding to the charm, tame resident mule deer wander among the campsites, and there's good birding for native waterfowl (with geese, of course). If you end up in Lakeview when Independence Day is being celebrated, you'll enjoy watching the annual Hang Gliding Festival, which launches off the summit of Black Cap Butte, above the northeastern side of town.

Lake Abert's briny shore, and Abert Rim beyond

Midday summer thunderstorm over Lake Abert

Long evening shadows in Big Basin, near Paisley

Lake Abert

Backtracking north of Lakeview along Highway 395 for about 25 miles brings into view another west-facing fault block escarpment similar to Hart Mountain's precipitous western edge. But it isn't just any fault block—this is Abert Rim, the largest exposed fault scarp in North America, and one of the most enormous of its type in the entire world. Below its thirty-mile-long, 2,500-foot-high, vertical face is Lake Abert, saltier than the Pacific Ocean and the third largest inland body of salt water in North America. Swarming in the lake's waters are many millions of tiny brine shrimp, which attract thousands of shorebirds that come to feast on this nourishing bonanza. On the white alkali flats at the northern end of Lake Abert is the state's largest nesting population of snowy plover. This is a place of immensities. The highway threads its way along the strip of land between the eastern lake shore and the base of the rim. Watch for two pullouts along Highway 395 that have excellent interpretive signs about the area's natural history, and use your binoculars to scan the

Alice Elshoff in Big Basin, proving that deserts are not the grimly forbidding places they're often believed to be.

towering cliffs for bighorn sheep and soaring birds of prey. On a hot summer day, when the lake has evaporated low and gulls scavenge dead shrimp at the water's edge, the strongly organic, briny smell is evocative of ocean tide-pools. To observe snowy plovers, turn left (west) on a dirt road at the northern end of the lake and drive slowly, using your car as a blind. About 15 miles farther north on 395 is the dry playa of Alkali Lake, where more snowy plover can sometimes be seen. Throughout these lake basins, watch for Native American petroglyphs on rocks, especially along the base of Abert Rim, where these intriguing aboriginal creations are common. Next, retrace Highway 395 to just south of Lake Abert, turning to the right where Highway 31 forks off to the northwest at the small community of Valley Falls.

For a great desert hike with a panoramic payoff, watch for a right-hand (northeast) dirt road within 8 miles after turning onto Highway 31. It crosses a shrubby alkali flat toward the rocky connective ridge of Coglan Buttes. If conditions are wet, do not pull off—there's a possibility of becoming stuck. If the weather is dry, though, and you have a vehicle with high ground clearance, proceed onward. Otherwise, park off the highway and walk. After approximately 1.5 miles, the dirt road leaves the flatlands and enters a large hollow within the southwesterly facing slopes of the ridge. This is Big Basin, which contains a typical Great Basin Desert ecosystem of saltscrub shrubs, desert horned lizards, long-nosed leopard lizards, giant desert hairy scorpions, black-throated sparrows, and white-tailed antelope squirrels. Shortly after entering the hollow, the road becomes rough; it's best to walk from that point. The ongoing jeep track traverses north through the basin, providing views of picturesque red rimrocks to the east. Proceed on this route for about 2 miles as it gradually climbs

to the head of Big Basin, and then another two miles to the ridgetop. At the crest, you'll be treated to marvelous views to the northeast, with Lake Abert and Abert Rim directly below, and beyond that are successive ranges and basins into the distance. When you've savored the grand scenery and solitude, return down the same jeep trail.

One cannot help but be moved by this land. Alice Elshoff, a long-time advocate for Oregon's arid wildlands, has given voice to the long view: "Having always enjoyed the beauty and dynamic precision of the natural world, what motivates me in my conservation efforts is the desire to make sure that generations to come will be able to see and know what I have known."

CONTINUING northwest on Highway 31 takes you through the Chewaucan Valley, the road paralleling the Chewaucan River and the Chewaucan Marsh (Chewaucan is Paiute for "Little Potato"). Several thousand years ago, during the Pleistocene era, this area was submerged under huge Lake Chewaucan. Present-day Lake Abert and Summer Lake are mere remnants from when Ice Age waters brimmed in these basins and connected through this narrow valley. The lofty Coglan Butte summit, where we hiked earlier, would have been a relatively low peninsula with lake waves nearly lapping at our feet.

Soon, the highway brings you to the ranching town of Paisley (population 250). It would be easy to just drive on through this quiet place. But looks can be deceiving. All kinds of community happenings are going on in this self-sufficient, community-spirited village. For one thing, tune into the local radio station as you drive through (KPAI-LP at 103.1 FM), run by the kids in the Paisley School District. Their K–12 public school includes a dormitory that houses up to twenty-four students from outside the area, including exchange students from other parts of the world. A new Paisley Wellness Center, important in a remote community, has a volunteer parish nurse provided by the town's United Methodist Church. Or check out their recently refurbished airport, with the comings and goings of small private jets belonging to the local headquarters of the J. R. Simplot Co. ZX Ranch. This historic ranching operation, dating from the 1800s, is the largest contiguous ranch in the nation—65 miles wide and 163 miles long, including a nature preserve at nearby Sycan Marsh that is co-managed with The Nature Conservancy. If you happen to be in Paisley during the last weekend in July, you'll be able take in the annual Mosquito Festival. Begun in 1984 to raise funds for control of these pesky insects, the two-day event has grown to include not only the usual hometown parade, quilt auction, craft fair, art show, barbecue, and horseshoe-throwing contest, but also a rodeo, fly-fishing contest, kids olympics, acrobatic airplane show, classic car show, and a live-music street dance. Before leaving, stock up on groceries or just about anything else you need at the classic Paisley Mercantile, and there's an equally classic, small-town café next door.

Summer Lake

Just a few miles to the northwest of Paisley is a fault scarp that differs greatly from what we saw at the more arid locations of Abert Rim, Hart Mountain, and Steens Mountain—it is topped by thick coniferous forest. This is Winter Rim, which like the Steens escarpment, faces east. In the large basin below is immense, shallow Summer Lake, which becomes largely dry alkali playa during drought years. The abrupt contrast between

the parched desert dunes at the east side of the lake and the green woods high above the western shore dramatically delineates the point at which Pacific winds lose much of their moisture. These bordering timberlands are part of the Fremont National Forest, where the 1.2 million acres of basalt tablelands are cloaked with ponderosa pine, lodgepole pine, Douglas fir, and white fir. Positioned between the Cascade Range to the west and the high desert on the east, these forests have been largely overlooked by the usual throngs of summer vacationers. The forested drainage of the Chewaucan River and the Gearhart Mountain Wilderness, west of Paisley, has remote campgrounds, trails, and trout streams that are relatively seldom visited.

Even more unknown and untrammeled is the desert country east of Summer Lake. Three or four rather vague and undependable jeep trails penetrate the margins of this vast landscape of saltscrub, sand, and rock—one of the largest roadless areas in the state. Just northwest of the Paisley Airport, a good dirt BLM road turns east off Highway 31 and then deteriorates into meandering sand tracks after several sun-bleached miles. For adventurous desert rats, here's the chance for delightfully wild solitude, afoot in the backside of beyond. Just bring plenty of water, a sensible hat, and a good map of the area. Shorter rambles along old, fading jeep trails into the Tenmile Butte area are a possibility. Watch for the same mix of Great Basin small wildlife mentioned earlier for Coglan Buttes—desert horned lizards, long-nosed leopard lizards, striped whipsnakes, black-throated sparrows, and white-tailed antelope squirrels. A longer trek to the crest of the Diablo Rim gives sweeping views into still more lonely desert lands farther to the east, and the possibility of seeing reintroduced bighorn sheep on the

Summer Lake during a high-water year

rocky heights. However, with the strenuous distances involved getting to Diablo Rim, an overnight backpacking trip might be in order. Just remember that all water needs (plenty, in this thirsty land) will have to be carried on your back. Spring or autumn, when temperatures are more comfortably low, are generally the best times for hiking in this region. Or consider backpacking under a summer night's full moon. Flick a flashlight on occasionally to discover a variety of nocturnal desert animals—kangaroo rats, pocket mice, gopher snakes, and perhaps a western rattlesnake—so watch your step, but realize that a rattler is just as wary of you as you are of it. If you observe a rattlesnake from a respectful distance, it will usually crawl away.

About 30 miles to the north is the diminutive community of Summer Lake, consisting of a store–gas station combination that sells groceries, ice, and other basic supplies. Directly across the road is a wayside picnic area with tables, restrooms, water, and pleasant shade from tall poplars. About a mile south, on the west side of the highway, is a lodge-style motel with cabins and a good quality restaurant. Across the road is the Oregon Department of Fish and Wildlife (ODFW) headquarters for the Summer Lake Wildlife Area. Although not as well known among birders as the famed Malheur National Wildlife Refuge, Summer Lake is also an important stopover along the Pacific Flyway for migrating waterfowl and spring nesting birds. Before grabbing your binoculars and heading for the marshes, check out the visitor center at the headquarters where bird checklists, maps, and restrooms are available, along with postings of the latest wildlife reports.

Here at the north end of the lake basin, the Ana River feeds marshes, canals, and a reservoir, accessed by a 9-mile loop road (sections are closed during fall hunting and spring nesting seasons—check with ODFW for schedule). Depending upon the time of year, driving slowly through these various wetlands might turn up Wilson's phalaropes, black-necked stilts, great blue herons, black-crowned night herons, American avocets, great and snowy egrets, double-crested cormorants, American white pelicans, Caspian terns, black terns, willets, cinnamon teal, blue-winged teal, and yellow-headed and red-winged blackbirds, among others on the list of approximately 250 bird species recorded for Summer Lake. During spring and autumn migration time, it's possible to see spectacular numbers of snow geese and Canada geese. Winter is a good time to observe tundra swans on the refuge, and trumpeter swans are a possibility, too. The trumpeter, once near the brink of extinction, has been reintroduced to Oregon and now breeds and winters at the Summer Lake Wildlife Area.

During their respective seasons, hunters flock to the area after deer and elk, ducks, and geese. Anglers gravitate to the spring-fed, trout-stocked Ana River and Ana Reservoir, which are open to fishing year-round. A privately operated RV park (with tent sites and laundry-shower facilities) is located by the reservoir. This is the only place in Oregon stocked with the "whiper," which reaches 20 pounds and is a hybrid between the oceangoing striped bass and the freshwater white bass. There are also campsites on the refuge, although they are a bit open and spartan, being better suited to pickup truck campers and travel trailers. For those desiring more comfortable overnight accommodations there's the previously mentioned motel with cabins in the community of Summer Lake. The more upscale Summer Lake Inn is located about 10 miles south of town, off Highway 31 along the shore. Elegantly rustic cabins have

views across Summer Lake, with the resort's emphasis being on relaxed recreation, such as birdwatching, petroglyph tours, hiking, bicycling, canoeing and fly-fishing. The cedarwood dining room in the main lodge serves fine cuisine meals, including to non-guests by reservation. For an affordable hot soak, just down the road is Summer Lake Hot Springs, a family-owned business that has a geothermally warmed swimming pool in a delightfully funky, barn-like building.

The Christmas Valley area

We'll wind up our explorations of Southeastern Oregon in an area known by early pioneers as the Great Sandy Desert. This vast bowl of aridity extends northward from the Abert and Summer Lake basins to the Millican Valley and the foothills of the Maury and Ochoco mountains. Highway 31 will take us there, north over Picture Rock Pass and down the other side into the Silver Lake Basin (the lake is more marsh than open water). At 13 miles north of downtown Summer Lake, there's a paved turnoff to the right that will take you northeast for 14 miles to the desert-surrounded town of Christmas Valley.

Incongruous as it may seem, situated in the middle of this open expanse, a small settlement clusters around an irrigated green golf course and a man-made lake. A California land development firm started the community in 1961 when it purchased 108 square miles of rangelands for a mere ten dollars per acre. After building the golf green and lake, the developer advertised lots to prospective out-of-state buyers. No doubt visualizing Oregon's famed green forests, several thousand people purchased, sight unseen, their own bits of paradise. Upon visiting their pieces of arid real estate, many disappointed buyers demanded refunds, and lawsuits proliferated. Christmas Valley, though lacking the evergreen trees its name might suggest, does abound in an invigorating, sunny climate with low land costs and taxes. This has attracted retirees, but the town of around a thousand people is mostly the hub for the surrounding ranching and farming community, which specializes in growing high-protein alfalfa crops. Christmas Valley has grown and now boasts a city park, two grocery markets, a hardware store, three restaurants, pizza-deli, video store, two motels, a bed-and-breakfast, a farm and auto supply, airfield, and a K–12 public school. Though its genesis was a bit shady, nearly a half-century later a solid community has emerged amid the sagebrush and greasewood.

About 20 miles northeast of Christmas Valley, the aptly named Fossil Lake preserves the dry remains of an Ice Age body of water. When ranchers reported seeing strange bones at the remote site, University of Oregon geologist and paleontologist Thomas Condon (see "Thomas Condon: frontier paleontologist" in Part I) made an expedition to the lake bed in 1877. He found the fossilized bones of Pleistocene horses, elephants, camels, birds, fish, and other animals. Some of these remains date back as far as two million years, and others are as recent as 10,000 years ago. At its eastern border, this ancient lake bed holds another surprise—12,000 acres of huge, barren, wind-whipped sand dunes. This is the most extensive shifting inland dune system in the state and it attracts many off-highway-vehicle enthusiasts who scoot across this Oregon sahara on oversized tires.

Fossil Lake has yet another surprise. At the northeastern edge of the dunes there is an interesting anomaly, the Lost Forest. This is a 9,000-acre stand of ponderosa pine grow-

A wind-rippled Fossil Lake dune

ing in an arid environment where the annual precipitation may dip below ten inches. Normally these trees require from fifteen to thirty inches of annual precipitation, with the nearest ponderosa timberlands being about fifty miles to the west. The Fossil Lake pines are a vestige of the large Pleistocene forests that once covered the entire region 10,000 years ago when climatic conditions were cooler and moister. Studies have shown that an impervious lake bed underlying the sand's surface traps the scant rainfall, allowing the pines to survive.

Our final hike in Southeastern Oregon will be here in the Lost Forest. The path leads through the ponderosas to a huge reddish-tan stone formation that abruptly juts upward, well above the tree crowns. This is Sand Rock, a lonely volcanic tuff ring, like a desert island in a vast sea of sand. As with Fort Rock to the west, Sand Rock was eroded by wave action from the now-vanished hundred-foot-deep Fort Rock Lake that covered nearly six hundred square miles of the surrounding country. When this enormous lake finally dried up some 13,000 years ago, Oregon's Great Sandy Desert was created.

Climbing to the top of Sand Rock provides wonderful views in all directions. This arid landscape encompasses many of the diverse elements that typify Southeastern Oregon. You're standing on a volcanic formation that was born of explosive eruptions, like so much of the terrain east of the Cascades. Below is an ancient lake bottom that ties the present to the prehistoric past, when anadromous salmon swam these ancient waters, which then had a river link to the sea, and wooly mammoths and horses foraged the shoreline meadows. Today's dry desert winds moan through the branches of the remnant pines of that long-ago era. Scattered throughout this surrounding high desert are basalt rocks bearing Native American petroglyphs, reminders of the first people here. To the south, you can hear the faint motorized sounds of joyriders in their sand buggies on the Fossil Lake dunes. Still farther away to the southwest, patches of green alfalfa fields can be seen, the irrigated agricultural lands of the Christmas Valley area. In the cloudless blue sky a red-tailed hawk soars, its telescopic vision searching the sagebrush flats for Merriam's ground squirrels. To the north, a small herd of pronghorn slowly moves across a flat, while a lone coyote watches from a ridgetop. Eastward is an opening of golden pumice sand, deposited here 7,600 years ago by the ash cloud from Mount Mazama's eruption in the distant southern Cascades. On its sun-warmed surface is a swarming anthill, where a pigmy short-horned lizard snacks on the frenetic little creatures.

The Big Land

Like the paleolithic artist who pecked the petroglyph into lava rock, we all leave our mark on this big land—whether you are a local fourth-generation rancher, a hiker from Portland, or a visiting Japanese tourist. Unfortunately, not all cultural traces are aesthetically pleasing art. The boot tracks, tire tread marks, campfire rings, tent-peg holes, pop cans, and cow pies accumulate. The largest portion of the high desert is composed of public lands, and sorting out how Americans (and international guests) use it all is becoming increasingly contentious. The differences in perspective can be light-years apart between an urban recreationist who views the backcountry as a place for nature study and the regional native who raises marketable cattle on the same land.

The opposing sides of a battle have been chosen, and woe to any middle-ground person caught in the heated crossfire. Many drysider families cling precariously to their fading traditional lifestyles of ranching, farming, and logging, feeling assaulted by environmental organizations. Preservationists, who envision the natural ecosystems of Oregon's dry side largely restored to original integrity, call for extensive restrictions of public land grazing and timber harvesting, if not complete cessation of these activities. They view such uses as being damaging to the health of the land and wasteful of taxpayer dollars that support the federal and state agencies entrusted with managing these resources.

Throughout the entire state, even the most remote locations are increasingly being visited by vacationing recreationists. With hoards of people enjoying the outdoors, conflicts of interest are bound to arise. Off-highway-vehicle enthusiasts who relish the exhilaration of roaring down a backcountry trail on a motorcycle are having altercations with birdwatchers and hikers seeking peaceful quietude in nature. Interpreting the concept of "multiple use" as meaning everyone does everything in the same places is not working. Consequently, the U.S. Forest Service and Bureau of Land

Christmas Valley sunset

Management have designated extensive trail systems for the OHV crowd, while setting aside other places as wilderness and natural areas where motorized vehicles are prohibited. Dividing up all the pieces of the public lands pie for various types of recreation, livestock grazing, and tree cutting is a daunting task that will become ever more complex to implement.

Despite the fact that most people prefer to recreate in green, wooded environments, Oregon's deserts are being increasingly visited. Hikers wishing to avoid the often crowded forest trails of the perennially popular Cascade and Wallowa mountains are discovering the delights of Steens Mountain and Hart Mountain. Many areas, such as the Alvord Desert, Owyhee Canyonlands, and Summer Lake are at relatively lower elevations and accommodate outings during the early spring and autumn seasons, and even winter. These desert alternatives may ease some of the strain on certain heavily used forest playgrounds that are currently being "loved to death."

Reflecting this increased interest, desert-oriented advocacy groups have arisen. For backpackers who prefer trekking through unfettered arid expanses, there's the Desert Trail Association (based in Madras, Oregon), dedicated to developing a long-distance trail system. Like the Pacific Crest and Continental Divide trails, the Desert Trail would extend from the Canadian border to Mexico, but traverse the arid regions of the American West. Eight sections are in place, mostly in Oregon, and the organization has published a separate trail guide for each. And just as the Oregon Cattlemen's Association was organized in 1913 to advance the interests of the beef industry, there's also an organization for desert aficionados. The Oregon Natural Desert Association was formed in 1987 by a group of like-minded desert rats to "protect, defend and restore the health of Oregon's native deserts." ONDA has been highly successfully in its efforts through educational outreach, litigation, and old-fashioned grassroots activism by a dedicated sagebrush fraternity. In 2000, the group was one of the major movers and shakers in a coalition of ranchers, conservationists, politicians, and government agencies that hammered out a plan that led to congressional approval for the Steens Mountain Cooperative Management and Protection Act. This resulted in Oregon's first cow-free wilderness. Along with other conservation groups, ONDA was instrumental in filing a lawsuit that forced an end to livestock grazing in Hart Mountain National Antelope Refuge. The group regularly organizes volunteer trips to remove barbed wire fences within these graze-free areas.

The high desert, far from centers of population, offers a refreshingly different outdoor alternative. Nevertheless, despite the region's unique beauty, this parched environment will probably never attract the same numbers of people as do forested mountains and ocean beaches. Much of Southeastern Oregon's outback will no doubt remain a sanctuary of quiet solitude. Even if one visits the high desert only rarely, it's reassuring to know that these wild places still exist. Bill Marlett, executive director of ONDA, has said that "Wilderness is nothing more than a spiritual desire, if not a biological necessity, for people to be whole with their past and connected to their future; like the gates of a temple, the boundaries of wilderness are artificial, yet crossing that threshold allows feelings of a larger self, a nod of respect for what was, and a sense of what should be."

Sentiments that anyone who loves wide open spaces and elbow room could probably agree with—whether urban environmentalist or rural cowboy traditionalist.

The eco-ranchers

The range wars didn't end with the closing of the nineteenth-century Old West. Skirmishes are still going on out there in the sagebrush country, and the outcome will ultimately shape the face of the entire Intermountain West—ecologically, culturally, and economically.

It would be convenient to paint things a simplistic black and white and say it's the environmentalists versus the ranchers. But it's more complex. There are many kinds of ranching—from conventional cattle operations that sell to the huge agribusiness corporations, to specialty natural and organic ranches, and those who raise sheep or buffalo.

Currently, the records of the American Meat Institute show that about 70 percent of all the beef sold in the nation is processed and marketed by just four enormous meatpacking companies. These megacorporations mechanistically churn out "factory beef" in a very successful but artificial manner. This is far different from the ranching scene during the 1800s and the early part of the 1900s when all cows grazed native grasses on the open range. Then it took three to five years to grow a calf to a mature, marketable steer. Now thousands of cows are jammed into corporate feedlots, which use growth-hormone injections and a diet of rich corn and protein supplements containing animal byproducts, plus prophylactic antibiotics, to achieve the same growth in just a year and a half. The resulting pumped-up steaks, roasts, and hamburger that end up being sold in the large supermarket chain stores are high in saturated fat and low in healthy Omega 3 and CLA fats. These beef products are produced so efficiently and in such massive quantities that the four big corporations hold the power and monopolize the market. A meager amount of the profits end up trickling down to small ranches and the little mom and pop feedlot-meatpacking companies.

In a bid for survival, some ranchers have gone around the big agribusiness industry and used a David versus Goliath strategy. Joining forces, they have formed cooperatives that produce grass-fed, hormone-free cattle, which they sell directly to the more profitable "natural beef" niche market. This return to a more independent traditionalism is proving increasingly profitable and points toward the future of small family ranching.

A pioneer in this movement, and the most successful, is Oregon Country Beef, initiated by Doc and Connie Hatfield, who have a small ranch near Brothers. It all began in 1986 when Connie had a conversation with a fitness instructor in Bend. Mentioning that he advised his clients to eat low-fat, additive-free beef, the instructor lamented that such products were difficult to find. A light went on in Connie's head, and in no time the Hatfields were planning a strategy born of necessity. "We were going broke!" During the early to mid 1980s, agriculture in general was experiencing one of the worst declines since the Great Depression. Product values were down because of a market glutted by overproduction, land prices declined while interest rates shot up, and dietitians were advising Americans to avoid eating red meat. Out of desperation, many ranchers began commuting to city jobs or selling off sections of their lands to developers of condos and housing subdivisions. Additionally, environmental organizations launched a vigorous campaign to abolish the practice of allowing grazing on public lands. They cited a century and a half of cow-related ecosystem degradation throughout the American West, particularly in riparian zones.

Amid this tumultuous climate, an initial small group of ranch folks met in the Hatfields' living room one February day in 1986. They were from various Oregon locations throughout the country east of the Cascades, most of them descendants of Oregon Trail homesteaders, and of varying ages, ranging from twenty-year-olds to elders of more than seventy. Doc and Connie shared their research: although records for the previous ten years showed that the prices they were all paid for their cattle drastically rose and fell, the retail price remained more or less steady. In the end everyone was in agreement that the days of profitable ranching based on the

Doc and Connie Hatfield, initiators of the innovative Oregon Country Beef ranching cooperative

commodity market were history. By producing a high-quality, natural product and selling directly to the consumer, the ranchers could set a price that covered their overhead and still make a fair profit.

Besides a consensus to produce animals that are primarily grass-fed and totally devoid of growth hormones and needless antibiotics, a manifesto of land stewardship was drafted. The resulting "graze well" principles draw somewhat from the holistic methods developed by wildlife biologist Allan Savory, as well as from other influences. Each family commits to manage their ranch in sustainable ways, the written code stating in part, "We recognize that truly healthy and productive land is biologically diverse. We prefer a diversity of grasses, forbs, shrubs, and trees over monoculture. Rodents, insects, birds, predators and other grazing animals all have their role in a healthy ecosystem. We adapt our management to fit our individual environments rather than fitting the environment to our management." An important component of their eco-ranching approach is to keep cows moving by rotating the animals through different sections of ranchlands, according to seasonal variation. Overgrazing is avoided in this way, particularly along easily damaged streamcourses.

From the original fourteen founding ranch families, Oregon Country Beef has grown to now include around a hundred participating ranches in Oregon, Washington, Idaho, California, Nevada, Wyoming, and Hawaii, and continues to expand. Their meats are sold in natural and independent food stores from California to Louisiana and north to Alaska— annual retail sales routinely amount to well over $40 million. Their products are served in a number of restaurants as well. With this expansion into other states, the name is now shifting back to Country Natural Beef, which is the original founding trademark.

Doc Hatfield, a veterinarian, fills the quality-control position within the cooperative. Third-party inspections are made by the Food Alliance, a nonprofit organization that promotes sustainable agriculture by recognizing farmers who produce food in environmentally and socially responsible ways. Humane treatment is a key component of the program. Because member ranches retain ownership of the beef until it reaches the retail level, they have direct oversight of the short feedlot finishing period, the slaughter and the processing. In keeping with the cooperative's grassroots, homegrown philosophy, the ninety-day finishing phase takes place at a small family-run feedlot company in Boardman, Oregon. There, Beef Northwest Feeders nourish the cattle on a custom, vegetarian-based diet, which completely avoids the contamination risks associated with animal byproducts. Their unique feed rations, composed of potatoes, corn and alfalfa are fortified with vitamin-mineral supplements—especially Vitamin E for its healthful antioxidant–immune system benefits.

Another important emphasis at Oregon Country Beef is the requirement that at least once a year representatives of each ranch family travel to a city store that retails Oregon Country Beef and visit with their customers by the meat counter. Doc Hatfield commented, "Our ranchers have found that the rural/urban split is considerably overstated . . . lots of folks in the city care about healthy rural communities surrounded by productive open space." Surprisingly, Japanese philosophy influenced the ranching cooperative in 1988 when the Kyotura Company (a huge restaurant empire) began importing Oregon Country Beef. Although the Kyotura Company failed in the Japanese economic crash of the early 1990s, the five-year-successful liaison allowed Oregon Country Beef to absorb the Japanese management concept of *shinrai*—that each link in a group of associated businesses must be successful for everyone to prosper. This symbiotic principle of commerce mirrors Oregon Country Beef's ecological philosophy of land stewardship. In 2004, this principle made a connection with Burgerville, a regional chain of fast-food restaurants based in Vancouver, Washington. Specializing in using localized Northwest ingredients, the company switched entirely to vegetarian-raised Oregon Country Beef for its hamburgers. Ironically, four years of communication between the two companies, while Oregon Country Beef grew large enough to supply Burgerville's needs, led to a partnership just before the mad-cow disease scare occurred. It was a mutually beneficial, *shinrai* meshing, not only for Oregon Country Beef and Burgerville but the consumer and environment as well.

Well intentioned as the eco-ranchers may be, environmentalists are still skeptical. From their point of view, whether the cattle are natural and hormone-free or not makes no difference. They're still cows, which muck up streams, trample the cryptobiotic crust soils of the sagebrush ecosystems, and require wildlife-hampering fences.

Nevertheless, Oregon Country Beef maintains that their innovative graze-well methods are not damaging to the environment. They add that in most situations it stimulates new vegetative growth when cows briefly graze through, stirring up dead, compacted duff and fertilizing as they go. Feeling caught between the eco-warriors and megacorporate-agribusiness, Doc Hatfield commented, "The extremes push the middle into solutions."

This commitment is exemplified at the historic Roaring Springs Ranch (a member of the Oregon Country Beef cooperative), where a full-time wildlife biologist is part of the crew. Manager Stacy Davies emphatically states:

> We're ecologically sound here—the sage grouse population is exploding. This ranch is proof that you can have healthy livestock, wildlife, and plant communities successfully existing together. Economically healthy ranches on the land and healthy ecosystems are codependent when you consider the long term. Looking at the world, and history, anytime economic times are tough the environment is sacrificed, as all economic wealth begins with raw natural resources. It all has to be sustainable.

In all these voices, eco-activist and eco-rancher alike, a longing can be heard—the ages-old dream of living in harmony with nature. This is reflected in the poetic words of Doc Hatfield and his daughter, Becky, in an Oregon Country Beef brochure:

> Our product is more than beef—it's the smell of sage after a summer thunderstorm, the cool shade of a ponderosa pine forest. It's the 80-year-old weathered hands saddling a horse in the Blue Mountains, the future of a 6-year-old in a one room school on the High Desert. It's a trout in a beaver-built pond, haystacks on an aspen-framed meadow. It's the hardy quail running to join the cattle for a meal, the welcome ring of a dinner bell at dusk.

PART IV

Northeastern Oregon

Northeastern Oregon

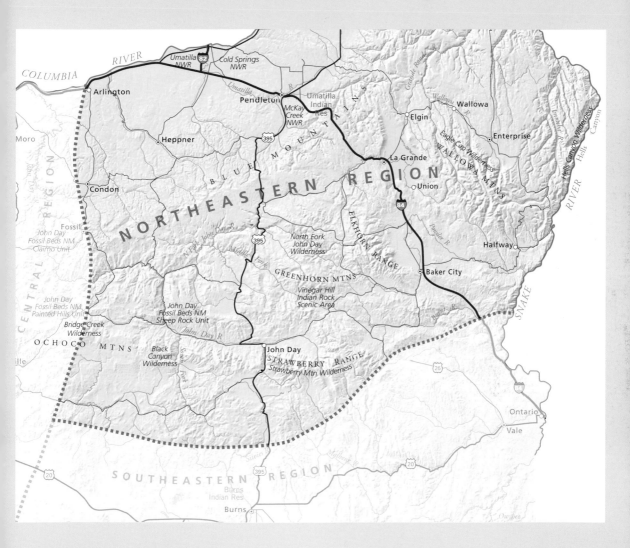

From Nez Perce Appaloosas to the Iron Horse Railroad

I could observe high rugged mountains in
every direction as far as I could see.

CAPTAIN WILLIAM CLARK
September 15, 1805
The Journals of Lewis and Clark

When Captains Meriwether Lewis and William Clark worked their way down the Snake and Columbia drainages in 1805, their route roughly traced Oregon's future northeastern boundaries. These famed expedition leaders and their men became the first whites to explore the interior sections of these rivers east of the Cascade Range. Clark's September 15 journal entry was made in complete awe and consternation. And with good reason—he and his crew were struggling for their lives to cross the snowbound Bitterroot Mountains and descend westward into the lower, warmer canyons of the Snake. If not for friendly Shoshone and Nez Perce Indians, who fed them and acted as their guides through this mountainous maze, they surely would have perished.

Northeastern Oregon's ranges, geologically and floristically, are a western offshoot of the Rocky Mountains of Idaho and Montana. Much the same mix of plant species and glaciated white granite crags that Lewis and Clark encountered during their crossing of the Continental Divide are found in this corner of Oregon. Carpeting the rolling, open foothills

Pages 242–243: Evening light bathes the Wallowa Mountains, near Joseph. Inset: Scarlet (Indian) paintbrush in the upper Imnaha River Canyon. Page 244: Clearing spring storm in upper Imnaha River Canyon

Opposite: January snow whitens Sheep Rock and the banks of the John Day River. Trapping in the winter when animal pelts are thick-furred and of the highest quality, a Hudson's Bay Company brigade worked its way through this river drainage in the early 1800s.

are mostly grasses, not the extensive sage-brush flats of the central and southeastern regions of the state. In fact, large level areas of any kind are rare here—most of Northeastern Oregon "stands on end." Except for the open Columbia Basin in the northern section, mountains rising between nine thousand and ten thousand feet dominate the landscape: the Wallowa, Elkhorn, Greenhorn, Strawberry, and Ochoco subranges that comprise the Blue Mountain complex. Like enormous jagged teeth, these upthrusts soar from green forest mantles to above timberline. Interlaced between these ranges are small to moderately sized valleys nestled into foothills. The spectacular Hells Canyon of the Snake River, the deepest gorge in North America, traces the eastern edges of this vast territory of wild peaks.

First encounters

The Native Americans met by the Lewis and Clark expedition had lived on this remote land for many hundreds of years. Divided into various tribes, Northeastern Oregon was inhabited by the Nez Perce of the Wallowa area, the Umatilla along the Columbia River, the Cayuse of the Columbia Basin plains and northern Blue Mountains, and the Northern Paiutes of the southerly portions of the Blue Mountains and the northern Great Basin. Most were seasonally nomadic, and their tribal boundaries were rather fluid and organic. To the communal Native American, the Euro-American concept of dividing and owning the land was alien.

Lewis and Clark discovered that the Indians of the region had already acquired horses many years before this initial contact with whites by trading with Indians from east of the Rocky Mountains. The Comanches of the southern plains had acquired horses in raids on Spanish settlements in Mexico during the 1700s. From this initial stock, horses soon spread throughout tribes of the interior American West. In a related development, Indians in the eastern portions of Oregon also adopted another plains tribe innovation, the tipi. With the combination of the horse and this portable shelter, Oregon Indians traveled to distant Montana to hunt buffalo and trade with other tribes.

After the Lewis and Clark expedition, the next white people to explore Northeastern Oregon were adventurous fur trappers, many of them tough French Canadian voyageurs. The Indians generally welcomed the first small groups of whites because they were merely passing through. Tribes trustingly fed these new light-skinned people, traded their furs to them, and showed the visitors ancient trails and hunting grounds. Unfortunately, the newcomers brought with them previously unknown diseases against which the Indians had no immunity. Thousands died and whole villages disappeared.

John Jacob Astor's Pacific Fur Company sent two groups to Oregon in 1811. One party went there first by ship, arriving in November, and constructed a fort and trading post on the coast near the mouth of the Columbia River. This became the settlement of Astoria. The second group traveled overland, led by Wilson Price Hunt. They started from St. Joseph, Missouri, on April 20, 1811, and reached the Snake River in December. The expedition included thirty-two white men, three Indians, and the family of a French trapper: two small children and his pregnant Indian wife. By the time the party reached Oregon Territory, they were short on food and exhausted

Cayuse mother and child in traditional dress.
Photo: Edward S. Curtis

died during this cold, arduous climb and was buried on the summit, above the Columbia Basin. The bedraggled group followed the Columbia River to the coast, arriving at the Pacific Fur Company post on February 15, 1812.

A few months later, seven of Astor's trappers, led by Robert Stuart, more or less retraced this route from west to east. They left Astoria on June 29, 1812, bound for New York to report their progress to Astor. Passing through Northeastern Oregon in August, they reached St. Louis on April 30, 1813. Here, again, was proof that a passable—though lengthy and difficult—route across the continent existed.

Within the next few years, other groups of trappers explored the watercourses of Northeastern Oregon for beaver and other fur-bearing mammals and traded with the Indian tribes. Hudson's Bay Company trapper Donald McKenzie led a large brigade of men across the Blue Mountains in 1818 and continued into Idaho and Wyoming. Peter Skene Ogden entered the John Day drainage in the western Blue Mountains with another group of Hudson's Bay Trappers in 1825–26 and again, on a later trip, approximated the route of the future Oregon Trail over the Blue Mountains.

First scientific and military surveys of the region

During June of 1826, Scottish botanist David Douglas traveled upriver from the Pacific Ocean into the bunchgrass-covered hills of the Columbia Basin. While collecting specimens of many previously undescribed plant species (the Douglas fir honors his name), the pioneer naturalist progressed to the northern slopes of the Blue Mountains. There he heard

from the long, hazardous trip. At first, they attempted to reach the Columbia River by passing through the gorge of the Snake River Canyon, but they soon abandoned the precipitous route when it proved too difficult for their trail-worn horses. They struck off to the northwest, following closely what would later be the Oregon Trail. In what probably was the Baker Valley, the woman went into labor and the trapper and his family, with newborn baby, caught up with the expedition in the Grande Ronde Valley. A friendly band of Indians invited the Astor brigade to camp with them there and they feasted on horse and dog meat to celebrate on New Year's day.

After a two-day rest, the trek resumed over the snowy Blue Mountains. Sadly, the baby

beguiling tales of a beautiful, level-floored valley beyond this forested range. Douglas made two attempts to reach the oval basin, what the French-speaking trappers called Grand Ronde, but deep snow on the summit of the Blue Mountains blocked his path.

By the 1830s, the U.S. Army was conducting explorations and began mapping this region of the Northwest. At least two expeditions crossed Northeastern Oregon during this period. Captain L. E. Bonneville, on leave of absence from the army, led his own exploratory group of twelve men through the Grande Ronde and Wallowa valleys in 1834. And that seemingly ubiquitous adventurer Captain John C. Fremont, on assignment to explore the Far West, led an 1843 army survey detail through this same remote corner of Oregon. He and his men spent time camping near the present site of the town of La Grande. In his later report, Fremont commented on the area's agricultural potential: "a place—one of the few we have seen in our journey so far—where a farmer would delight himself to establish, if he were content to live in the seclusion which it imposes." But many years would pass before settlers tilled the rich soils of this mountain-sequestered valley. Tantalizing reports describing the wonders of the American West in general and an Eden-like Willamette Valley were beginning to circulate in the East by the end of the 1830s. The increasing allure of the Oregon Trail thus focused upon reaching and settling the Willamette drainage of Western Oregon; emigrants were merely passing through most parts of the interior regions of the Northwest, so that Northeastern Oregon remained a largely unexplored, primitive wilderness inhabited only by Indians and a few hardy trappers—literally, blank spaces on the sketchy maps of the region during that period.

The Oregon Trail emigrants

Before 1843, only a small trickle of emigrants from the East had attempted to make the long, challenging trip to the Oregon country. But in the spring of that year, the first large wagon train was organized. Consisting of nearly a thousand people, 120 wagons, and five thousand head of livestock, the expedition left Independence, Missouri, on May 22. With Jesse Applegate as the primary leader, they crossed the plains, deserts, and mountain passes to reach the Oregon Trail's goal of the Willamette Valley in slightly less than six months. The Great Emigration, as it was called, had begun. Enterprising people from all walks of life caught "Oregon fever," committing to the arduous journey not only for the purpose of building a new life but to some extent for patriotic reasons as well. Peter H. Burnett, a leader on the premier 1843 wagon train, wrote about the motivations involved in the formative days of the Oregon Territory in his memoir, *Recollections and Opinions of an Old Pioneer*: "At that time the country was claimed by both Great Britain and the United States, so that the most ready and peaceable way to settle the conflicting and doubtful claims of the two governments was to fill the country with American citizens."

Wagon trains grew ever larger. There was a continuing procession of emigrants from the East, with their possessions, hopes, and dreams crammed into canvas-covered wagons that soon swelled into a flood. These early caravans of pioneers enjoyed plentiful hunting and rich forage for their stock along the way, but the Oregon Trail gradually became a wide swath of overhunted, overgrazed land.

The trail entered the state near present-day Ontario, where the Snake River flowed more slowly and provided several crossing places.

Wallowa Mountains foothills at the northeastern edge of the Baker Valley, near the route of the Oregon Trail

One of these, where the Snake takes a wide swing around a high, rocky point, became a traditional camping spot on the Oregon side, and travelers named it Farewell Bend. From this point, the trail progressed toward the northwest, through the Baker and Grande Ronde valleys, over a 4,193-foot pass in the forested Blue Mountains, then down into the open grasslands of the Columbia Basin and westward to The Dalles. Beyond that point, reaching the Willamette Valley required a treacherous float through the narrow portal of the Columbia River Gorge—the region's only breach through the formidable Cascade Range. There the emigrants transported their belongings lashed to rafts or any available watercraft that served the purpose of navigating the hair-raising rapids.

At first, these great caravans of people only passed through the northeastern region, intent on reaching the fabled productive soils and mild climate of the Willamette Valley in Northwestern Oregon. Possibly, the dry, open country and rugged mountain ranges

east of the Cascades in Oregon were too reminiscent of the difficult lands they had already struggled through while crossing the continent; and indeed, few were tempted to settle in the isolated, mountainous wilds of the northeastern corner of the state. Only the Columbia Basin, with its lower elevations, good soils, and a climate more beneficial for growing crops, enticed a relatively small number of settlers away from the westbound wagon trains. During the 1840s, The Dalles remained the only white Oregon community along the Columbia River east of the Cascades. Farther eastward the land remained the domain of Indian tribes. A lone white outpost appeared in 1847 when a Catholic Mission was built along the Umatilla River.

The Oregon Trail had penetrated the heart of the traditional lands of all major Indian tribes of Northeastern Oregon. The first small parties of white explorers and trappers were met with friendly interest; now this growing influx of large wagon trains bringing hordes of white emigrants through the region

Farmlands near Summerville, Grande Ronde Valley. White settlers first came to this oval, mountain-surrounded basin in 1861.

took on the threat that it was. Realizing that the new invaders would settle more and more of the region, some Indians began harassing wagon trains.

The Cayuse War

Resentment toward whites was particularly inflamed in 1847 when emigrant wagon trains brought an epidemic of measles. The Cayuse lacked resistance to this disease and approximately half of their tribe died. On November 28, 1847, their anguish and rage was

vented upon the Waiilatpu Mission in the vicinity of Fort Walla Walla, Washington. Believing that the Christians had purposefully stricken the tribe with sickness to clear the way for more white settlement, the Cayuse attacked. They killed Marcus and Narcissa Whitman, who oversaw the Protestant outpost, along with more than a dozen other residents of the mission. Although several individuals escaped into the surrounding hills, nearly fifty whites were kept as hostages. This sparked the beginning of the Cayuse War.

After receiving word of the massacre, Peter Skene Ogden and an armed troop of Hudson's Bay Company men quickly traveled eastward up the Columbia River from Fort Vancouver and managed to successfully bargain with the Cayuse for release of their captives. Within a few days, a volunteer army of forty-eight soldiers from the Willamette Valley, called the Oregon Rifles, also made its way into the region. Under the leadership of Colonel Cornelius Gilliam, a fort was established at The Dalles. Further recruitment from the territory significantly increased the ranks of men willing to fight Indians, but the hastily composed military had meager funding and lacked sufficient supplies of such needed items as gunpowder and food. For the next six months, the army chased Indians ever eastward in the Columbia Basin, encountering combatant bands that not only included Cayuse but Umatilla as well. After several battles in which Gilliam's men were the victors, this show of force was eventually sufficient to quell the war. However, Oregon's first army had their triumphant glory somewhat diminished when Colonel Gilliam accidentally shot himself and died at the campaign's culmination.

With varying peaceful lulls, Native American unrest continued in the northeastern region for several more years. The final battles of the Cayuse War occurred in 1856 along the Burnt River and in the Grande Ronde Valley. With the Indian danger subsided, white pioneers increasingly began to settle along the Columbia River. By the early 1850s, the Catholic Indian Mission on the plains between the Blue Mountains and the Columbia had been joined by a nearby way-station trading post. With more additions, the cluster eventually grew into the town of Pendleton. As the Cayuse Indians had earlier feared, more and more emigrants traveling the Oregon Trail were tempted by promising land along the route and abandoned their goal of the Willamette Valley. In 1861, several adventurous settlers agreed with John Fremont's earlier positive assessment of the Grande Ronde Valley's agricultural potential and built cabins in the secluded basin. Within a few short years, the population there grew and the villages of La Grande, Union, Cove, and Elgin sprang up.

Gold fever

In 1861 the discovery of gold near the present site of Baker City launched a gold rush, and would-be miners swarmed into the region, many coming north from the gold fields of California. Auburn, the first white settlement in the new gold fields of the southern Blue Mountains, mushroomed to a population of nearly six thousand exuberant placer miners. As more gold strikes were made in the area, other mining boomtowns burst into existence. Canyon City, along the upper John Day River, started as a mining camp in 1861, and by 1864 was a full-fledged, lively town with stage service from The Dalles. During this period John Day, Prairie City, Dayville, Mitchell, Greenhorn, Granite, Sumpter, Bourne, and Baker City were born. The dis-

covery of gold on the south slope of the Wallowa Mountains in the late 1860s swelled Sparta to three thousand residents. Many inhabitants of the new towns were Asian, as miners imported large numbers of Chinese laborers to do the backbreaking work.

With most of the region overrun by brash, zealous miners, it was inevitable that hostilities between whites and Native American Indians would be reignited. A number of massacres during this period took advantage of the absence of local army troops, which were fighting in the Civil War. Chief Paulina's band of Northern Paiutes caused considerable bloodshed throughout the southern Blue Mountains, until ranchers ambushed them in 1867. When the army returned at the end of the war, military camps were established at a number of locations in Oregon east of the Cascades. This resulted in a decline of Indian unrest by 1870.

Growth throughout Oregon during this period was phenomenal, and the northeast-

Digging for gold in the Bonanza Mine, 1894, near Greenhorn, Oregon. Courtesy of Baker County Library

The Greenhorn Mountains of Baker and Grant counties, with their rich mineral deposits, fostered many mining boomtowns during Northeastern Oregon's gold rush of the 1860s.

ern region experienced its share of rapid civilizing. Thriving gold towns demanded supplies: entrepreneurs built roads, started stage lines, and plied steamboats up and down the Columbia River between Portland and Umatilla City (with portages of supplies around rapids and falls).

Local farmers and ranchers within the region found the hardworking, hungry miners a lucrative market for agricultural produce. With irrigation, the rich soils of the prairies along the Columbia River and the mountain-rimmed Grande Ronde, Baker, and John Day valleys all began producing crops of grains, vegetables, and fruits. Cattle, sheep, and horse ranching, underway since the first settlers arrived, expanded greatly during the

1860s. Lumber, too, was in demand for homes and businesses in booming communities during this exuberant phase in Oregon's youth. Small sawmills, a longtime fixture in many communities, expanded to serve a huge timber industry that came into its own around 1870. Cutters extended their logging operations farther from towns, certain that the supply would never end, so limitless seemed the vast old-growth forests at that time.

The final Indian wars

In 1877 and 1878, two final battles erupted between Indians and whites. The first occurred when the government ordered Chief Joseph's Nez Perce band to leave their ancestral home in the Wallowa Valley and relocate on a reservation in Idaho. When a few young, impetuous braves rebelled by killing some white settlers, all the Nez Perce from the area were drawn into an ongoing series of battles with the U.S. Army as they fled eastward for 1,300 miles. They finally surrendered in Montana on October 5, 1877.

A second uprising, the Bannock War of 1878, came about when the government opened an important food-gathering area on the Bannock reservation in southern Idaho to white settlement. Enlisting the aid of the Paiutes in Southeastern Oregon, the large band of Indians moved north through the John Day country, killing whites. The war lost its momentum, however, when other tribes along the Columbia River refused to join the Bannocks and Paiutes. When a group of Umatilla Indians sided with the white army and killed one of the Paiute chiefs, the war came to an end.

Chief Joseph, 1903. Photo: Edward S. Curtis

Chief Joseph and his "Land of Winding Waters"

Visitors to the Wallowa Valley will readily see why Chief Joseph struggled so valiantly to keep this beautiful place for his people. However, because of the famous series of Nez Perce battles that occurred when unfortunate events eventually forced them from their ancestral Wallowa homelands, it is often assumed that Joseph was an aggressive warrior chief. Nothing could be further from the truth.

He was born in 1840 in a canyon just north of the mountain valley that the Indians called the Land of Winding Waters, named for the meandering watercourses that flow through the wide, grassy flats there. His Nez Perce name, Hin-mah-too-yah-lah-ket, means "Thunder Rolling in the Mountains." Tu-eka-kas, chief of the Wallowa band of Nez Perce, was his father. But the first white settlers in the valley called the father Old Chief Joseph, so they naturally referred to his son as Young Joseph.

When Young Joseph was thirty-one years old, his father died, leaving him with these final words of counsel: "A few years more and white men will be all around you. They have their eyes on this land. My son, never forget my dying words. This country holds your father's body. Never sell the bones of your mother and father." Joseph, now the chief, was later to say, "I pressed my father's hand and told him I would protect his grave with my life. . . . I buried him in that beautiful val-

Chief Joseph's "Land of Winding Waters," the Wallowa Valley. Photo: David Jensen

ley of the winding waters. I love that land more than all the rest of the world."

For centuries, Joseph's people had fished, hunted, gathered useful plants, and camped in the Wallowa area. They spent summers in the high, cool valley at the base of the snowy, white granite peaks and retreated to warmer, lower canyons along the nearby Snake River during winter. The valley's stunning jewel was a large blue lake nestled in a glacial trough at the foot of the towering mountains. In summer, Joseph's people constructed willow-pole fish traps across the lake's outlet to capture salmon swimming upstream. The tripod of poles that supported each end of the trap was called a wallowa, hence the Nez Perce name for the lake.

After Europeans brought cattle and horses to North America, the Nez Perce acquired herds of these domesticated animals. They quickly became expert horsemen and de-

veloped their own unique breed, the Appaloosa, with its distinctive speckled markings. Horses allowed them to make long journeys east, beyond the Rocky Mountains, to hunt buffalo and trade with plains tribes.

The Nez Perce people were proud that none of their tribe had ever killed a white man or woman. They had aided the Lewis and Clark expedition in 1805 and had befriended all other whites traveling through their country. For many years the Wallowa Valley's remote location sheltered these Indians from the negative aspects of white settlement, such as new diseases, liquor, and usurpation of their lands. The Wallowa band of Nez Perce continued to maintain their traditional lifestyle.

Settlers began pressuring other Nez Perce bands in Washington and Idaho for their lands and, in 1863, the government requested the entire Nez Perce tribe to give up their homelands and move to a reservation in

Idaho. Although some Nez Perce leaders in more settled areas acquiesced and took their people to the reservation, Chief Joseph the Elder, as he has come to be known, and the leaders of several nearby bands in this remote area refused. They called the peace treaty a "thief treaty" and refused to sign away their heritage.

However, by 1871, when the elder Chief Joseph died, the new young chief faced the first white settlers moving into the valley. Again, the government requested that the Indians relocate to the Idaho reservation, but Joseph refused and moved his people instead to a less-settled section of the valley to avoid conflicts with their new neighbors.

Unscrupulous white ranchers often claimed unbranded Indian cattle as their own, but Joseph overlooked these injustices to maintain peace. Even when two ranchers murdered a young Nez Perce, claiming he had stolen their horses, Joseph calmed his people.

Nevertheless, settlers feared the Nez Perce and asked for military protection. Army troops dispatched to the Wallowa Valley in May of 1877 ordered all non-treaty bands of Nez Perce to move to the Idaho reservation. With sad hearts, the Indians left their homeland, meeting other neighboring Nez Perce bands across the Snake River in Idaho. Unfortunately, before Joseph's people could continue to the reservation, hotheaded young men from one of the other bands left the encampment without the knowledge of their chiefs and went on a rampage, killing a number of whites. Army troops rushed to the area and the peace-loving, diplomatic Joseph and his people were unwillingly drawn into war. A four-month-long series of skirmishes progressed through 1,300 miles of rugged, mountainous country. The long ordeal ended with the Nez Perce surrendering during a freezing October snowstorm on a bloody battlefield in Montana. It was there that Joseph spoke his famous words: "My heart is sick and sad. From where the sun now stands, I will fight no more forever."

Joseph and his people never returned to live in their beloved mountain valley. The dispossessed Indians were restricted to reservations, first in Oklahoma and, later, in Washington and Idaho. Joseph was allowed to make one brief visit to the Wallowa Valley in 1900 to visit his father's grave. While there, he asked the local whites to give the Nez Perce a small amount of land where they could live and build a school. The whites refused.

During a visit to Washington, D.C., to tell officials of his people's grievances, the patriarch eloquently presented his point of view:

> If the white man wants to live in peace with the Indian, he can live in peace. There need be no trouble. Treat all men alike. Give them all the same law. Give them all an even chance to live and grow. All men were made by the Great Spirit Chief. They are all brothers. The earth is the mother of all people and all people should have equal rights upon it.

Chief Joseph died on September 21, 1904, on the Colville Reservation in eastern Washington. ▪

Lumber and agriculture prosper

The 1880s brought a new form of transportation to Northeastern Oregon. With the construction of railroad lines east of the Cascade Range, the region was opened to the "great iron horse," as train engines were commonly referred to during this era. Two rail systems, one from Western Oregon and one from the east, finally connected at Huntington on the

An engineer stokes the fires of a restored classic steam locomotive at the Sumpter Valley Railroad's McEwen Station. During the late 1800s and early 1900s, Sumpter trains transported logs and other cargo from the Greenhorn and Elkhorn ranges to Baker City.

Snake River on November 24, 1884, linking Portland with the East Coast of America by rail. Many communities along the railroads became shipping centers and prospered; others that were bypassed often lost population or disappeared completely.

The stimulus of railroad connections with the outside world boosted agriculture and the lumber industry enormously, just as the gold rush period waned and many mines began to play out. Wheat soon became the leading crop of the Columbia plateau country. Not only did rail exports greatly expand marketing potential, but also revolutionary farm machinery could cultivate the soil, seed, harvest, and thresh, magnifying the productive potential of farms. These amazing machines, first pulled by horses or mules, soon were powered by another innovation, the gasoline engine.

The wild days of the Old West drew to a close in Northeastern Oregon. Trains from the east brought a new wave of emigrants and even remote areas like the isolated Wallowa Valley were settled. With the Nez Perce Indians relocated to Washington and Idaho, the white communities of Joseph and Enterprise were growing. After a brief economic downturn in the 1890s, Northeastern Oregon entered the twentieth century with renewed prosperity: World War I in 1914 spurred demand for lumber, and by 1930 all of Oregon's modern railroad lines were in place and an increasing number of automobiles were creating a demand for improved roads.

The 1940s and 1950s saw a network of modern highways begin to probe the state's backcountry areas. Indian trails up forested ravines, where moccasin-clad feet once stalked deer, now were traced by the paved pathways of an automated age. The Oregon Trail had become Interstate 84. This once remote, seemingly untamable region of soaring mountains and deep canyons was no longer a pristine wilderness.

Bustling Main Street in Baker City, circa 1910, during a period of prosperity in Northeastern Oregon. Courtesy of Baker County Library

Buffalo Bill and Indians from his famous Wild West Show visit Baker City, 1914.
Courtesy of Baker County Library

Land of Gold-Bearing Mountains and Golden Wheat

*Climb the mountains and get their good tidings. Nature's
peace will flow into you as sunshine flows into trees. The
winds will blow their freshness into you, and the storms
their energy, while cares will drop off like autumn leaves.*

JOHN MUIR, *Our National Parks*, 1901

The stifling summer heat of the low-elevation Columbia Basin
tempts visitors to accept John Muir's invitation to climb the
mountains and flee eastward to the cooler, forested heights of
the Blue Mountains that beckon on the green horizon. Northeastern Oregon is mostly mountains, many soaring to above
timberline. However, this wide, open wheat country beckons,
too, with explorations on I-84's side roads into patchwork fields
and quiet farming communities.

From a speeding car, the view from Interstate 84 seems
a golden blur. Fields of ripe, yellow wheat mount the rolling
Columbia Basin hills to the blue skyline. Heat waves of the
midday summer sun keep the distance out of focus. Billow-
ing clouds of wheat dust follow huge harvesting machines as
they crawl back and forth across the croplands. Dust devils
spin through cut fields, vacuuming large columns of straw and
chaff high above the baking countryside.

The broad, modern roadway of I-84 cuts east–west along the
Columbia River through the Oregon Wheat Belt. It also follows the Old Oregon Trail. To emigrants crossing as quickly

Farmlands near Summerville,
in the Grande Ronde Valley

Contrasting opposites: the lowland wheat country and the cool-aired heights of Northeastern Oregon's many mountain ranges. Wheat harvest near Condon (top); Mirror Lake in the Eagle Cap Wilderness of the Wallowa Mountains (above)

Land generating both food and electrical energy, near Condon

as their slow wagons allowed, the dry, open Columbia plains of the 1800s appeared lifeless and harbored potentially hostile Indians. Now irrigation and proper dryland farming methods have transformed a seemingly sterile environment into the state's breadbasket. The rich glacial deposits of loess silt soils in the Palouse Hills northeast of Pendleton produce bumper crops of fruits and vegetables. The Columbia Basin also grows famous Hermiston watermelons, a refreshing delight after a long, hot harvest workday in August.

The region's smaller settlements usually consist of at least a grocery store–gas station combination, and perhaps a school, a grange hall, a church, and some homes. Reflecting the local economy, a large grain elevator may dwarf the cluster of structures below it. The history of the Oregon Trail and of the first Columbia Basin settlers comes alive in the small museums many of these towns contain. Having a meal in a hometown café alongside the locals may acquaint visitors with the flavor and personality of the land and its people.

The wheat heartland

When you see a huge grain elevator below the freeway, crowding the Columbia River edge and sporting a sign saying "Arlington," take the exit onto Highway 19. It leads due south into the heartland of wheat country through treeless, rolling terrain. For long distances you'll drive across flat plateau tops until reaching a previously unseen brink. Then the road will suddenly wind down into the head of a stream canyon (probably dry in August), a green riparian zone of black hawthorn snaking along the creek bottom. The route spans a small bridge and climbs the other side of the ravine, and it's back to traversing the open levels again. Perhaps another harvest crew will be seen, two trucks waiting to be filled with golden grain when the combine swings in from the field. After 38 miles of agricultural expanses, with the occasional repeated dip into a stream drainage, the startling forms of enormous windmills sprout from fields southwest of the highway—all eighty-three of them. This wind farm was completed in 2002 and does an admirable job of double-tasking the land. Not only do the surrounding fields produce wheat crops, they now generate environmentally clean power to the area as well. Just beyond these rather futuristic-looking structures, which stand like alien sentinels along the hillcrests, is the contrastingly old-fashioned town of Condon.

It would be easy to just cruise on through this seemingly fading little community of nearly eight hundred souls, but looks can be deceiving. There's more going on here than first meets the eye. For instance, there's the nice old brick, three-story building on the east side of the main street. That's Hotel Condon, dating from 1920 and now completely restored to its former elegance by a group of Condonites who raised the needed funds. Local craftspeople donated their time and expertise, and following three years of renovation, the hotel reopened in 2001. After many years of neglect, luxurious guest rooms and suites are again available, along with fine cuisine in the dining hall. If you're in the mood for entertainment, next door is the historic, completely restored Liberty Theatre, which shows first-run movies. Stroll across the street to the mercantile and have a treat at their soda fountain or browse the boutique. In the rear is another surprise: an eastern outpost of Portland's world-renowned Powell's Books, but greatly scaled down to small-town size. Condon is becoming reinvigorated. To learn something of the past glory days of the area

visit the Gilliam County Museum, located in the old 1905 train depot. During the 1920s, Condon was a bustling railroad shipping hub for local farms. The village welcomed many road-weary, dusty travelers who lodged and dined at the hotel.

Launching eastward, Highway 206 crosses mile after mile of more undulating wheatlands until the road meanders into the town of Heppner. You'll notice green shamrocks throughout the city, reflecting the ancestral family pride of the area's many pioneer Irish farmers and ranchers. Tragedy is also part of this community's past history. In 1903, after an enormous June cloudburst, a forty-foot-high wall of floodwater swept down Willow Creek through the center of town, killing nearly 250 people. The Morrow County Museum, by the city park, tells of these events, along with displaying one of the finest collections of homesteader memorabilia in the Northwest. Continuing east on Highway 74, and later connecting with U.S. 395, the route passes through the community of Pilot Rock. This town's name comes from an adjacent basalt prominence that served as a landmark for pioneers on the nearby Oregon Trail. After Pilot Rock, U.S. 395 swings north for 14 miles and reconnects you with I-84 in the city of Pendleton.

Pendleton

With a population of more than sixteen thousand, this is the largest city in Northeastern Oregon. Spending some time exploring the downtown streets will quickly show that, besides wheat farming and wool production, cattle ranching is a major segment of the local economy and culture. Cowboy hats and boots are much in evidence. The Pendleton Chamber of Commerce promotes such slogans as,

Pendleton, situated amid rolling agricultural lands, is the largest city in Northeastern Oregon, but up close it still exudes an Old West flavor. Photo: David Jensen

"Not the New West, not the Old West, but the Real West." But this is not merely tourism hyperbole; Pendleton has been a classic frontier-style cow town since the 1850s. Colorful historic facts indicate that besides being the real West, Pendleton was real wild as well. The town reportedly once contained thirty-two saloons and around eighteen assorted bawdy houses. But that was just the street-level revelry. Additionally, in the late 1800s Chinese railroad workers dug a several-mile-long maze of tunnels beneath the historic district. This underground secondary town contained bordellos, saloons, opium dens, and card-gambling rooms, along with a subterranean Chinatown of living quarters, laundries, a butcher shop, and a jail. Some historians think the Chinese excavated this alternate neighborhood to separate themselves from the persecution they received on the streets of rough and tough Old Pendleton. Entertaining tours of this netherworld are conducted, complete with actors in period costumes. More insight into the region's history is available at the Heritage Station, an old train depot that houses the exhibits of the Umatilla County Historical Society, including a one-room schoolhouse, caboose, and homestead.

The cowboy persona dominates the town during four days every September when the nationally famous rodeo, the Pendleton Round-up, takes place. Dating from 1910, it attracts hundreds of cowboys, including some of the nation's top rodeo stars. Native American Indians from the nearby Umatilla Indian Reservation and other visiting tribes participate in the celebrations by performing traditional ceremonial dances. Other related festivities include a parade, cowboy breakfasts and barbecues, concerts, dances, and art shows. The Round-up Hall of Fame, located under the south grandstands, features Pendleton Round-up history as well as exhibits about buckaroo and Native American culture.

There's more to Pendleton than the rip-roaring Old West, though. In the downtown area are many art galleries and antique stores, and the Pendleton Center for the Arts features the work of local artists. The 800-seat Vert Auditorium hosts concerts by the Oregon East Symphony, and on a hillside overlooking the town is the campus of Blue Mountain Community College.

Besides farming and ranching, the Columbia Basin is also sheep country. The famed Pendleton Woolen Mills, producer of fine blankets, shirts, sweaters, and other products, got its start in 1909. The company originally produced blankets and robes for Native Americans; the colorful patterns were based on tribal designs from throughout the Northwest and Southwest. These soon became highly prized for basic wearing apparel, trading, and ceremonial use. In 1924, the company also began production of shirts. Until that time, the only wool shirts available on the market for outdoorsmen were rather drab.

However, the Pendleton shirts borrowed their colorful designs from the Indian blankets and became immediately popular, remaining so until present day. Now the Pendleton Woolen Mills name is synonymous with the Pacific Northwest region. Tours of the facility are available on weekdays.

Just east of Pendleton, off I-84, the Confederated Tribes of the Umatilla operate two facilities. One is the Wildhorse Resort and Casino, which besides gambling offers a hotel, restaurant, RV park, and Scottish links-style golf. Nearby is their excellent Tamastslikt Cultural Institute, with museum displays that trace their tribe's history from many hundreds of years in the past to the present. A store sells Native American art, crafts, apparel, music, and books; and a café serves soup, sandwiches, salads, and pastries. This museum is refreshingly unique in offering a chronicle of not only their own tribal heritage but also in giving the Native American perspective on the impact of Euro-American western migrations on their culture and lives.

During the Lewis and Clark Bicentennial celebrations, the institute's director, Roberta "Bobbie" Conner, clarified her people's point of view: "There is little that is celebratory about the expedition from the Native perspective. It is in fact the case that the Lewis and Clark Expedition is the harbinger of all adverse change that will come subsequent to the mapping and charting of our homeland."

For those inclined toward birdwatching, three wildlife sanctuaries nestled within the farmlands attract a rich variety of bird life: the Umatilla National Wildlife Refuge along the Columbia River, between Boardman and Umatilla; the Cold Springs National Wildlife Refuge east of Hermiston; and the McKay Creek National Wildlife Refuge just south of Pendleton. Although there's good birding at these preserves just about any season, all three areas are particularly noted as wintering places for waterfowl; and migration times bring many thousands of geese, ducks, and swans. During warm weather, hike the refuge trails that skirt the shorelines and watch for sunning painted turtles. Through binoculars, you'll see the attractive red markings on their shell undersides (plastron) and yellow stripings on their legs and necks. Watch your step; prickly pear cactus are common in the area.

Just southeast of Pendleton, I-84 ascends to the top of the Blue Mountains on Deadman Pass over Emigrant Hill where an incredible view to the west across the Columbia Basin unfolds at an overlook turnout. An even more interesting and scenic alternative is to drive the parallel Emigrant Hill Road (take the Mission exit north off I-84, just east of Pendleton), which for 36 miles closely follows the route of the Oregon Trail before reconnecting with the Interstate. An emigrant on the Oregon Trail, describing this spot in his journal, wrote, "The sight from this mountain top is one to be remembered while life lasts. It affects me as did my first sight of the ocean . . . from this point north and south there are no bounds in sight." When pioneers crossed this pass, they tied logs behind their covered wagons to slow their descents down the steep slope.

The Grande Ronde Valley

Interstate 84 continues east for 50 miles through pine and fir forests until it suddenly emerges from a canyon into a wide, oval basin surrounded by mountains. The initial impression is of a timber-bordered, great green bowl. This is the Grande Ronde Valley, where the highway immediately enters the city of La Grande. With a population of 12,600, it serves

Morning sunbeams flood the Grande Ronde Valley. Photo: David Jensen

as the cultural center for the intermountain region of Northeastern Oregon. The presence of Eastern Oregon University, established in 1929 (initially as a college for women studying to be teachers), invigorates the intellectual life of La Grande. A good example is the university's Community Concert Series, which "showcases local, regional, and international talent in an effort to bring diverse musical presentations to the region."

An interesting mix of the modern and the old permeates the downtown section, where up-to-date buildings stand side by side with brick and stone structures out of the nineteenth century. It's easy to imagine miners, trappers, ranchers, and farmers coming to town via horses and wagons to do business in stores that fronted dirt streets. The arrival of the railroad in 1884 made La Grande the area's prime trade center. The train station, yards, and roundhouse, busy with trains coming and going, still functions as an integral part of the community. Besides agriculture, logging is a part of the local economy and a

large lumber mill at the eastern edge of town has been a longtime part of La Grande. The historic downtown brick buildings now house an assortment of retail shops, galleries, and restaurants (three are listed in the guidebook *Northwest Best Places*).

A walk through the university's 215-acre campus, perched on the wooded slope of a west-side neighborhood, provides vantage points from which to see the lay of the land below. The grounds of Eastern Oregon University are quite lovely, with green lawns and many shading maples. In autumn, the reds and yellows of these trees complement the pale stucco walls and red tile roofs of the classic Mediterranean-style architecture of the campus. While strolling the university sidewalks, be sure to see the interpretive exhibit marking where the Oregon Trail passed along the hillside to avoid marshy areas on the valley floor. Through openings in the campus trees, views to the east encompass the city below and the patchwork farmlands of the broad valley floor that extend to the foothills of the snowcapped Wallowa Mountains. The Grande Ronde River can be seen meandering north through the miles of green, irrigated crops; and Mount Emily, at 6,000 feet in height, dominates the northern horizon.

Nestled along the Wallowa foothills at the eastern edge of the valley are two small communities that are well worth visiting. Cove, as its name suggests, is tucked into a pocket where Mill Creek flows out of the mountains into the valley. The small community of six hundred people is located 17 miles east of La Grande on Highway 237. This sheltered area is considered by locals to be favored with a "banana belt" microclimate that produces some of the best fruit crops in the region. It also boasts the only winery in Eastern Oregon. The grape rows of the Gilstrap Brothers Winery can be seen on a hillside above the town, where wine tasting and tours are available on Saturdays during the summer months. Another treat to be sampled is the Cove Hot Springs Pool, where you can swim and soak in warm waters that well up from thermal springs through a rock fissure. A Cove must-see is the beautifully maintained small Ascension Chapel, built in 1869. The picturesque white church features a bright red door and a stained-glass window that was brought by sailing ship from the East, "around the Horn" of South America.

Eight miles farther south along Highway 237 is the other small community. Driving into Union, population two thousand, is like entering an Americana time warp. There's an impression of returning to the 1920s as you pass stately Victorian-style homes and the grand red-brick Union Hotel; then comes the Union Carnegie Public Library and on through the downtown area's collection of vintage brick buildings. But this isn't a community drifting toward ghost-town sta-

Autumn on the Eastern Oregon University campus, La Grande

High school football game in Cove

The 1869 Ascension Chapel in Cove

Driving down Union's Main Street is like taking a trip back to the 1920s.

Railroad depot for the Hot Lake Sanitarium, circa 1920s. Courtesy of Baker County Library

tus. Nearly every building contains a business—grocery, drugstore, hardware, banks, cafés, barbershop, lumberyard—and all of them local, mom-and-pop owned. Travelers are checking in at the hotel. The town readily brings to mind fictional Mayberry, North Carolina, of the classic 1960s television series *The Andy Griffith Show*. And glancing in the window of the barbershop, you do a double take because the gentleman getting a haircut resembles Sheriff Andy Taylor.

Union and its hotel are a good example of what has happened since the 1920s to many small American towns. Originally Highway 237, Union's Main Street, was also the primary route between Boise and Portland. In 1921, when the Union Hotel opened its doors, people traveled in slower-moving autos that leaked dust. After hours of driving, travelers arrived in town tired, grimy, and hungry. The new hotel and other businesses prospered. Then the Great Depression struck, and later the age of modern, high-speed autos arrived, complete with freeways. Interstate 84 was constructed 14 miles to the west, bypassing Union, and the town began to wither. Now, however, more and more people are getting out of the fast lane, desiring to live in smaller, quieter towns that provide a sense of community for families. Reflecting this trend, many villages like Union are gradually becoming revitalized. The commercial area has been granted National Historic District status, and the city is working with the businesses there to restore the downtown buildings. In 1996 the Union Hotel was purchased by folks who discerned its potential—and the vacant, run-down structure was completely refurbished to its former elegance. The hotel's restaurant serves breakfast, lunch, and dinner, with a brunch on Sundays. Each guest room has a theme, including one named the Clark Gable Room and another called the Annie Oakley Suite. Reportedly, these famous people stayed at the Union Hotel during its heyday. To learn more about the local history, visit the Union County Museum. Located on Main Street, it has exhibits pertaining to the pioneer settlement of the area, along with an excellent section titled "Cowboys Then and Now."

About 6 miles northwest of Union, along Highway 203, another renovation is underway. This is a major, long-range project to resurrect the huge, brick Hot Lake Resort, which had fallen into terrible disrepair. Renowned Wallowa Valley artist and sculptor David Manuel and his wife, Lee, acquired the property in 2003 and are progressively transforming it into an art museum, art gallery, foundry, hotel, day spa, restaurant, bed-and-breakfast, art school, and gift shop. Standing beside the steaming lake, the 1908 three-story, 105-room hotel-and-health sanitarium–hospital combination was referred to as the Mayo Clinic of the West. The resort became world famous under the direction of Dr. W. T. Phy, a friend of the Mayo brothers, who both frequently visited Hot Lake. At its peak of success, between 1924 and 1932, the facility often hosted the arrival of more than a hundred guests per day, many coming by train via the Union Pacific Railroad Transcontinental line that ran through the grounds. A surgical ward contained sixty beds, and X-ray radiation treatments, considered innovative at the time, were given to patients. However, bathing in the lake's hot waters and applying poultices composed of sediments from the lake bottom were the featured treatments.

With the coming of the Depression years and extensive damage from a large fire in 1934, the Hot Lake Sanitarium fell into decline and was finally closed. For untold hundreds of years Native Americans of several regional tribes came to this enormous geothermal pool to amicably bathe. Many were avowed enemies in other settings, but this was Cop Copi, the Valley of Peace. The first white explorers and trappers discovered the warm waters of this lush, green basin and were camping here in the early 1800s. By the 1840s, emigrants on the nearby Oregon Trail were routinely stopping at Hot Lake to rest and refresh themselves. With the reopening

of the rejuvenated resort, the procession of visitors resumes.

Just to the west of Hot Lake is Ladd Marsh Wildlife Area, managed by the Oregon Department of Fish and Wildlife. This wetland was enlarged to over four thousand acres in 2004 when The Nature Conservancy and Ducks Unlimited donated 136 adjoining acres to the state. Hot Lake feeds into this new section, providing unfrozen, open waters for winter waterfowl. During spring migration twenty thousand ducks and geese are often present at Ladd Marsh, and the area is also a nesting ground for sandhill cranes and bobolinks. An observation-photography blind is provided off Highway 203, and a viewpoint and nature trail can be accessed along Foothill Road. When you're at Ladd Marsh looking out across the dense tules, consider that this is only a small portion of the wetlands that originally extended throughout most of the Grande Ronde Valley. These waters, remnants of a Pleistocene lake that once existed in the basin, were channeled away during the 1800s and the lands converted to farming.

Another interesting historical stop is 12 miles west of La Grande along I-84. This is the Blue Mountain Crossing Interpretive Park, which brings to life the struggles of the Oregon Trail. Graphic signboards along a paved, wheelchair-friendly trail guide visitors through old-growth conifers to some of the state's most well-preserved Oregon Trail wheel ruts. On summer weekends and holidays, "living history characters"—actors in pioneer dress—perform daily camping chores by their covered wagon to demonstrate what life was like on the trail. The journals of these settlers indicate that they considered this crossing of the Blue Mountains to be the most difficult section of the entire 2,000-mile trek.

Another exhibit shows a frontier-era logging operation. The park has a picnic area, restrooms, and drinking water.

Taking Highway 82 northeast from La Grande leads 20 miles through the valley, passing through the village of Imbler, over a rise, and down to Elgin, population 1,700. Close to vast timberlands, this is a classic mill town—among the few remaining in the state. Immediately upon entering the southern city limits, you'll see the log piles and stacks of lumber, and catch the scent of fresh-cut pine in the air. The cultural center is the restored 1912 Elgin Opera House, where first-run movies are shown daily, plays are performed, and a variety of community events take place. The Colonial-style building is listed on the National Historic Register and is noted for its excellent acoustics. Elgin sits in a beautiful basin where Indian Creek flows into the Grande Ronde River. The area is known as Indian Valley, and many generations of Nez Perce camped in this location, calling the spot Lochow Lochow—"Lovely Little Forest." Now it's a gathering place for river rafters to launch float trips down the Grande Ronde. Every June the Elgin Riverfest takes place, with model boat races and a Ride-Run-Raft Triathlon.

Elgin is also a departure point for the Eagle Cap Excursion Train, which operates on the historic Wallowa Union Railroad Line. Scenic rides of various lengths, complete with meals, travel through spectacular canyons to the Wallowa Valley. To reach this famed valley by road, continue east 45 miles on Highway 82. The route first crosses Minam Hill, quickly descends into the Minam River Canyon, and then gradually climbs up the Wallowa River Canyon from the confluence of the two watercourses.

The Wallowa Valley

After a few miles, the road breaks free of confining stone walls and enters an expansive landscape of green meadows, cottonwoods, and aspen groves. Lofty, snow-clad mountains soar abruptly upward on the south, whereas grassland plateaus gently rise to meet the northern skyline. Highway 82 progresses southeast across the mostly level valley floor, where the Wallowa River meanders in languid loops—the Land of Winding Waters, as the Nez Perce Indians call their ancestral home.

Although towns and farmlands linked by modern paved roads now replace Native American tipi villages and Appaloosa horse trails, nature still takes center stage. Few locations in the Northwest exceed the Wallowa Valley for scenic grandeur. However, for those driving up the valley, the crown jewel is saved for last. Topping the crest of a small ridge, just beyond the edge of the town of Joseph, visitors suddenly see the entirety of Wallowa Lake. This five-mile-long body of water lies in a gigantic, glacially excavated furrow that extends back into the mouth of a large canyon in the mountains. The ridge that provides this initial, almost startling view is actually the terminal moraine deposited by a Pleistocene glacier, creating a natural dam.

On this gentle rise of ground, just off the roadside, is the grave of Chief Joseph the Elder. It's a simple stone monument and plaque, situated to overlook the lake and mountains this man loved so dearly. Here in the quiet of this place, the poignancy of what the Nez Perce lost is readily apparent. At a 1997 ceremony on the rim of Joseph Canyon, where lands have been returned to the fractured and dispersed tribe, Agnes Andrews Davis gave testimony with a trembling voice.

Farmlands in the Wallowa Valley

Wallowa Lake

She reflected upon memories of growing up on the Colville Reservation in Washington, and of her friendship with one of Young Chief Joseph's wives:

> I used to wonder as a little girl, how come she's so lonesome for someplace else? Seems like she doesn't like it where we're at. Then when I first came here with my brother Joe, I sat at that lake and I looked out and I realized why that old lady used to sit there telling stories and crying. . . . She'd cry about Wallowa, wishing she was home. She never got the chance to come here.

Clustered at the south end of the lake are rental cabins, restaurants, gift shops and other resort-style accommodations. Prominent is the classic Wallowa Lake Lodge, built in the 1920s and restored during the late 1980s. Well-known to generations of vacationers, it offers twenty-two rooms furnished in a 1920s-style lodge decor, along with eight adjacent cabins. Overstuffed chairs by the stone fireplace provide lake views out the lobby windows, and the dining hall serves breakfasts and dinners. A popular large state park has both picnicking and camping areas (with showers) and tame mule deer and red squirrels. This resort village is situated at the base of the mountains where the Wallowa River flows into the lake. Watch the huge, old cottonwood trees at the river's mouth, where bald eagles and osprey are often seen. At the end of Highway 82, trails lead off into the Eagle Cap Wilderness, and during summer it's common to see entire families or scout groups hoisting backpacks in readiness for a trek into the backcountry. Commercially operated horse-packing stations are situated here, and a llama-trekking business in nearby Halfway offers guided wilderness tours.

The High Wallowas

If you lack the time or stamina for these more strenuous explorations, there's the Wallowa Lake Tramway lift, which carries passengers in enclosed gondolas to the 8,256-foot alpine summit of Mount Howard. This Swiss-made tram has the steepest lift of any four-passenger gondola in North America (open June through September). At the top, the views are nothing short of spectacular, giving an eagle-eye perspective into the adjacent high peaks of the wilderness area. From this height, it can be clearly seen why geologists consider Wallowa Lake to be a textbook-perfect example of a glacial moraine lake. It appears to be a gargantuan furrow, gouged out by the heel of a giant and filled with water—which, glacially speaking, is more or less what it is. There are 2.5 miles of trails leading from the tramway terminus, with the highest summit point affording a panorama of neighboring Idaho and Washington, and reportedly on clear days, distant peaks in Montana. If the fresh mountain air stimulates your appetite, there's the Summit Grill and Alpine Patio—at 8,150 feet, the highest restaurant in the Northwest region. If it's a sunny day, sit at one of the outdoor tables and savor both the view and one of the grill's gourmet hamburgers, deli sandwiches, tacos, or burritos.

While munching, doing some scenery gazing toward the south and west will disclose the vast alpine realm of the Eagle Cap Wilderness. Comprising more than 360,000 acres and 500 miles of trail, this is the largest wilderness area in the state. This well-maintained network of paths winds through wildflower-sprinkled meadows, penetrates deep, shadowy forests, follows rushing streams, climbs awesome gorges, and crosses high passes above timberline that offer top-of-the-world views. Cradled among the peaks at the heart of the wilderness, the Lake Basin contains a collection of subalpine, sky blue lakes.

The Wallowa Mountains differ from all the other high ranges of Oregon. When viewed from high above in an airplane, the outer perimeters are seen to form a giant oval, with 9,595-foot Eagle Cap Peak rising from the center like the hub of a stupendous wheel. Radiating all directions from this alpine crest are the main watercourses of the range: Wallowa River, Sheep Creek, Imnaha River, Pine Creek, Eagle Creek, Catherine Creek, Minam River, Lostine River, and Hurricane Creek. Other prominent peaks of the Wallowas, all ranging between 9,000 and 10,000 feet in height, include the Matterhorn, Aneroid Mountain, and Petes Point. During the Ice Age, glaciers covered the entire range and carved steep-walled canyons, knife-edged ridges, hanging cirque valleys, and hornlike peaks and rounded knobs. The Wallowas, being more or less a western extension of the Northern Rockies, have many characteristics of that range, both geologically and floristically. Nevertheless, there are visual qualities reminiscent of California's Sierra Nevada Range as well—glacially sculpted, dome-shaped mountaintops and an abundance of polished white granite outcroppings and boulders. Hollywood noticed this Sierran resemblance in 1967 when East Eagle Creek served as the location to film the musical *Paint Your Wagon*, which supposedly takes place in the California gold fields of the 1800s.

Because of the attractive qualities of the Eagle Cap Wilderness, hundreds of people visit the popular Lake Basin each year. As a result, many prime camping locations are showing wear and tear, some of the lakes have become slightly polluted, and "traffic jams" between backpackers and commercial horse-packing caravans occasionally occur on nar-

The Eagle Cap Wilderness in the Wallowa Mountains is one of the most heavily used recreation areas in the state. This backpacker is hiking the popular East Fork Lostine River Trail.

Mirror Lake is nestled in a subalpine, glacially scoured basin below the 9,595-foot granite dome of Eagle Cap.

row sections of trail. To help protect these fragile places, the Forest Service requires that all camps be at least two hundred feet from lakes. The limitations are even more stringent at some of the higher-elevation lakes that have been impacted by overuse, where the minimum camping distance is one-quarter mile away from the shorelines. These areas have very little remaining firewood and need time to recover. In any wilderness area, practice "leave no trace" camping tech-

West Eagle Meadow, southern Wallowa Mountains

Hikers in the Wallowas are familiar with the Columbian ground squirrel, which can be seen scurrying about throughout the wilderness, often up to quite high elevations.

Tom Ferron, a Wilderness Steward from Salem volunteering for the U.S. Forest Service in the Wallowas. He provides visitor information, checks wilderness passes, and patrols Lake Basin campgrounds—always prepared to shovel over illegal fire rings found in no-camping zones.

niques: build small fires (or none at all—enjoy the stars instead), scatter and cover your fire ring before leaving, pack out all garbage, and properly bury toilet paper.

If experiencing solitude is your goal, get a good map and find trails and camping spots in the less-used sections of the wilderness. The nearest Forest Service office will give you good advice. Most people enter the wilderness at trailheads leading from the Wallowa Val-ley area; the southern and eastern sides of the range receive much less use. A free wilderness permit is required, obtained at a self-service box provided at each trailhead. Be aware, too, that before leaving your auto to stride off into the wilds, you may have to purchase a parking permit at some sites (likewise, there's a self-service box on site), or leave an in-car-visible annual Forest Pass or other valid recreation pass.

◆ TRAILPOST
Lostine Meadows

The East Fork Lostine River Trail offers an excellent family day-hike into the Eagle Cap Wilderness that most children can successfully undertake. In slightly less than three miles, it takes you to the subalpine zone of the high Wallowas, and offers numerous delightful picnicking spots in the green, wildflower-filled Lostine Meadows. The river—creek-like at this elevation—mean-ders through this long, grassy-floored glacial trough, with stunning views of the white granite summit of Eagle Cap.

Begin your outing at Two Pan Trailhead (wilderness and parking permits required), which is reached by driv-ing 18 miles up the Lostine River Road, south from the town of Lostine. The trail as-cends a series of switchbacks through shady coniferous for-ests along the river and, with a final cresting, levels out as the route enters the sunny mead-ows. Depending upon your available time, hiking ability, and inclination, your explo-rations can include the entire two-mile section of trail that continues on through the Los-tine Meadows. For a more ex-tensive trip, shoulder a back-pack outfitted with camping gear and proceed farther into the heart of the wilderness for a few days—Mirror Lake and the Lake Basin are only about two miles up a set of switchbacks beyond the end of the mead-ows. During the summer vaca-tion months, this trail is often crowded with other day-hikers, backpackers, and horse-pack-ers, so don't expect to experi-ence solitude here. By Sep-tember and early October the crowds thin out considerably, so you may want to plan an au-tumn visit.

A packer pauses to water her horses in one of the series of meadows along the East Lostine River, Eagle Cap Wilderness.

Wallowa Valley towns

Descending from the gondola lift and backtracking north on Highway 82 returns you to the small town of Joseph (population 1,000). An historic frontier motif along the main street attracts vacationers and outdoor recreationists to the several galleries, espresso shops, ice cream parlors, fly-fishing stores, boutique gift shops, a bookstore, and motels, along with the more traditional small-town convenience store, cafés, and gas station. Tourism boosters tout the area as the "Switzerland of America" and "Oregon's Alps." One journalist humorously described the Wallowa Lake–Joseph district as a mixture of *The Sound of Music* and the old TV Western series *Gunsmoke*. Despite the summer crowds these enticements bring, Joseph still prefers maintaining its relaxed pace, a sign at the city limits proclaiming, "This little town is heaven to us. Don't drive like hell through it."

The Wallowa Valley has become well known for being a flourishing center of bronze statue casting, which supports three foundries. Examples of local artists' works can be viewed along Joseph's Main Street, ranging from bronzes of Nez Perce Indians and cowboys to eagles and horses. Glenn Anderson and artist David Manuel opened the area's first foundry, Valley Bronze, in 1982. Following on the heels of their success, other entrepreneurs established Joseph Bronze, and the Enterprise art scene soon had the addition of Park Bronze. This art form has become a thriving local industry, and laid-off loggers and cowboys now work as polishers, weld statue parts, and are involved in the processing of plaster and wax models required in bronze casting. Reflecting this cultural shift, Joseph's annual events now include both the Chief Joseph Days Rodeo (late July) and the Bronze, Blues, and Brews Fest (mid-August). Prearranged tours of the foundries are available.

Enterprise, 6 miles to the northwest and more removed from the resort atmosphere of the lake, is a traditional Eastern Oregon community with a large stone 1910 courthouse in a central square, surrounded by retail businesses, cafés, churches, schools, motels, a supermarket, and residential neighborhoods. At the eastern edge of town, down quiet School Street, Terminal Gravity Brewing is receiving rave reviews. If this indicates a trend, the Wallowa Valley may soon become known as much for its high-quality craft beers as for bronze sculptures. The pub is tucked into a Craftsman-style bungalow alongside an aspen-bordered creek and meadow, and offers both indoor and outdoor seating. Sometimes accompanied by live music, waiters serve excellent foods, along with an India pale ale that is considered by many connoisseurs to be the finest in the state. To meet popular demand, Terminal Gravity has expanded, and its bottled brews are being shipped throughout the Northwest region. As with the bronze foundries, this successful addition to the Wallowa economy has given a significant boost to the local workforce.

Northeast of Enterprise about 10 miles, along Highway 82, is the community of Lostine, population 260. Consisting of a couple of secondhand stores, a church, and post office, at its core are two rock-solid businesses. M. Crow and Co., one of the few remaining genuine mercantiles in Oregon's dry side, sells the no-frills basic needs of a rural area: groceries, hardware, small appliances, clothing, hats, fishing gear—you name it. This general store has been owned by the Crow family since 1906. There's also the Lostine Tavern, ensconced in a stone building that dates from the town's beginnings at the turn of the last century. This establishment is authentic Eastern Oregon culture—no tourism-oriented, cappuccino-coffee ploys here. Just good, honest meals and beer. Driving through town some evening after sundown, you'll see the local worthies enjoying each other's hunting and fishing tales, gathered around tables in the warmly lit interior. If you want to soak up some friendly, native atmosphere, stop in for dinner and conversation. Although usually very quiet, on the Fourth of July the entire main street becomes a lively flea market, with booths selling antiques, crafts, and odds-and-ends. This town is also the turnoff for the Lostine River Road, which leads to campgrounds and trailheads in the Wallowa Mountains. The road up this federally designated Wild and Scenic River passes a wildlife area where bighorn sheep are frequently seen, so remain alert.

Traveling farther to the northeast 8 miles is the slightly larger town of Wallowa (population about 800), another traditional American community with locally owned stores and cafés, along with a post office, schools, and library. It's also host to a significant, long-needed cultural transformation. In July of each year, the three-day TamKaLiks Celebration (Nez Perce Friendship Feast and Pow Wow) is held northeast of town at a site along Whiskey Creek Road. After the Nez Perce people were exiled from the valley in 1877, they experienced more than a century of subsequent hostile rebuffs. But there has gradually been cross-cultural healing.

Beginning in 1989, contemporary inhabitants of European ancestry reached out to welcome descendants of the Wallowa Band of the Nez Perce back to their original homelands. A plan was initiated for acquiring land that would serve as a place to celebrate the reconciliation, and to provide their own account of

Visitors to Joseph are greeted by this humorous request to slow down when entering the laid-back community.

Valley Bronze was the first foundry to open in Joseph, launching a flourishing statue-casting art scene in the Wallowa Valley.

Nez Perce history in the Wallowa Valley. At an early meeting, Taz E. E. Conner, a relative of Chief Joseph the Elder, said:

> It is time once again to let the land hear the familiar sounds that have been developed over thousands of years here in the land of winding waters, the rhythm of the drumbeat, the songs, the language, the prayers, the people, and all creation joined to coexist and respect Mother Earth and this law of the land. . . . It has fallen upon

the shoulders of this generation to capture the history and through cultural understanding, respect this land that we live in.

Funds were raised, and the 320-acre Wallowa Homelands site along the Wallowa River now contains a permanent dance arbor and a 1.5-mile long trail to a scenic overlook on a hilltop. It has been designated as a Nez Perce National Historic Park site and trailhead for the Nez Perce (Nee-mee-poo—"we the people") National Historic Trail. Ongoing projects include construction of an interpretive center, longhouse, cooking facilities, caretaker residence, and campground. The Nez Perce word *TamKaLiks*, from which the celebration draws its name, means "From where you can see the mountains." The event regularly attracts more than 1,500 people and includes a parade, dancing, drumming, songs, speeches, potluck feast, and a tipi encampment. Jo Hallam, born and raised in the Wallowa Valley, commented, "My mother's family were 1880s pioneers here and their homestead came from the Nez Perce lands. We should honor these people, their homeland, and all that they've been through."

Canyon country of the Snake drainage

The region to the north and east of the Wallowa Valley takes in steep-sided ridges, broad, level benches, open grasslands, and forests. If you're in the Wallowa Valley during early June, be sure to take a drive north from Joseph on the gravel Zumwalt Road. This route leads through the heart of the rolling landscape of Zumwalt Prairie. Covering 200 square-miles, this is the largest remaining bunchgrass ecosystem in North America, and it is sublimely green and flower-sprin-

kled during the spring season. Also watch for hawks, eagles, and falcons. This area supports one of the largest concentrations of breeding birds of prey in North America.

As the Zumwalt Road continues northward, it gradually ascends into pine timber and onward to the Buckhorn Overlook. This is an excellent vantage point from which to see the immensity of the canyon country of the Snake River drainage. Directly below is the awesome gorge of the Imnaha River at its confluence with the even deeper Hells Canyon of the Snake. To the northwest are the canyons of other Snake tributaries—Joseph Creek and the Grande Ronde and Wenaha rivers. All of these contain substantial stretches designated as Wild and Scenic River. Here, at the verge of these breaks, everything, land and water, plunges downward to the main canyon of the Snake River—the deepest chasm in North America. This mile-deep rent in the earth's surface forms the Oregon-Idaho border and contains the Hells Canyon Wilderness. Only two communities exist within this vast district of canyonlands—the tiny outpost of Troy, located at the confluence of the Wenaha and Grande Ronde rivers, and Imnaha, along the banks of the Imnaha River.

Reaching Troy is an adventure into one of the less traveled parts of Oregon's dry side. After topping off your gas tank, turn north in Enterprise on Highway 3 and keep going due north for 34 miles. Just short of reaching the Washington state line, watch for a road sign pointing toward Troy and Flora. Turn left (west) onto this paved road and follow it through Flora, where the route turns to gravel. This community has faded away, but at the turn of the last century Flora was a boomtown with a population that exceeded the total number of people living in today's

As a spring storm clears, sunshine breaks through onto Zumwalt Prairie and a rancher's far-flung feed shed.

Wallowa County. Continuing on this 14-mile stretch of road soon brings you to the rim of the Grande Ronde Canyon, where the route steeply switchbacks downward. Be forewarned that these are precipitous, narrow turns with occasional widened turnouts to allow an oncoming auto to pass. Upon reaching the canyon bottom, the road crosses the Grande Ronde River before arriving in Troy. The minuscule community has the outpost basics: a general store, café, lodge, RV park, gas pump, bath–laundry house, and several homes and cabins. This is a hunting and fishing hub for restocking and refueling in an otherwise sparsely populated, largely roadless chunk of rough backcountry. Surprisingly, Troy has a one-teacher, one-room school; it is listed among the most remote public schools in the state.

The Grande Ronde River is noted among fishermen for its autumn steelhead run, with fish routinely weighing in at seven pounds or more. If your interests tend more toward

A fisherman casts for steelhead in the Grande Ronde River, near Troy.

Land of Gold-Bearing Mountains and Golden Wheat **279**

The Imnaha post office has been in operation since 1885.

A lone backpacker traverses the scenic Eagles Nest section of the Snake River Trail in the Hells Canyon Wilderness. Photo: David Jensen

largely untrodden places, this wild river canyon fits the bill. Watch your step, though. Rattlesnakes are very common throughout, but these fascinating reptiles are not as dangerous as is commonly believed.

Returning to Highway 3, be sure to pull off the east side of the road at the Joseph Canyon Overlook. This site provides views two thousand feet down to the canyon bottom, which was the ancestral wintering home for the Wallowa Band of the Nez Perce, and reportedly where Young Chief Joseph was born. You also may want to stop for dinner at the RimRock Inn, just a quarter-mile south of the Flora-Troy turnoff. Perched on the edge of Joseph Canyon, this refurbished roadhouse has become known as one of the finest restaurants in Northeastern Oregon (closed during the winter months). The views from their tables (both inside and outside) are dramatic. Besides offering RV spaces, RimRock Inn also rents fully equipped tipis with canyon views and doors oriented to catch the morning sun.

Back in Joseph, fill up your gas tank before heading east to Imnaha. This is the last available fuel for many miles. Highway 350 provides a good, paved route all of the 37 miles to Imnaha. This village sits in the canyon bottom at the confluence of Sheep Creek and the Imnaha River. Besides a store-tavern combination, a small elementary school, and several homes, there's also a tiny post office. Postmasters have been sorting mail in the snug interior since 1885, and the pole outside still flies the American flag to proclaim it's open for business. If you enjoy the unusual, join the festivities at the Imnaha Canyon Days Bear and Rattlesnake Feed, held on the third Saturday of every September. The event harkens back to the mountain-man trapper days of the frontier era when these rugged individualists

wildlife watching than hunting and angling, the local Wenaha Wildlife Area is a good place to see Rocky Mountain elk, mule deer, and somewhat unusual for Oregon, white-tailed deer as well. It's not uncommon to see elk and both species of deer all feeding in the same meadow. Be sure to scan the rocky canyon sides for bighorn sheep. Another remote preserve, the little-visited Wenaha–Tucannon Wilderness, is reached from a trailhead located just west of Troy, at the mouth of the Wenaha River. For those desiring to hike in

would have a rendezvous celebration. Wild revelry would ensue and wild meat feasts were savored. Food doesn't get much wilder than bear and rattlesnake meat, and it's on the Imnaha menu for this happening. Locals contribute bear from their hunting season successes, and decapitated rattlers are collected throughout the warm months and frozen in anticipation of this communal barbecue at the rustic store. The proceeds raised from the feed go to a scholarship fund for the area's youngsters. There's also a parade (a short one), tug-of-war contests, a bean-spitting competition for the kids, rodeo events, and a dance.

Imnaha is a good jumping off point to explore some of Oregon's truly wild outback. Depending on the ground clearance of your auto, there are two roads that offer drives showing off the spectacularly deep canyons of this far northeastern corner of Oregon. For those with a vehicle suited to rough roads, the gravel-dirt route leading down the Imnaha Canyon is well worth the time it takes to slowly negotiate the twists, turns, and rough spots. Your rewards include views of the Imnaha Gorge as the road winds along its brink, and probable up-close sightings of bighorn sheep. On the western flanks of Cactus Mountain, the reason for its name are apparent—clumps of prickly pear are seen everywhere on the open, grassy slopes. And just when you think the chasms can't get any deeper, the road finally breaks over the edge of Hells Canyon of the Snake River and makes a sinuous descent to the shore at Dug Bar. There are primitive camping spots, pit toilets, and a boat ramp, but no drinking water, so come fully self-sustained. This historical site is where Chief Joseph and his band of Nez Perce crossed the Snake River in 1877, attempting to outmaneuver the U.S. Army and escape to Canada.

Dug Bar is the only trailhead that provides a river-level entry into the Hells Canyon Wilderness in Oregon. All other trailheads begin high above the river at the canyon rim and switchback 7 or 8 miles down, down, down. Backpacking in this deepest gorge in North America entails traversing elevations ranging from subalpine zones at seven thousand feet to about a thousand feet in the canyon bottom. Therefore, unless you hike in on the river trail from Dug Bar and merely backtrack out again, continuing on through to any other trailhead will involve an arduous climb up several miles of switchbacks. Another alternative is to begin at one of the high trailheads and backpack downward and out to Dug Bar. However, depending upon the route, this may involve walking distances of 50 miles or more. No getting around it, if you want to penetrate the core of this wilderness by foot, resign yourself to the fact that long, tough miles will come with the trek. This is some of the roughest, most inaccessible backcountry in North America, which effectively thins out the crowds. Solitude is assured. Spring or autumn are the best seasons to hike in Hells Canyon. During summer, the stone-walled gorge holds heat like an oven, frequently exceeding 100 degrees F for many days in succession.

Exploration on horseback is another way to experience Hells Canyon, but the river trail is rather overgrown and narrow in many places, making passage for pack stock difficult. Trails in the mid- and upper levels of the canyon are generally better suited to horse-packing. If time or athletic ability does not allow backpacking or horse trips, consider taking a jet boat tour through Hells Canyon, or try a more leisurely float trip by rubber raft. Commercial jet boat services and rafting outfitters are available in Oxbow, Oregon; Clarkston,

If you'd like a taste of the remote Hells Canyon Wilderness that doesn't require mile after mile of up and down trekking, there's a relatively short footpath that switchbacks down the canyonside below the Hat Point fire lookout tower. In June and early July these grassy slopes are abloom with wildflowers, and it would be difficult to find a more pleasant hike. Following this trail downward for 3.5 miles will place you at the 5,000-foot mid-elevation level in the canyon on a broad, grassy bench edged with old-growth ponderosa pines. This is Smooth Hollow, a lovely place for a picnic or an overnight backpacking jaunt. Keep in mind, though, that returning to the trailhead requires regaining over two thousand feet in elevation up a very steep trail. But the climb back to the parking area is worth the delights of Smooth Hollow—towering pines that provide shade for lunch-munching or pleasant campsites, with burbling Hat Creek by an old, picturesque sheepherder cabin. For backpacking enthusiasts desiring a more "in-depth" experience of this vertical wilderness, connecting trails lead outward from Smooth Hollow and continue ever downward into Hells Canyon.

Smooth Hollow, below Hat Point, is situated on a broad bench at the mid-elevation level of Hells Canyon.

An inviting trail leads across grassy Smooth Hollow, and then steeply switchbacks down to the Snake River. By turns, the path progresses deeper and deeper into the Hells Canyon Wilderness.

Washington; and Lewiston, Idaho. Prearranged jet boat shuttle services are available for backpackers desiring to be dropped off and/or picked up at certain places in the canyon.

While you are in the area, Hat Point is a must see, as it provides some of the best views of Hells Canyon available from a roadside. Drivers in more conventional passenger cars with low ground clearance will have no problem driving there. Although consisting of 24 miles of gravel surface, it is generally in good shape. However, this winding road climbs to near seven thousand feet in elevation, so the

The Nature Conservancy's Clear Lake Ridge Preserve protects a large section of native grasslands and three shallow lakes. Perched atop a broad plateau that straddles the canyons of Little Sheep Creek and Big Sheep Creek, it is located between Joseph and Imnaha.

highest final section is usually closed by snow until early June. At the road's end, there's a parking area (with pit toilets, but no drinking water) where a short trail wends its way to a spot that gives new meaning to the word *overlook*. More than a mile below is the Snake River and east beyond the yawning gorge are the snowy peaks of Idaho's Seven Devils Mountains. For an even better vantage point, a trail leads up the near hillside to a fire lookout tower where stairs climb sixty feet to a public observation deck.

RETURNING to Imnaha, turning south on gravel Forest Road 3955 traces the Imnaha River upstream through a beautiful section of forested ridges. There are several nice Forest Service campgrounds and picnic areas along the way. After about 30 miles, this route connects with paved Forest Road 39. Shortly after, a turnoff to the east leads 3 miles through stands of ponderosa pine and

The south entrance to Hells Canyon, just below Hells Canyon Dam

flower-sprinkled meadows to Hells Canyon Overlook. There are interpretive displays and restrooms, and of course, breathtaking views. Note that, unlike 7,000-foot Hat Point, from this 5,400-foot elevation it is not possible to look down upon the Snake River far, far below. If you quietly listen, though, you can faintly hear the flowing water, along with the murmuring wind in the pines and the soft "beep, beep, beep" calls of nuthatches.

Continuing southwesterly, Forest Road 39 connects with Highway 86. Turning left (northeast) on 86 leads to three Snake River Dams—the Brownlee, Oxbow, and Hells Canyon. This area is well known among fishermen and upland-game bird hunters. A worthwhile side trip north through the small community of Oxbow leads 30 miles to a dead-end at Hells Canyon Dam. Just below the dam, the Hells Canyon Creek Visitor Center has informative natural history displays. Behind the visitor center, steps descend to the boat launch area, where a one-mile-long trail follows the river into Hells Canyon. The path soon fades away at the mouth of Stud Creek, but the short hike gives a dramatic glimpse into the depths of this magnificent gorge. As you walk back to the trailhead, it's entertaining to watch the jet boats negotiating rapids below the dam.

Pine Valley and the southern Wallowas

Returning to Highway 86 and progressing southwest for about 15 miles will bring you to a right-hand (northwest) turnoff to Halfway. Don't miss this mellow little town of some 350 people, located about 2 miles off the main highway. Largely an agriculturally based community, it's pleasantly nestled into the green farmlands of Pine Valley, with

the snowy heights of the Wallowas presiding above. Because of localized weather patterns and its geographical orientation to the mountains, this small valley receives abundant snow each winter. Consequently, the environment is more moist and lush compared to most areas in Eastern Oregon. Besides farming and ranching, the town's economy is increasingly receiving a boost from recreationists. The heavy winter snowfall attracts snowmobilers, and summer brings campers and hikers. The town's small collection of gift boutiques and bed-and-breakfast establishments are a sure sign of greater interest from tourists. Visiting fishermen are commonly seen in Halfway's friendly stores and cafés, while the fall sporting season attracts many hunters.

Everyone asks locals how the town's name originated. According to historical lore, after a few initial settlers arrived in the valley during the 1860s, small communities began to grow by the 1880s. When Alex Stalker built a store with a post office on his farm, the budding village needed a name. Because the new Stalker establishment was located about midway between a post office in Pine at the lower end of the valley and another one in Jimtown at the upper end, christening the hamlet as Halfway just seemed like the natural choice. Nevertheless, many residents will tell you the name refers to the obvious fact that the town is halfway to heaven. For more facts about the area's pioneer past, check out the well-maintained and informative Pine Valley History Museum, a half block off Main Street.

Continuing northwest out of Halfway leads 12 miles to the mining ghost town of Cornucopia in the Wallowa Mountains. The drive passes through the upper valley's countryside, where roadside fencerows are abloom with wild roses during summer and crickets chorus

The small community of Halfway is nestled in the farmlands of Pine Valley, below the Wallowa Mountains.

A June storm passes across the eastern flanks of the Wallowas.

Land of Gold-Bearing Mountains and Golden Wheat **285**

Sparta Ridge, with the lofty Wallowas to the north

Clyde Makinson, of Richland, Washington, restorer of this 1872 Old Sparta store building, enjoying the late-evening June air on the front porch of his unique vacation home

in the surrounding meadows. Before long, the road becomes gravel and enters the Wallowa Whitman National Forest, ascending to Cornucopia. When gold was discovered at this site in 1885, a boomtown of about a thousand miners quickly grew, with the usual attendant saloons and bordellos. Twenty million dollars worth of gold was mined from Cornucopia's thirty-six miles of tunnels, along with silver, copper, and lead. It was the region's last operating mine, continuing production until the beginning of the 1940s, when the quality of its ore decreased. The closing of Cornucopia's post office in 1942 marked the culmination of Oregon's gold rush period. Today, despite the harsh, 7,000-foot elevation, many of the original buildings still stand and it's a historically interesting place to visit.

Westward from Halfway, Highway 86 meanders along the southern flanks of the Wallowas, through the small town of Richland, where fruit orchards grow on sunny slopes above cattle ranches and hayfields.

At the western edge of Richland, turn right (north) on the paved road that leads up the Eagle Creek drainage to the tiny settlement of New Bridge, another fruit growing area. From here, there's a wonderful secondary gravel road that loops west along the top of Sparta Ridge, and after about 25 miles reconnects with Highway 86. The Sparta Road offers top-of-the-world, exquisite views north across Eagle Creek Canyon to thick forests and the lofty masses of the Wallowa peaks. Along the crest of Sparta Ridge and sweeping downward to the Powder River on the south are miles and miles of open, rolling foothills. Driving this route in early June is a visual feast of velvety, spring green slopes, accented with the bright yellow blooms of arrowleaf balsamroot. Pronghorn frequent these bunchgrass prairies, along with many birds of prey, such as golden eagles, red-tailed hawks, and ferruginous hawks. Burrowing owls stand guard over their subterranean nests and rattlesnakes occasionally cross the road.

Unlike the north side of the range, where recreationists flock to Wallowa Lake, the southern and eastern portions of the Wallowas draw fewer visitors. Forest Service roads that lead north from Sparta Ridge penetrate the upper reaches of the Eagle Creek drainage, where trailheads provide jumping-off points to adventures in the Eagle Cap Wilderness. These forest paths are comparatively lightly used and offer greater opportunities for solitude.

Along this stretch of little-traveled ridgetop road, you'll find a lone surviving stone building that marks all that remains of the once-thriving mining town of Sparta. In this peacefully rural spot, it's difficult to comprehend that when gold was discovered here in 1869, a mining town of three thousand people sprang into existence. After a century of several incarnations as a general store or dance hall, this beautifully crafted old structure has been painstakingly restored by the present owner.

Following the Oregon Trail to Baker Valley

After you rejoin Highway 86, more local history is to be found about 20 miles farther west. Where the highway crosses a rise at the western end of Virtue Flat, watch for signs indicating a right-hand (north) turnoff for the National Historic Oregon Trail Interpretive Center. After a fee booth, the entrance road climbs to the crest of Flagstaff Hill where there's a parking area. The 23,000-square-foot building commands a panoramic view west, across Baker Valley, to the craggy backbone of the Elkhorn Range. Maintained by the U.S. Bureau of Land Management (BLM), this high-quality facility is well worth at least two hours of your time, if not more. Inside, the excellent walkthrough, interactive displays include audio and video components along with "living history" enactments to bring to life the struggles of pioneers along the 2,000-mile route. Quotations from Oregon Trail diaries are used extensively to great effect. Many visitors, though, find that the most compelling experience of the entire interpretive center is to be found outside. A 1.5-mile footpath leads down the slope, allowing you to walk the same sagebrush-covered hill that the emigrants crossed. At the bottom, you reach the actual wheel ruts of the Oregon Trail. A covered wagon has been placed on the route to accentuate the experience.

Driving 5 miles west, you connect with Interstate 84, and shortly thereafter will enter Baker City, which is the valley's largest cen-

On Flagstaff Hill, near Baker City, a covered wagon sits in the actual wheel ruts on the Oregon Trail at the National Historic Oregon Trail Interpretive Center. Photo: David Jensen

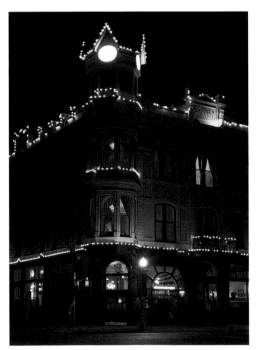

Refurbished to its former elegance, the Geiser Grand Hotel graces Main Street in Baker City.

ter of commerce. The architecture and general personality of the town evoke small midwestern farming communities of Kansas and Missouri. This influence can be traced to many early pioneer residents of Baker City who had their roots in mid-America. All in all, the community exudes an ambiance of traditional stability reminiscent of an earlier era. You'll see quarried-stone buildings, a tall courthouse clock tower, Victorian-style brick homes, and shady, tree-lined streets. Although Baker City got its start during the gold rush of the 1860s, this was no short-lived boomtown. Before the mines played out, it was established as a railroad trade center for cattle ranching, farming, and timber. Baker City's population of around ten thousand people has remained remarkably constant since the turn of the last century.

However, as trends and economies have changed, conservative Baker City has realized its need to adapt. As with many other Oregon dry side communities that have experienced varying degrees of decline linked to the faltering timber and agricultural markets, Baker City has made an attempt to attract tourism dollars. Capitalizing upon its rich history, the entire downtown business district has been designated a National Historic Site with more than a hundred reconstructive face-lifts.

The plan is succeeding. After experiencing an economic slump when empty stores seemed to outnumber solvent businesses, Baker City steadily made a comeback through the 1990s. Ironically, as the revamped town entered the twenty-first century, its appearance decidedly took on that of the nineteenth century. Although not yet having a booming expansion similar to Bend in Central Oregon, it is increasingly welcoming families seeking a more traditional quality of life. Promoting this appeal as a slice of more affordable, slower-paced Americana, the city bills itself as "The premier rural living experience in the Pacific Northwest." A large part of this metamorphosis can be attributed to the 1992 opening of the nearby Oregon Trail Interpretive Center on Flagstaff Hill, which has attracted more visitors to Baker City.

A stroll through the downtown historic district will quickly clarify why tourists are coming to this retro community. In fact, the city provides a free self-guided walking tour (you can pick up the informational pamphlet from just about any shopkeeper). Immediately the Geiser Grand Hotel on Main Street catches the eye. Once considered the finest hotel between Seattle and Salt Lake City, the 1889, thirty-room establishment, with its impressive clock turret, was completely refurbished in 1998. When the hard work was done and the dust had settled, the cost had topped six million dollars. Walk inside for a meal in the hotel's restaurant and you'll see the results of this investment. Polished ornate mahogany and Viennese crystal gleam everywhere. Take a table in the Palm Tea Court area and then look up. Overhead is a huge colorful stained-glass skylight. Although Geiser Grand is unquestionably the most elegant place to dine in Baker County, this is still an Eastern Oregon ranch town. The ambiance is better described as casual elegance. Among several selections on the menu are buffalo steak and their signature mesquite-smoked prime rib.

Across Main Street is an 1888 store building that is home to Betty's Books, one of the friendliest and largest booksellers in Northeastern Oregon. A couple of doors down is the U.S. Bank, with its display of mining artifacts and a huge, 80.4-ounce gold nugget dug up near Baker City in 1913. Near the shady city park and library is the Oregon Trail Regional Museum. This large building houses an eclectic collection of pioneer memorabilia; classic antique autos; and notably, a rock, mineral, and fossil collection that's ranked among the best in the nation. At the west end of Main Street is the ten-story Baker Hotel, a recognizable feature of the city skyline since 1929. The tallest building in Eastern Oregon, it, too, had become run-down but is now listed among the downtown's restoration successes. The new, improved version is called the Baker Tower, with offices on the lower floors and residential condos in the upper levels.

One of Baker City's most appealing qualities, however, has nothing to do with all these civic improvements. Despite the extensive remodeling to attract tourists, the trap of becoming an artificial, theme-park characterization of itself has been avoided. Baker City remains a rock-solid, genuine community.

DRIVING north on old Highway 30 toward the small town of Haines provides a pleasant excursion. There are views across the broad Baker Valley, bounded on the west by the jagged Elkhorn Range, and to the east are the shining white peaks of the Wallowas. Here the Powder River supplies irrigation to farmlands, but a large portion of the area remains dry, devoted to extensive rangelands for beef production. A number of large, prospering ranches will be seen along Highway 30. To learn more about the colorful regional history, make a stop in Haines (population about 300) to take in the Eastern Oregon Museum. Housed in a former high school gymnasium, it displays an impressive collection of relics from pioneer days. Afterward, if you want to savor the local ranching flavor literally, try the rustic Haines Steak House, a longtime fixture in the area. This is where cattlemen come to eat, because it's the real deal and is considered by many to serve the best steaks in the entire state. Just be aware that this definitely isn't a vegetarian restaurant; but if a classic western-style meal with huge steaks sounds good, you've walked into the correct cowboy eatery. The barbecue beans are rated topnotch, too.

North of Haines about 8 miles, Highway 30 connects with I-84 at the town of North Powder (population 480) . However, instead of continuing north to La Grande on the Interstate, turn west. This leads 19 miles on Forest Road 73 to one of the Northwest's highest-elevation ski facilities, located in a glaciated granite basin at between seven and eight thousand feet in the Elkhorn Range. The Anthony Lakes Ski Resort explains that they don't offer high-speed lifts or high-priced tickets—instead you get some of the best powder skiing in the Northwest. Groomed cross-country ski trails are provided as well, along with snowboarding and snowshoeing. Although no overnight accommodations are available at the ski area, there's a day lodge with a café-saloon and a retail ski shop that rents equipment.

Anthony Lakes is also a haven for snowmobilers, with many miles of trails throughout the area. During summer, this beautiful basin is a hiking, camping, fishing, canoeing, and kayaking delight, with lakes surrounded by flower-filled meadows. Forest Service campgrounds and picnic areas with toilets and drinking water are available, and a trailhead offers several excellent hiking options (parking fee or passes required). Shorter excursions lead to Hoffer Lakes (.6 mile) or Black Lake (.5 mile). For the more industrious, there's an 8-mile-loop trail that encircles Gunsight Mountain and gives spectacular views in all directions. For hard-core backpackers, this loop also connects with the Elkhorn Crest Trail, which traces the dramatic, razor-edged

summit of the range. This lightly visited route affords a trek of nearly 30 miles through an alpine world of gnarled whitebark pine and glacial cirque lakes, with mountain goats likely to be the only other trekkers you'll see.

The Sumpter Valley area

Continuing west on Forest Road 73 takes you over a mountain pass into the upper Powder River drainage, a fascinating region of mining ghost towns that date from Northeastern Oregon's gold rush era. There, between the Elkhorn and Greenhorn Ranges, is the Sumpter Valley with its village of Sumpter. This is a good central location from which to explore; almost any drive or hike reveals the remains of old mine shafts, dilapidated cabins, and abandoned boomtowns where thousands of people once lived.

Sometimes described as "The liveliest ghost town in Oregon," Sumpter has accommodations that include the Sumpter Bed and Breakfast (housed in what was originally the town hospital), two RV parks, and a barracks-style hostel that offers low-cost beds and bathroom facilities. Other needs, ranging from food and gasoline to browsing, can be met at Sumpter's cafés, general store, galleries, gift shops, and museums. This revitalized former mining town is also known for having extravagantly huge flea markets on the holiday weekends of Memorial Day, Independence Day, and Labor Day.

A mining history tour can begin at the edge of Sumpter. Extensive areas of mounded gravel and rock along the river extend eastward the entire length of the valley floor. These were created long ago by the filtering and disgorging action of the Sumpter Gold Dredge. This huge, long-necked, mechanical monster operated until 1954, and now rests just off the highway at the edge of town. Designated as a state heritage park, the site includes interpretive displays and a path leading to the dredge for viewing. The valley's dredged areas are gradually being reclaimed by nature and a state wildlife area provides protected habitat for birds and other animals attracted by cattail-lined ponds among the rock piles.

Something else not to be missed is the Sumpter Valley Railroad, which boasts two beautifully restored steam locomotives. Visitors are taken on scenic excursions up and down the valley for 5 miles between train depots at Sumpter and McEwen. The historic narrow-gauge railroad was initially constructed in 1890 to haul logs from the Sumpter area's timber camps to the mill in Baker City. This proved so successful that the train was soon shuttling all manner of freight, including ore, mining equipment, lumber, mail, and livestock, as well as human travelers. Eventually, the line was extended eighty miles southwest to Prairie City in the John Day Valley. After the coming of more roads with competing truck transportation, this mountain railway line declined and was finally closed in 1947. The railroad's long resurrection process began in 1971, when a group of dedicated Baker City volunteers organized the nonprofit Sumpter Valley Railroad Restoration, Inc. As the train chugs through the wildlife area while you enjoy views of the Elkhorn Mountains, think of the countless hours of hard work these volunteers have contributed.

West of Sumpter, steep roads climb into the outback sections of the Greenhorn Mountains. Hidden in this rugged terrain, the relic mining towns of Bourne, Granite, and Greenhorn stand like bleached skeletons after weathering more than a century of harsh, high-elevation weather. However, pri-

A beautifully restored locomotive of the Sumpter Valley Railroad waits for passengers at the McEwen train depot.

A snowbound log cabin in a remote section of the Greenhorn Mountains

vately owned summer cabins are in use, and a few hardy, year-round residents still live in some of these outposts and the surrounding canyons. When the price of gold increases, miners reactivate claims throughout the region, and the backwoods population rises and falls in harmony with the fluctuating values.

In these remote parts of the Blue Mountains, lesser-known wilderness retreats are to be found where day hikers and backpackers have the trails mostly to themselves. The 121,800-acre North Fork John Day Wilderness encompasses sections of both the high

Greenhorn Mountains and the Elkhorn Range. This prime wildlife habitat supports large populations of Rocky Mountain elk; and steelhead and chinook salmon spawn in a Wild and Scenic stretch of the North Fork John Day River. The Vinegar Hill–Indian Rock Scenic Area features 8,000-foot alpine zones, where paths traverse open, grassy summits. Early miners called a huge greenish point of serpentine rock on Vinegar Hill the Green Horn, thus bestowing a name upon this subrange of the Blue Mountain complex.

Mining ghost towns

It is nearly impossible to drive through the mountainous sections of Northeastern Oregon without noticing the almost palpable aura of the gold rush that swept through the region in the late 1800s. After the initial 1861 gold strike in Griffin Gulch, near the present site of Baker City, thousands of men swarmed into the area from the Willamette Valley and California. Small wilderness mining camps of tents soon became "boomtowns," filled with zealous miners enjoying saloons and bawdy houses that lined the streets. But shortly after the turn of the century, the gold was running out and the mining towns began to fade.

These fascinating and picturesque old town sites resurrect an exciting era of Oregon's history. Many are not true ghost towns because they retain year-round residents, sometimes with one or two operating stores and cafés. Others have only seasonal occupants in summer cabins. Nevertheless, they all have weathered buildings full of echoes from the 1800s and are well worth exploring. The Blue Mountains to the west of Baker City offer the largest concentration of historical mining sites in Northeastern Oregon. Highway 7, a pleasantly scenic route, leads west toward Sumpter into the heart of the old mining fields and some particularly interesting ghost towns.

Auburn

During its heyday, Northeastern Oregon's first boomtown ranked as the largest city in Oregon, with a population of more than five thousand brawling, energetic miners, all suffering gold fever. Shortly after the first strike in Griffin Gulch in 1861, Auburn sprang into existence and quickly became the original Baker County seat. However, by 1868, when the diggings played out, places of commerce moved a few miles northeast to Baker City on the railroad line. Virtually no remnants of Auburn remain today.

Sumpter

Five southerners discovered gold at this site in 1862. With slight misspelling, they honored their native South by naming the town after Fort Sumter, South Carolina. Initially, Sumpter remained a mining camp until the Sumpter Valley Railroad arrived in 1896. Then the town quickly grew from a small village of three hundred to a bustling city of four thousand, and was called Golden Sumpter at the height of its fame. By 1900, it boasted sixteen saloons, seven hotels, six restaurants, seven general stores, and many other businesses, including an opera house that hosted dress balls. In 1917, fire leveled most of the town in just three hours. Today, Sumpter is a small, quiet community with stores, cafés, and a bed-and-breakfast housed in a renovated century-old building. Sumpter also boasts a relict gold-mining dredge. Resembling a huge, landlocked riverboat, it slumbers like an old

The old Granite School is now used as the city hall.

The Sumpter dredge

A snowplow makes its way along a rural road near Bates, at the southern base of the Greenhorn Mountains.

retiree at the edge of town by one of its formerly churned gravel piles.

Bourne

Few buildings remain of this hard-rock mining center along Cracker Creek, 7 miles north of Sumpter. In 1937, the stream flooded and swept away most of the town, originally called Cracker City.

Granite

The dirt streets of this community, located high in the Blue Mountains 17 miles west of Sumpter, lend authenticity. Granite has retained more of an atmosphere of the old days than any of the other mining towns of Northeastern Oregon. Many original buildings still stand, hinting of better times when residents prided themselves on a fifty-room hotel, a few smaller hotels and boarding houses, a dance hall, school, church, four saloons, a jail, and a Chinatown district. An old stone marker at the foot of the hill below town proclaims,

"Gold was discovered here July 4, 1862." Approximately thirty year-round residents reside in Granite at present. A combination café and grocery store sells gas and diesel, and a new lodge offers overnight accommodations.

Greenhorn

Located 14 miles south of Granite in a remote section of the Greenhorn Mountains, Oregon's highest and smallest incorporated town sits at a 6,271-foot elevation. Property owners with summer cabins in Greenhorn reactivated the town charter in the 1970s, making it a legally incorporated city with a mayor and other officials. Thus, Greenhorn has been protected by its city council from commercialization and retains its authentic qualities. Founded in 1891, it never exceeded a population of around seven hundred. Only a few buildings remain today.

Whitney

Located 11 miles southwest of Sumpter in a large meadow along Highway 7, Whitney utilized the Sumpter Valley Railroad to transport lumber from its mill, as well as some ore from nearby mines. Always a small town, it dates from 1901. Old mill buildings and a few cabins, some occupied by full-time residents, remain. ■

The John Day River drainage

Westerly from the Greenhorn-Elkhorn ranges, the vast headwaters of the John Day River drainage feeds 280 miles of undammed water—second only to Montana's Yellowstone River for claiming longest free-running river status in the lower forty-eight states. To explore the many-faceted faces of the John Day country, drive southwest on Highway 7 out of the Sumpter Valley. The route climbs southwest over timbered Larch Summit, down through broad meadows and aspen groves at the ghost town of Whitney, and then climbs again into forests before connecting with Highway 26 at Austin Junction. Turning west on this road soon takes you over Dixie Pass, and with a swing to the south it leaves the dense conifers to reveal a commanding vista. Spread out below are prairies and farmlands in the long east-west trough of the John Day Valley. Beyond this open landscape, the green heights of Strawberry Mountain form the valley's southern boundary. This range holds

the headwaters of the main stem of the John Day River, which can be seen flowing westward through the basin.

Several communities line Highway 26 along the valley floor, most of them originally mining towns or way stations along the old stage road in the 1800s. Shortly after descending to the valley floor, the highway arrives in Prairie City, with a population of just over a thousand. Whatever Prairie City may lack in size, it makes up for in small-town charm. There's nothing complicated here. Highway 26 doubles as the main business street—all two blocks of it. Whether a general store, bank, café, barbershop, bakery, or western-wear store, each building has been carefully restored to enhance its historical qualities; nineteenth-century-style red brick, natural pine siding, and stone are accented by flower-filled hanging baskets and storefront awnings in cheery colors. As with the well-intentioned face-lifts of historical districts in Baker City and Union, this frontier persona is not merely hucksterism to lure tourists. It's readily apparent that the residents of Prairie City have genuine pride in their mining, ranching, farming, and logging history and want to share it with visitors.

Side streets are mostly tree-lined rows of homes, perhaps with a nearby park, church, or school. Another historical touch is to be seen on Bridge Street at the DeWitt Museum and Depot Park. This two-story 1910 building originally served as the train depot when the Sumpter Valley Railroad then extended from Baker City to Prairie City. Now it displays era-specific memorabilia and antiques in the ground floor's waiting room, agent's office, and freight areas. Upstairs, the agent's living quarters also contain furnishings typical of the period. Although the glory days of unlimited logging of old-growth trees may now

East of Prairie City, a country road leads to double rainbows.

Weathered corrals and Strawberry Mountain, near Prairie City

be history as well, there's still the presence of a mill in this community. Prairie Wood Products is a computerized stud-mill operation that specializes in 2×4s, along with supplying custom-cut lumber. Additionally, because the local ponderosa pine is nationally noted for being fine-grained, this mill markets lumber suited to the making of quality doors, windows, and cabinetry.

Outdoor recreation, fishing, and hunting are increasingly boosting the Prairie City economy; and a slogan describes the area as the "Gateway to the Strawberry Wilderness." This town offers the last chance to stock up on groceries, fishing tackle, maps, ice, and gas before seeking a campsite on Strawberry Mountain. Besides several Forest Service campgrounds along roads that skirt the mountain's lower slopes, more than 100 miles of trails traverse the wilderness. These range from a family-friendly, 1-mile hike to Strawberry Lake, to a backpacking trek of nearly 20 miles that loops through the heart of the wilderness. The rewards of this strenuous enterprise include high, grassy summits with wonderful views, remote, little-visited lakes, and possible sightings of bighorn sheep. If you take the Strawberry Lake jaunt, be sure to continue another mile beyond to lovely Strawberry Falls, which drops sixty feet over a rock cliff. And if you're stiff and achy after hiking, visit the Blue Mountain Hot Springs (privately owned, with a fee) 10 miles southeast of Prairie City along County Road 62.

Continuing west from Prairie City for 13 miles on Highway 26 will bring you to John Day. With a population of nearly two thousand, this is the valley's largest city. As in Prairie City, the timber industry has not faded away here, and two mills, Malheur Lumber and Grant Western Lumber, currently operate in John Day. However, as with many of the smaller communities of Oregon's dry side, government employment with the Forest Service, Bureau of Land Management, Fish and Wildlife Service, or state agencies provides livelihoods for many residents. John Day is also a ranching and farming hub, and the Old West doesn't seem so old when a local tradition takes place each year: come spring, buckaroos on horses drive cattle through downtown John Day, moving livestock from winter pasture to higher summer ranges. When fall arrives—you guessed it—the cows come back through town on the return trip.

Mining history permeates this community, including the town of Canyon City, which is more or less a southern extension of John Day. In June of 1862 gold was discovered along Canyon Creek, and the boom that ensued created John Day and Canyon City—where 26 million dollars worth of gold was mined from the area during this wild period. Hundreds of Chinese immigrants came to the area to work in the mines, and by 1879 they greatly outnumbered Euro-Americans in the gold fields of Eastern Oregon. The Kam Wah Chung building and museum in John Day, a stone Chinese trading post built in 1867, was operated by Ing Hay and Lung On. Besides selling groceries and other supplies, it served as an herb pharmacy, opium den, and religious temple. Now the oldest structure in John Day, it is a fascinating museum of Chinese artifacts from that period, and is listed as a National Historic Landmark.

Traveling 8 miles west on Highway 26, you'll pass through the quiet ranching and farming community of Mount Vernon (population 645). Just east of town there's a nice state park that's a combination rest area and picnic-campground. The John Day River runs along the southern edge of the park, where you'll find shady tables that provide a good

Strawberry Lake in the Strawberry Mountain Wilderness

place to have lunch and take a short break from driving. Continuing on another 23 miles brings you to the village of Dayville (population 185). If you haven't filled your gas tank recently, do so here at the friendly general store. Beyond this point in the journey, it's a long way to the next gas pump.

Before returning to the highway, however, seekers of solitude may want to take an 11-mile side trip south from Dayville on Forest Road 74. This leads up the South Fork of the John Day River to the Black Canyon Wilderness. This relatively small (13,400 acres) preserve is not well known, and you'll be assured of uncrowded paths. The 14.5-mile trail accesses rugged, varied terrain, including dry juniper woodlands, forests of pine, fir and mountain mahogany, and grassy benches. Nearly three hundred species of wildlife have been recorded from Black Canyon—including mule deer, Rocky Mountain elk, black bear, and cougar. Reportedly, rattlesnakes are common in this rocky habitat, so be alert.

Strawberry Falls

Land of Gold-Bearing Mountains and Golden Wheat **297**

The John Day River, with Sheep Rock on the skyline. John Day Fossil Beds National Monument, Sheep Rock Unit

From Dayville, Highway 26 takes you to the westernmost extent of the valley, where the John Day River and the road squeeze between the sheer walls of Picture Gorge. Just beyond the narrow aperture, the route forks. Turn right on Highway 19, which ventures north along the river into a startling landscape of eroded, multicolored badlands. This is the Sheep Rock Unit of John Day Fossil Beds National Monument. Two smaller sections of the monument, the Painted Hills and Clarno Units, are situated more than 50 miles to the west in the Central Oregon region.

First studied in the 1860s by Thomas Condon, this unique area is characterized by the National Park Service as "an archive of ancient life." The ash beds, with their bands of red, yellow, and green, hold a 50-million-year-old continuous fossil record of flora and fauna. This is unique on the entire planet, as most fossil beds provide only a two- to three-million-year snapshot. The world scientific community regards the John Day Fossil Beds as being one of the finest sites known for studying mammalian evolution. Nearly every species of the region's past eras is represented. Additionally, the volcanic ash layers can be precisely dated by radioisotopes. Ted Fremd, the monument's head paleontologist, likened this timeline accuracy to "page numbers in a book with a 45-million-year-long plot." A perfect combination of conditions created the fossil beds—a rich variety of species coexisting in the same place, all quickly buried by ash from volcanic eruptions that contained the right preserving minerals, and the location in a basin where erosion could not dislodge and scatter the plant and animal remains far downstream.

This ash bed Book of Genesis tells of past ages when the now semiarid landscape was a lush subtropical forest, inhabited by such exotic creatures as rhinoceroses, saber-toothed cats, and small, primitive horses. Over vast spans of time, the John Day River cut its way through these colorful layers, revealing the

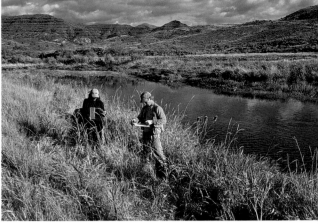

After setting live traps the evening before, biologists return the following morning to inspect the captured native mice. Data is recorded for an ongoing wildlife survey in the monument, and then the rodents are released.

story of the long-vanished ecosystems. Before taking a tour, it's advisable to visit the monument's headquarters along Highway 19 for a quick educational orientation. There are no admission fees for anything within the monument. Watch for the Thomas Condon Paleontology Center, off the west side of the highway. Half of the 11,000-square-foot, state-of-the-art building houses a fossil museum and bookstore, and the other half is a research facility. The excellent interpretive displays and an eighteen-minute movie describe both the area's paleontology and the work of the scientists, from past to present. There's even a viewing window that provides a chance to observe a paleontologist working on fossil specimens. Across the road is the old Cant Ranch House, a former sheep operation dating from the homestead era of the early 1900s. The pleasant tree-shaded yard has picnic tables, and inside are exhibits explaining the history of the region's Native Americans, pioneers, and livestock ranchers.

Trails providing self-guided hikes through the fossil-bearing ash beds (no collecting allowed) are located north of the headquarters along Highway 19. The Blue Basin trailhead (restrooms, but no water) offers the choice of the one-mile long Island in Time walk or the Blue Basin Overlook, a more strenuous 3-mile hike that affords wonderful views of the ash beds from above. Farther north is the Foree Picnic Area, with shaded tables, restrooms, and drinking water. Leading off the park-

ing area are two trails, both a quarter mile in length. The Flood of Fire path (dirt) ascends a low ridge to a viewpoint overlooking basalt cliffs and the John Day River. A paved, wheelchair-accessible trail, called the Story in Stone, provides interpretive displays along the route.

In many ways, the John Day country embodies the richly varied contrasts that are characteristic of the state's regions east of the Cascades. Here, in the heartland of it all, brightly colored ash beds adjoin muted greenish-gray sagebrush. Gnarled, stocky junipers grow at the margins of towering ponderosa pines. Prickly cacti grow side by side with delicate wildflowers. And the farmlands of level-floored valleys repose below vertical basalt rimrock. There's no place quite like Oregon's dry side.

Scientific Names of Plants and Animals in This Book

Plants

FERNS
bracken fern, *Pteridium aquilinum*
pumice grape fern, *Botrychium pumicola*
western swordfern, *Polystichum munitum*

SHRUBS
bartonberry, *Rubus bartonianus*
big sagebrush, *Artemisia tridentata*
bitterbrush, *Purshia tridentata*
black greasewood (big greasewood), *Sarcobatus vermiculatus*
black sagebrush, *Artemisia nova*
bud sage, *Artemisiu spinescens*
Cascades blueberry, *Vaccinium deliciosum*
common rabbitbrush, *Ericameria nauseosa*
common snowberry, *Symphoricarpos albus*
creeping Oregon-grape, *Berberis repens*
four-winged saltbush, *Atriplex canescens*
green ephedra (Mormon tea), *Ephedra viridis*
green manzanita, *Arctostaphylos patula*
green rabbitbrush, *Ericameria viscidiflora*
grouse huckleberry, *Vaccinium scoparium*
iodine bush (pickleweed), *Allenrolfea occidentalis*
kinnikinnick, *Arctostaphylos uva-ursi*
low sagebrush, *Artemisia arbuscula*
Nevada ephedra (Mormon tea), *Ephedra nevadensis*
nootka rose, *Rosa nutkana*
Owyhee sagebrush, *Artemisia papposa*
Packard's sagebrush, *Artemisia packardiae*
pinemat manzanita, *Arctostaphylos nevadensis*
saltsage, *Atriplex gardneri*

serviceberry, *Amelanchier alnifolia*
shadscale, *Atriplex confertifolia*
silver sagebrush, *Artemisia cana*
smooth sumac, *Rhus glabra*
spiny hopsage, *Grayia spinosa*
spiny horsebrush, *Tetradymia spinosa*
stiff sagebrush, *Artemisia rigida*
threetip sagebrush, *Artemisia tripartita*
wax currant, *Ribes cereum*
western poison oak, *Toxicodendron diversilobum*
winterfat, *Krascheninnikovia lanata*

TREES
Alaska cedar, *Chamaecyparis nootkatensis*
arroyo willow, *Salix lasiolepis*
bigleaf maple, *Acer macrophyllum*
birchleaf mountain mahogany, *Cercocarpus betuloides*
black cottonwood, *Populus trichocarpa*
black hawthorn, *Crataegus douglasii*
California black oak, *Quercus kelloggii*
curlleaf mountain mahogany, *Cercocarpus ledifolius*
Douglas fir, *Pseudotsuga menziesii*
Engelmann spruce, *Picea engelmannii*
grand fir, *Abies grandis*
incense cedar, *Calocedrus decurrens*
Klamath plum, *Prunus subcordata*
lodgepole pine, *Pinus contorta*
mountain alder, *Alnus incana*
mountain hemlock, *Tsuga mertensiana*
narrow-leaved willow (coyote willow), *Salix exigua*

noble fir, *Abies procera*
Oregon white oak, *Quercus garryana*
Pacific silver fir, *Abies amabilis*
Pacific willow, *Salix lucida*
Pacific yew, *Taxus brevifolia*
paper birch, *Betula papyrifera*
ponderosa pine (yellow pine), *Pinus ponderosa*
quaking aspen, *Populus tremuloides*
red fir, *Abies magnifica*
Rocky Mountain juniper, *Juniperus scopulorum*
scouler willow, *Salix scouleriana*
Sitka alder, *Alnus viridis*
subalpine fir, *Abies lasiocarpa*
sugar pine, *Pinus lambertiana*
thinleaf alder, *Alnus incana*
vine maple, *Acer circinatum*
water birch, *Betula occidentalis*
western juniper, *Juniperus occidentalis*
western larch, *Larix occidentalis*
western mountain maple (Rocky Mountain maple), *Acer glabrum*
western red cedar, *Thuja plicata*
western white pine, *Pinus monticola*
whitebark pine, *Pinus albicaulis*
white fir, *Abies concolor*

GRASSES, SEDGES & RUSHES

Asian crested wheatgrass, *Agropyron desertorum*
Baltic rush, *Juncus balticus*
bluebunch wheatgrass, *Pseudoroegneria spicata*
bulrush (tule), *Scirpus acutus*
burreed, *Sparganium* species
cattail, *Typha latifolia*
cheatgrass, *Bromus tectorum*
giant wild rye, *Leymus cinereus*
Idaho fescue, *Festuca idahoensis*
Indian ricegrass, *Achnatherum hymenoides*
Sandberg's bluegrass, *Poa sandbergii*

CACTI

black-spined hedgehog cactus, *Pediocactus nigrispinus*
brittle prickly pear, *Opuntia fragilis*
plains prickly pear, *Opuntia polyacantha*
Simpson's hedgehog cactus, *Pediocactus simpsonii*

WILDFLOWERS

alpine forget-me-not, *Eritrichium nanum*
alpine laurel, *Kalmia microphylla*

alpine lily, *Lloydia serotina*
alpine paintbrush, *Castilleja rhexifolia*
arrowleaf balsamroot, *Balsamorhiza sagittata*
beargrass, *Xerophyllum tenax*
bitterroot, *Lewisia rediviva*
blazing star, *Mentzelia laevicaulis*
bluebell, *Mertensia paniculata*
Blue Mountain lomatium, *Lomatium oreganum*
Blue Mountain penstemon, *Penstemon venustus*
camas, *Camassia quamash*
Cascades lily, *Lilium washingtonianum*
cushion buckwheat, *Eriogonum ovalifolium nivale*
Cusick's camas, *Camassia cusickii*
Cusick's milkvetch, *Astragalus cusickii*
Cusick's monkeyflower, *Mimulus cusickii*
desert evening primrose, *Oenothera caespitosa*
desert paintbrush, *Castilleja angustifolia* var. *dubia* (*C. chromosa*)
dwarf golden daisy, *Erigeron chrysopsidis* var. *brevifolius*
dwarf lousewort, *Pedicularis centranthera*
fireweed, *Chamerion angustifolium*
fraternal paintbrush, *Castilleja fraterna*
glacier lily, *Erythronium grandiflorum*
golden bee plant, *Cleome platycarpa*
hairy yellow paintbrush, *Castilleja pilosa* var. *pilosa*
Hazel's prickly phlox, *Leptodactylon pungens* var. *hazeliae*
large-flowered tonella, *Tonella floribunda*
large-leaved (meadow) lupine, *Lupinus polyphyllus*
long-leaved phlox, *Phlox longifolia*
Malheur wire lettuce, *Stephanomeria malheurensis*
McFarlane's four-o'clock, *Mirabilis macfarlanei*
mountain lady's slipper, *Cypripedium montanum*
orange globemallow, *Sphaeralcea munroana*
orange honeysuckle, *Lonicera ciliosa*
Oregon twinpod, *Physaria oregana*
Packard's mentzelia, *Mentzelia packardiae*
pearly everlasting, *Anaphalis margaritacea*
Peck's penstemon, *Penstemon peckii*
pinedrops, *Pterospora andromedea*
pink spiraea (hardhack), *Spiraea douglasii*
prickly poppy, *Argemone munita*
prince's plume, *Stanleya pinnata*
purple alpine paintbrush, *Castilleja rubida*
purple sage, *Salvia dorrii*
red columbine, *Aquilegia formosa*

sand penstemon, *Penstemon acuminatus*
scarlet (Indian) paintbrush, *Castilleja miniata*
shooting star, *Dodecatheon pulchellum*
silky lupine, *Lupinus sericeus*
skyrocket (scarlet gilia), *Ipomopsis aggregata*
small-leaved lupine, *Lupinus lepidus* var. *lobbii*
Snake River phlox, *Phlox colubrina*
snowline spring parsley, *Cymopterus nivalis*
spreading phlox, *Phlox diffusa*
Steens Mountain paintbrush, *Castilleja pilosa* var. *steenensis*
Steens Mountain penstemon, *Penstemon davidsonii* var. *praeteritus*
Steens Mountain thistle, *Cirsium peckii*
sulphur buckwheat (umbrella buckwheat), *Eriogonum umbellatum*
tiger lily, *Lilium columbianum*
Wallowa lewisia, *Lewisia columbiana* var. *wallowensis*
Wallowa penstemon, *Penstemon spatulatus*
Wallowa primrose, *Primula cusickiana*
western iris, *Iris missouriensis*
western prairie clover, *Petalostemon ornatum*
western trillium (wake robin), *Trillium ovatum*
wide-stemmed onion (pink star onion), *Allium platycaule*
wooly sunflower (Oregon sunshine), *Eriophyllum lanatum*
yellow columbine, *Aquilegia flavescens*

Animals

INSECTS & ARACHNIDS
American copper, *Lycaena phlaeas*
ant lion, *Myrmeleon immaculatus*
cicada, *Okanagana*
desert marble, *Euchloe lotta*
giant desert hairy scorpion, *Hadrurus arizonensis*
harvester ant, *Pogonomyrmex* species
Jerusalem cricket, *Stenopelmatus fuscus*
sagebrush checkerspot, *Chlosyne acastus*
western tiger swallowtail, *Papilio rutulus*
white-lined sphinx moth, *Hyles lineata*

FISH
Alvord chub, *Gila alvordensis*
Borax Lake chub, *Gila boraxobius*
Bull trout, *Salvelinus confluentus*
Catlow tui chub, *Gila bicolor* subspecies

chinook salmon, *Oncorhynchus tshawytscha*
Foskett speckled dace, *Rhinichthys osculus* subspecies
Lahontan cutthroat trout, *Oncorhynchus clarki henshawi*
redband (rainbow) trout, *Oncorhynchus mykiss*
    Columbia River Basin subspecies, *O. mykiss gairdneri*
    northern Great Basin subspecies, *O. mykiss newberrii*
sockeye salmon, *Oncorhynchus nerka*
steelhead (Columbia River Basin redband subspecies), *Oncorhynchus mykiss gairdneri*
Summer Basin tui chub, *Gila bicolor* subspecies
Warner sucker, *Catostomus warnerensis*

AMPHIBIANS
Columbia spotted frog, *Rana luteiventris*
Great Basin spadefoot, *Spea intermontana*
long-toed salamander, *Ambystoma macrodactylum*
Pacific treefrog, *Pseudacris (Hyla) regilla*
tailed frog
    coastal, *Ascaphus truei*
    Rocky Mountain, *Ascaphus montanus*

REPTILES
desert horned lizard, *Phrynosoma platyrhinos*
gopher snake (bullsnake), *Pituophis catenifer*
Great Basin collared lizard, *Crotaphytus bicinctores*
ground snake, *Sonora semiannulata*
long-nosed leopard lizard, *Gambelia wislizenii*
painted turtle, *Chrysemys picta*
pigmy short-horned lizard, *Phrynosoma douglasi*
racer, *Coluber constrictor*
rubber boa, *Charina bottae*
sagebrush lizard, *Sceloporus graciosus*
side-blotched lizard, *Uta stansburiana*
striped whipsnake, *Masticophis taeniatus*
western fence lizard, *Sceloporus occidentalis*
western rattlesnake, *Crotalus viridis*
    Northern Pacific form, *C. viridis oreganus*
    Great Basin form, *C. viridis lutosus*
western whiptail, *Cnemidophorus tigris*

BIRDS
American avocet, *Recurvirostra americana*
American bittern, *Botaurus lentiginosus*
American dipper, *Cinclus mexicanus*

American bittern, *Botaurus lentiginosus*
American dipper, *Cinclus mexicanus*
American kestrel (sparrow hawk), *Falco sparverius*
American robin, *Turdus migratorius*
American white pelican, *Pelecanus erythrorhynchos*
Anna's hummingbird, *Calypte anna*
bald eagle, *Haliaeetus leucocephalus*
barn owl, *Tyto alba*
barred owl, *Strix varia*
belted kingfisher, *Ceryle alcyon*
black-backed woodpecker, *Picoides arcticus*
black-billed magpie, *Pica hudsonia*
black-chinned hummingbird, *Archilochus alexandri*
black-crowned night heron, *Nycticorax nycticorax*
black-necked stilt, *Himantopus mexicanus*
black rosy finch, *Leucosticte atrata*
black tern, *Chlidonias niger*
black-throated sparrow, *Amphispiza bilineata*
blue grouse, *Dendragapus obscurus*
blue jay, *Cyanocitta cristata*
blue-winged teal, *Anas discors*
bobolink, *Dolichonyx oryzivorus*
broad-tailed hummingbird, *Selasphorus platycercus*
burrowing owl, *Athene cunicularia*
California quail, *Callipepla californica*
calliope hummingbird, *Stellula calliope*
Canada goose, *Branta canadensis*
canyon wren, *Catherpes mexicanus*
Cape May warbler, *Dendroica tigrina*
Caspian tern, *Sterna caspia*
chukar, *Alectoris chukar*
cinnamon teal, *Anas cyanoptera*
Clark's nutcracker, *Nucifraga columbiana*
common grackle, *Quiscalus quiscula*
common nighthawk, *Chordeiles minor*
common poorwill, *Phalaenoptilus nuttallii*
common raven, *Corvus corax*
Cooper's hawk, *Accipiter cooperii*
double-crested cormorant, *Phalacrocorax auritus*
downy woodpecker, *Picoides pubescens*
ferruginous hawk, *Buteo regalis*
flammulated owl, *Otus flammeolus*
Franklin's gull, *Larus pipixcan*
golden eagle, *Aquila chrysaetos*
gray-crowned rosy finch, *Leucosticte tephrocotis*
gray jay, *Perisoreus canadensis*

great blue heron, *Ardea herodias*
great egret, *Ardea alba*
great gray owl, *Strix nebulosa*
great horned owl, *Bubo virginianus*
greater sage grouse, *Centrocercus urophasianus*
greater white-fronted goose, *Anser albifrons*
green-tailed towhee, *Pipilo chlorurus*
horned lark, *Eremophila alpestris*
indigo bunting, *Passerina cyanea*
loggerhead shrike, *Lanius ludovicianus*
long-billed curlew, *Numenius americanus*
long-eared owl, *Asio otus*
magnolia warbler, *Dendroica magnolia*
mallard, *Anas platyrhynchos*
marsh wren, *Cistothorus palustris*
mountain bluebird, *Sialia currucoides*
mountain chickadee, *Poecile gambeli*
mountain dove, *Zenaida macroura*
mountain quail, *Oreortyx pictus*
northern flicker, *Colaptes auratus*
northern harrier (marsh hawk), *Circus cyaneus*
northern hawk owl, *Surnia ulula*
northern parula, *Parula americana*
northern pintail, *Anas acuta*
northern saw-whet owl, *Aegolius acadicus*
osprey, *Pandion haliaetus*
painted bunting, *Passerina ciris*
pileated woodpecker, *Dryocopus pileatus*
pinyon jay, *Gymnorhinus cyanocephalus*
prairie falcon, *Falco mexicanus*
pygmy nuthatch, *Sitta pygmaea*
red-breasted nuthatch, *Sitta canadensis*
red-eyed vireo, *Vireo olivaceus*
red-naped sapsucker, *Sphyrapicus nuchalis*
red-tailed hawk, *Buteo jamaicensis*
red-winged blackbird, *Agelaius phoeniceus*
ring-necked pheasant, *Phasianus colchicus*
rock wren, *Salpinctes obsoletus*
rose-breasted grosbeak, *Pheucticus ludovicianus*
Ross's goose, *Chen rossii*
rough-legged hawk, *Buteo lagopus*
ruddy duck, *Oxyura jamaicensis*
ruffed grouse, *Bonasa umbellus*
rufous hummingbird, *Selasphorus rufus*
sage sparrow, *Amphispiza belli*
sage thrasher, *Oreoscoptes montanus*
sandhill crane, *Grus canadensis*
scarlet tanager, *Piranga olivacea*
sharp-shinned hawk, *Accipiter striatus*

Steller's jay, *Cyanocitta stelleri*
Swainson's hawk, *Buteo swainsoni*
Townsend's solitaire, *Myadestes townsendi*
trumpeter swan, *Cygnus buccinator*
tundra swan, *Cygnus columbianus*
turkey vulture, *Cathartes aura*
western grebe, *Aechmophorus occidentalis*
western kingbird, *Tyrannus verticalis*
western meadowlark, *Sturnella neglecta*
western screech-owl, *Otus kennicottii*
western tanager, *Piranga ludoviciana*
white-breasted nuthatch, *Sitta carolinensis*
white-faced ibis, *Plegadis chihi*
willet, *Catoptrophorus semipalmatus*
Wilson's phalarope, *Phalaropus tricolor*
Wilson's snipe, *Gallinago delicata*
yellow-billed cuckoo, *Coccyzus americanus*
yellow-headed blackbird, *Xanthocephalus xantho-*
cephalus

MAMMALS
American badger, *Taxidea taxus*
American beaver, *Castor canadensis*
American bison (buffalo), *Bison bison*
American marten, *Martes americana*
American mink, *Mustela vison*
American pika, *Ochotona princeps*
Belding's ground squirrel, *Spermophilus beldingi*
bighorn sheep, *Ovis canadensis*
black bear, *Ursus americanus*
black-tailed jackrabbit, *Lepus californicus*
bobcat, *Lynx rufus*
Canadian lynx, *Lynx canadensis*
canyon mouse, *Peromyscus crinitus*
chisel-toothed kangaroo rat, *Dipodomys microps*
Columbian ground squirrel, *Spermophilus colum-*
bianus
common muskrat, *Ondatra zibethicus*
cougar (mountain lion), *Puma concolor*
coyote, *Canis latrans*
dark kangaroo mouse, *Microdipodops megacephalus*
deer mouse, *Peromyscus maniculatus*
desert wood rat, *Neotoma lepida*
Douglas' squirrel (chickaree), *Tamiasciurus doug-*
lasii
elk, *Cervus elaphus*
fisher, *Martes pennanti*
golden-mantled ground squirrel, *Spermophilus*
lateralis

gray fox, *Urocyon cinereoargenteus*
gray wolf, *Canis lupus*
Great Basin pocket mouse, *Perognathus parvus*
grizzly bear, *Ursus arctos*
kit fox, *Vulpes macrotis*
least chipmunk, *Tamias minimus*
little brown bat, *Myotis lucifugus*
little pocket mouse, *Perognathus longimembris*
long-legged bat, *Myotis volans*
long-tailed weasel, *Mustela frenata*
Merriam's ground squirrel, *Spermophilus canus*
mountain cottontail, *Sylvilagus nuttallii*
mountain goat, *Oreamnos americanus*
mule deer, *Odocoileus hemionus*
northern flying squirrel, *Glaucomys sabrinus*
northern grasshopper mouse, *Onychomys leuco-*
gaster
northern raccoon, *Procyon lotor*
northern river otter, *Lontra canadensis*
Ord's kangaroo rat, *Dipodomys ordii*
pallid bat, *Antrozous pallidus*
pinyon mouse, *Peromyscus truei*
North American porcupine, *Erethizon dorsatum*
pronghorn, *Antilocapra americana*
pygmy rabbit, *Brachylagus idahoensis*
red fox, *Vulpes vulpes*
red squirrel (pine squirrel), *Tamiasciurus hud-*
sonicus
sagebrush vole, *Lemmiscus curtatus*
short-tailed weasel (ermine), *Mustela erminea*
spotted bat, *Euderma maculatum*
striped skunk, *Mephitis mephitis*
water shrew, *Sorex palustris*
water vole, *Microtus richardsoni*
western gray squirrel, *Sciurus griseus*
western harvest mouse, *Reithrodontomys mega-*
lotis
western pipistrelle, *Pipistrellus hesperus*
western small-footed bat, *Myotis ciliolabrum*
western spotted skunk, *Spilogale gracilis*
white-tailed antelope squirrel, *Ammospermophi-*
lus leucurus
white-tailed deer, *Odocoileus virginianus*
white-tailed jackrabbit, *Lepus townsendii*
wolverine, *Gulo gulo*
yellow-bellied marmot, *Marmota flaviventris*
yellow pine chipmunk, *Tamias amoenus*
Yuma bat, *Myotis yumanensis*

Resources

General references

Barnes, Christine. 1996. *Central Oregon: View from the Middle*. Helena, Montana: Farcountry Press.

Brogan, Phil F. 1965. *East of the Cascades*. Portland, Oregon: Binford and Mort, Publishing.

Ferguson, Denzel and Nancy. 1982. *Oregon's Great Basin Country*. Bend, Oregon: Maverick Publications.

Hatton, Raymond R. 1978. *Bend in Central Oregon*. Portland, Oregon: Binford and Mort Publishing.

———. 1997. *High Desert of Central Oregon*. Portland, Oregon: Binford and Mort Publishing.

———. 1988. *Oregon's Big Country: A Portrait of Southeastern Oregon*. Bend, Oregon: Maverick Publications.

———. 1996. *Oregon's Sisters Country: A Portrait of Its Lands, Waters and People*. Bend, Oregon: Maverick Publications.

Jackman, E. R., and R. A. Long. 2003. *The Oregon Desert*. Caldwell, Idaho: Caxton Press.

Kerr, Andy. 2004. *Oregon Wild: Endangered Forest Wilderness*. Portland, Oregon: Oregon Natural Resources Council.

Olson, L. N., and J. Daniel. 1997. *Oregon Rivers*. Englewood, Colorado: Westcliffe Publishers.

Oregon Biodiversity Project. 1998. *Oregon's Living Landscape*. West Linn, Oregon: Defenders of Wildlife.

Wuerthner, George. 1987. *Oregon Mountain Ranges*. Helena, Montana: Farcountry Press.

Literature

Abbey, Edward. 1984. *Beyond the Wall*. New York, N.Y.: Henry Holt and Co.

———. 1985. *Desert Solitaire: A Season in the Wilderness*. New York, N.Y.: Ballantine Books.

Adams, Melvin R. 2001. *Netting the Sun: A Personal Geography of the Oregon Desert*. Pullman, Washington: Washington State University Press.

Anderson, Jim. 1992. *Tales from a Northwest Naturalist*. Caldwell, Idaho: Caxton Press.

Bayles, David. 2005. *Notes on a Shared Landscape: Making Sense of the American West*. Eugene, Oregon: Image Continuum Press.

Dagget, Dan. 2005. *Gardeners of Eden: Rediscovering Our Importance to Nature*. Santa Barbara, California: The Thatcher Charitable Trust—EcoResults!

Douglas, William O. 1960. *My Wilderness: The Pacific West*. Garden City, N.Y.: Doubleday and Company, Inc.

Egan, Timothy. 1999. *Lasso the Wind: Away to the New West*. New York, N.Y.: Knopf Publishing Group.

Houle, Marcy. 1996. *The Prairie Keepers: Secrets of the Grasslands*. New York, N.Y.: Perseus Books Group.

Kittredge, William. 2000. *Balancing Water: Restoring the Klamath Basin*. Berkeley, California: University of California Press.

———. 1993. *Hole in the Sky: A Memoir*. New York, N.Y.: Vintage Books.

———. 2002. *Owning It All*. Saint Paul, Minnesota: Graywolf Press.

———. 1995. *Who Owns the West?* San Francisco, California: Mercury House.

Leopold, Aldo. 1989. *A Sand County Almanac.* New York, N.Y.: Oxford University Press.

McCall, Tom. 1977. *Tom McCall: Maverick.* Portland, Oregon: Binford and Mort Publishing.

McPhee, John. 1981. *Basin and Range.* New York, N.Y.: Farrar, Straus and Giroux.

Muir, John. 2001. *The Wilderness World of John Muir.* Editor, Edwin Way Teale. Boston, Massachusetts: Houghton Mifflin Co.

Murie, Margaret and Olaus. 1987. *Wapiti Wilderness.* Boulder, Colorado: University Press of Colorado.

Putnam, George P. 1942. *Wide Margins: A Publisher's Autobiography.* New York, N.Y.: Harcourt, Brace and Co.

Service, Robert. 1907. *The Spell of the Yukon.* Reprint. New York, N.Y.: G. P. Putnam's Sons, 1992.

Sullivan, William L. 2000. *Listening for Coyote: A Walk Across Oregon's Wilderness.* Corvallis, Oregon: Oregon State University Press.

Walth, Brent. 1994. *Fire at Eden's Gate: Tom McCall and the Oregon Story.* Portland, Oregon: Oregon Historical Society Press.

Young, James A. 2002. *Cattle in the Cold Desert.* Reno, Nevada: University of Nevada Press.

Recreation and travel

Barstad, Fred. 2001. *Hiking Hells Canyon and Idaho's Seven Devils Mountains.* Guilford, Connecticut: A Falcon Guide, The Globe Pequot Press.

———. 2002. *Hiking Oregon's Eagle Cap Wilderness.* Guilford, Connecticut: A Falcon Guide, The Globe Pequot Press.

Cole, L., and J. Yuskavitch. 2002. *Insider's Guide to Bend and Central Oregon.* Guilford, Connecticut: The Globe Pequot Press.

Davis, James L. 1996. *Seasonal Guide to the Natural Year: Oregon, Washington and British Columbia.* Golden, Colorado: Fulcrum Publishing.

Devine, Bob. 2000. *National Geographic Guide to America's Outdoors: Pacific Northwest.* Washington, D.C.: National Geographic Society.

Hayse, Bruce. 1979. *Unobscured Horizons, Untravelled Trails: Hiking the Oregon High Desert.* Portland, Oregon: self-published.

Highberger, Mark. 2003. *An Explorer's Guide: Oregon.* Woodstock, Vermont. The Countryman Press.

Kerr, Andy. 2000. *Oregon Desert Guide: 70 Hikes.* Seattle, Washington: The Mountaineers Books.

Lorain, Douglas. 2004. *100 Classic Hikes in Oregon.* Seattle, Washington: The Mountaineers Books.

Smith, Giselle, editor. 2004. *Best Places Northwest.* Seattle, Washington: Sasquatch Books.

Sullivan, William L. 2002. *Exploring Oregon's Wild Areas.* Eugene, Oregon: Navillus Press.

———. 2005. *100 Hikes in the Central Oregon Cascades.* Eugene, Oregon: Navillus Press.

———. 2001. *100 Hikes Travel Guide: Eastern Oregon.* Eugene, Oregon: Navillus Press.

———. 2003. *Trips and Trails Oregon.* Eugene, Oregon: Navillus Press.

Yuskavitch, Jim. 2000. *Oregon Nature Weekends.* Helena, Montana: Falcon Publishing, Inc.

Natural history

Acorn, John. 2001. *Bugs of Washington and Oregon.* Edmonton, Alberta: Lone Pine Publishing.

Alden, P., and D. Paulson. 1998. *National Audubon Society Field Guide to the Pacific Northwest.* New York, N.Y.: Alfred A. Knopf, Inc.

Bailey, Vernon. 1936. *The Mammals and Life Zones of Oregon.* Washington, D.C.: North American Fauna No. 55, U. S. Dept. of Agriculture, Bureau of Biological Survey.

Baughman, Mel, editor. 2002. *National Geographic Field Guide to the Birds of North America.* Washington, D. C.: National Geographic Society.

Behnke, Robert J. 2002. *Trout and Salmon of North America.* New York, N.Y.: Simon and Schuster.

Bever, Dale N. 1981. *Northwest Conifers.* Portland, Oregon: Binford and Mort Publishing.

Bishop, Ellen Morris. 2004. *Hiking Oregon's Geology.* Seattle, Washington: The Mountaineers Books.

———. 2003. *In Search of Ancient Oregon: A Geological and Natural History.* Portland, Oregon: Timber Press.

Botkin, Daniel B. 1996. *Our Natural History: The Lessons of Lewis and Clark*. New York, N.Y.: Perigee Books.

Bowers, N., R. Bowers, and K. Kaufman. 2004. *Mammals of North America: Kaufman Focus Guides*. New York, N.Y.: Houghton Mifflin Co.

Brock, J. P., and K. Kaufman. 2003. *Butterflies of North America: Kaufman Focus Guides*. New York, N.Y.: Houghton Mifflin Co.

Burrows, R. and J. Gilligan. 2003. *Birds of Oregon*. Edmonton, Alberta: Lone Pine Publishing.

Corkran, C. C., and C. Thoms. 1996. *Amphibians of Oregon, Washington and British Columbia*. Edmonton, Alberta: Lone Pine Publishing.

Crawford, J. A., et al. 2004. Ecology and Management of Sage-grouse and Sage-grouse Habitat. *Journal of Range Management* (January) 57: 2–19.

Eastman, Donald C. 1990. *Rare and Endangered Plants of Oregon*. Beautiful America Publishing Co.

Eaton, E., and K. Kaufman. 2007. *Kaufman Field Guide to Insects of North America*. New York, N.Y.: Houghton Mifflin Co.

Eder, Tamara. 2002. *Mammals of Washington and Oregon*. Edmonton, Alberta: Lone Pine Publishing.

Evanich, Jr., Joseph E. 1990. *The Birder's Guide to Oregon*. Portland, Oregon: Portland Audubon Society.

Franklin, J. F., and C. T. Dryness. 1988. *Natural Vegetation of Oregon and Washington*. Corvallis, Oregon: Oregon State University Press.

Jensen, E. C., and C. R. Ross. 1999. *Trees to Know in Oregon*. Corvallis, Oregon: Publication EC-1450, Oregon State University and Oregon Dept. of Forestry.

Johnson, Charles G. 1998. *Common Plants of the Inland Pacific Northwest*. Publication R6-NR-ECOL-TP-04-98, USDA - Forest Service, Pacific Northwest Region.

———. 2004. *Alpine and Subalpine Vegetation of the Wallowa, Seven Devils and Blue Mountains*. Publication R6-NR-ECOL-TP-03-04, USDA Forest Service, Pacific Northwest Region.

Johnson, D. H., and T. A. O'Neil, editors. 2001. *Wildlife-Habitat Relationships in Oregon and Washington*. Corvallis, Oregon: Oregon State University Press.

Jolley, Russ. 1988. *Wildflowers of the Columbia Gorge*. Portland, Oregon: Oregon Historical Society Press.

Jones, L. C., W. P. Leonard, and D. H. Olson, editors. 2005. *Amphibians of the Pacific Northwest*. Seattle, Washington: Seattle Audubon Society.

Kaufman, Kenn. 2000. *Kaufman Field Guide to Birds of North America*. New York, N.Y.: Houghton Mifflin Co.

Lanner, Ronald M. 1983. *Trees of the Great Basin: A Natural History*. Reno, Nevada: University of Nevada Press.

Littlefield, Carroll D. 1990. *Birds of the Malheur National Wildlife Refuge*. Corvallis, Oregon: Oregon State University Press.

Mansfield, Donald H. 2000. *Flora of Steens Mountain*. Corvallis, Oregon: Oregon State University Press.

Marshall, D. B., et al. 2003. *Birds of Oregon: A General Reference*. Corvallis, Oregon: Oregon State University Press.

Matthews, Daniel. 1999. *Cascade-Olympic Natural History: A Trailside Reference*. Portland, Oregon: Raven Editions.

Miller, R. F., et al. 2005. *Biology, Ecology, and Management of Western Juniper*. Technical Bulletin 152, Oregon State University Agricultural Experiment Station, Corvallis, Oregon.

Mozingo, Hugh N. 1987. *Shrubs of the Great Basin: A Natural History*. Reno, Nevada: University of Nevada Press.

Orr, E. L., and W. N. Orr. 1999. *Oregon Fossils*. Dubuque, Iowa: Kendall/Hunt Publishing Co.

Orr, William L., E. L. Orr, and E. M. Baldwin. 1999. *Geology of Oregon*. Dubuque, Iowa: Kendall/Hunt Publishing Co.

Page, L. M., and B. M. Burr. 1991. *Freshwater Fishes, North America North of Mexico: Peterson Field Guide Series*. New York, N.Y.: Houghton Mifflin Co.

Peck, Morton E. 1961. *A Manual of the Higher Plants of Oregon*. Portland, Oregon: Binford and Mort Publishers.

Peterson, Roger Tory. 1990. *Peterson Field Guide to Western Birds*. Boston, Massachusetts: Houghton Mifflin Co.

Petrides, George A. 1992. *Western Trees: Peterson Field Guide Series*. New York, N.Y.: Houghton Mifflin Co.

Pyle, Robert Michael. 2002. *The Butterflies of Cascadia*. Seattle, Washington: Seattle Audubon Society.

Ryser, Fred A. 1985. *Birds of the Great Basin: A Natural History*. Reno, Nevada: University of Nevada Press.

Sibley, David Allen. 2003. *The Sibley Field Guide to Birds of Western North America*. New York, N.Y.: Alfred A. Knopf, Inc.

Sigler, W. F., and J. W. Sigler. 1987. *Fishes of the Great Basin: A Natural History*. Reno, Nevada: University of Nevada Press.

Spivey, Terry, et al. 2004. *Fremont Flora Field Guide*. Publication FS/OR/FRE-WIN/2004/03, USDA - Forest Service, Fremont-Winema National Forests.

Stebbins, Robert C. 2003. *Western Reptiles and Amphibians: Peterson Field Guide Series*. New York, N.Y.: Houghton Mifflin Co.

St. John, Alan. 1989. *Amphibians and Reptiles of the Sunriver Area*. Sunriver, Oregon: Sunriver Nature Center.

————. 2002. *Reptiles of the Northwest: California to Alaska—Rockies to the Coast*. Edmonton, Alberta: Lone Pine Publishing.

Strickler, Dee. 1993. *Wayside Wildflowers of the Pacific Northwest*. Columbia Falls, Montana: The Flower Press.

Taylor, Ronald J. 1992. *Sagebrush Country: A Wildflower Sanctuary*. Missoula, Montana: Mountain Press Publishing Company.

Trimble, Stephen. 1989. *The Sagebrush Ocean: A Natural History of the Great Basin*. Reno, Nevada: University of Nevada Press.

Turner, M., and P. Gustafson. 2006. *Wildflowers of the Pacific Northwest*. Portland, Oregon: Timber Press.

Vallier, Tracy. 1998. *Islands and Rapids: A Geologic Story of Hells Canyon*. Lewiston, Idaho: Confluence Press.

Verts, B. J., and L. N. Carraway. 1998. *Land Mammals of Oregon*. Berkeley, California: University of California Press.

Human history

Billington, Ray Allen. 2001. *Westward Expansion: A History of the American Frontier*. Albuquerque, New Mexico: University of New Mexico Press.

Boyd, Robert, editor. 1999. *Indians, Fire and the Land in the Pacific Northwest*. Corvallis, Oregon: Oregon State University Press.

Burnett, Peter. 1880. *Recollections and Opinions of an Old Pioneer*. Reprint. Lebanon, Oregon: The Narrative Press, 2004

Carey, Charles Henry. 1922. *History of Oregon*. Portland, Oregon: The Pioneer Historical Publishing Co.

Chatters, James C. 2002. *Ancient Encounters: Kennewick Man and the First Americans*. New York, N.Y.: Simon and Schuster, Inc.

Clark, Robert D. 1989. *The Odyssey of Thomas Condon*. Portland, Oregon: Oregon Historical Society Press.

Coe, Urling C. 1940. *Frontier Doctor: Observations on Central Oregon and the Changing West*. Reprint. Corvallis, Oregon: Oregon State University Press, 2003.

d'Azevedo, Warren L., editor 1986. *Handbook of North American Indians*. Volume 11, Great Basin. Washington, D. C.: Smithsonian Institution.

Deschutes County Historical Society. 2004. *Bend: 100 Years of History*. Bend, Oregon: Deschutes County Historical Society.

DeVoto, Bernard, editor. 1997. *The Journals of Lewis and Clark*. Boston, Massachusetts: Houghton Mifflin Co.

Gulick, Bill. 1994. *Chief Joseph Country: Land of the Nez Perce*. Caldwell, Idaho: Caxton Printers.

Hanley, Mike, with Ellis Lucia. 1974. *Owyhee Trails: The West's Forgotten Corner*. Caldwell, Idaho: Caxton Printers.

Josephy, Alvin M. 1997. *The Nez Perce Indians and the Opening of the Northwest*. New York, N.Y.: Houghton Mifflin Co.

Lanham, Url. 1973. *The Bone Hunters: The Heroic Age of Paleontology in the American West*. New York, N.Y.: Dover Publications, Inc.

Lavender, David. 2001. *Land of Giants: The Drive to the Pacific Northwest 1750–1950*. Edison, New Jersey: Castle Books.

Laycock, George. 1996. *The Mountain Men*. Guilford, Connecticut: The Lyons Press.

MacGregor, Carol Lynn, editor. 1997. *The Journals of Patrick Gass, Member of the Lewis and Clark Expedition*. Missoula, Montana: Mountain Press Publishing Co.

McCornack, Ellen Condon. 2001. *Thomas Condon, Pioneer Geologist of Oregon*. Eugene, Oregon: University of Oregon Press.

Moulton, Gary E., editor. 2003. *The Lewis and Clark Journals: An American Epic of Discovery*. Lincoln, Nebraska: University of Nebraska Press.

Parkman, Francis. 1994. *The Oregon Trail*. Lincoln, Nebraska: University of Nebraska Press—Bison Books.

Potter, Miles. 1985. *Oregon's Golden Years: Bonanza of the West*. Caldwell, Idaho: Caxton Printers.

Ruby, R. H., and J. A. Brown. 1992. *A Guide to the Indian Tribes of the Pacific Northwest*. Norman, Oklahoma: University of Oklahoma Press.

Sharp, Dallas Lore. 1914. *Where Rolls the Oregon*. Reprint. Whitefish, Montana: Kessinger Publishing, 2004.

Walker, Deward E., editor. 1998. *Handbook of North American Indians*. Volume 12, Plateau. Washington, D. C.: Smithsonian Institution.

Maps and atlases

Loy, William G., editor. 2001. *Atlas of Oregon*. Eugene, Oregon: University of Oregon Press.

Lyons, Guy. *Pictorial Landform Maps Series*. Graphic Adventures, P.O. Box 865, Christmas Valley, Oregon 97641.

Oregon Road and Recreation Atlas. 2005. Medford, Oregon: Benchmark Maps.

Index

Al St. John photographing a Great Basin collared lizard. Owyhee Reservoir, Southeastern Oregon. Photo: Jan St. John

About the author

Native Oregonian Alan D. St. John resides in Bend. He is a freelance interpretive naturalist who uses writing, photography, drawings, and paintings to teach about the natural world. A specialist in herpetology, Al wrote the field guide *Reptiles of the Northwest*. His work has also appeared in *National Geographic*, *Outdoor Photographer*, *Ranger Rick*, *Natural History*, *Nature Conservancy*, *The New York Times*, and other periodicals. He has worked as a reptile keeper at Portland's zoological park and conducted extensive reptile and amphibian field surveys for the Oregon Department of Fish and Wildlife, the USDA Forest Service, the U.S. Department of the Interior's Bureau of Land Management, and the National Park Service.